POST-ŚAṀKARA DIALECTICS OF THE ADVAITA VEDĀNTA

POST-ŚAṀKARA DIALECTICS
OF
THE ADVAITA VEDĀNTA

BY

A. BHATTACHARYYA SHASTRI

BHARATIYA KALA PRAKASHAN
DELHI (INDIA)

First Edition : 1936
Revised Edition : 2009

Published by **C.P. Gautam**
BHARATIYA KALA PRAKASHAN
3421-A, IInd Floor Narang Colony, Tri Nagar,
Delhi-110035. Ph. : 32967505, Telefax : 01127393083
E-mail : 3241bkp@yahoo.co.in
Website : www.bkpbooks.com

ISBN : 978-81-8090-004-4

Printed By :
Laxmi Offset Process, Delhi

To

THE SACRED MEMORY

of

MY FATHER

CONTENTS

PREFACE

In these pages an attempt has been made to give a systematic presentation of post-Śaṁkara dialectics of the Advaita-Vedānta. The work is substantially based upon my thesis approved for the Degree of Doctorate in Philosophy by the Calcutta University in 1933.

Advaita-Vedānta may be studied purely from a religious standpoint as an intuitive principle of realisation as well as conceptual dialectics. In the former aspect, it unfolds to us the highest art of life, brings solace in affliction and holds out a promise of self-realisation and transcendental bliss. It is also a science of thinking, abounding in philosophic boldness and in this respect it has exhibited the keenest logical subtleties and is on the same footing with the Science of Reasoning. Though the Vedāntic teachers render allegiance to the infallibility of the Śruti, still, the free natural growth of Philosophic thinking has not been checked in the Vedānta literature. And in the history of the development of Vedāntic concepts, the more we advance the more we are impressed by the diversity of thoughts, the complexity of concepts and the subtlety of reasoning. Advaitism in its later development has become the pyramid of conceptual construction. Contributions of Śrīharṣa, Citsukha and Madhusūdana, open a new era in the domain of the Advaita-Vedānta and add a new page in the history of the development of monistic thought. Contributions of the Neo-Vedāntic teachers have novel features which originate a new form of dialectology to test the growth of Vedāntic concepts and thus make the system a living one in Indian Philosophy.

The main object of the dialectics as developed by the Neo-Vedāntic teachers is to carry thought to perfection by a critical examination of the concepts and categories of the opposing sister schools so as to expose their untenability on the ground of their inherent contradictions and antinomies. This paved the way for the establishment of their own position on a sound logical basis which was made stronger still by a further dialectical refutation of the charges and criticisms that might conceivably be levelled by the opponents against their own position. The Neo-Vedāntic dialectic has thus a twofold destructive-constructive aspect— refutation of the opponents' thesis and the establishment of the true Vedāntic position by a refutation of its refutation by the opponent. In some teachers, the former, destructive or offensive, aspect is predominant while in others there is a harmonious combination of destruction with construction. Madhusūdana in his *Advaitasiddhi* is mainly preoccupied with a refutation of Vyāsarāja's *Nyāyāmṛta* almost line by line and Śrīharṣa in his *Khāṇḍanakhaṇḍakhādya* is more busy in demolishing the *Nyāya-Vaiśeṣika* categories than in propounding his own thesis. Citsukhācāryya however in his monumental *Tattva-pradīpikā* tries to hold the balance even between these two aspects. These three thinkers carry post-Śaṁkara dialectic to the perfection and predominance it has reached in Indian thought. Hence in the present study these three remarkable dialecticians have come in for attention.

The present volume comprises eight chapters bearing mainly on the epistemology of post-Śaṁkara thought. Of eight chapters, the first three deal with the nature and validity of knowledge and the next five are concerned mainly with an explanation of appearance and its implication from the standpoint of epistemology.

In the first chapter, nature of knowledge has been examined and analysed so as to bring out the problems involved therein. This enables us to grasp the fundamental problem of Vedāntic epistemology, and thus serves as an introduction to it. The second chapter deals with the important and unique Indian conception of self-luminosity of knowledge—the problem of self-luminosity being studied from two sides, *viz.*, its nature and its validity, n I developing the definition, mainly following Citsukhācāryya an attempt has been made to show how by an inner dialectic movement, thought arrives at the most perfect definition of its object by discovering and discarding the inherent contradictions of inadequate definitions. With regard to the validity of the conception, it has been shown how Vedāntic thinkers establish their position by a dialectical refutation of the opponent's arguments in such a perfectly Socratic manner as to lead gradually and inevitably to its establishment on an irrefutable logical basis. The third chapter is concerned with the validity of knowledge, and deals mainly with the formidable arguments of the Navya-Nyāya school as represented by Gaṅgeśa in his *Tattva-cintāmaṇi* and discusses how the Mīmāṁsā and Vedānta schools refute the neo-logicians by their own dialectic.

In the fourth chapter, Śrīharṣa's famous dialectic in the refutation of the *Nyāya-Vaiśeṣika* categories has been studied while the fifth and sixth chapters deal with Madhusūdana's refutation of Vyāsarāja's arguments against the Vedāntic conception of the universe as unreal. Epistemology of illusion or *Adhyāsa* has been discussed in the seventh chapter where an attempt has been made to study the monistic theory of illusion or super-imposition in a comparative way by analysing different theories of illusion advanced by the sister schools of Indian Philosophy. The last chapter deals with Nescience or *Avidyā* and the famous *anupapattis* of Rāmānuja and the charges of Mādhva have been examined and an effort has been made to show how the Advaita-teachers refute their opponents by their irresistible dialectics and finally establish their own position on the bedrock of irrefutable logic.

I owe an apology to students of modern philosophy for my following the logical technique of original authors whose views have been represented by me in this book. This will, I am afraid, give an undesirable impression of scholasticism, the days of which are irrevocably past. But a twofold consideration led me to run the gauntlet of criticism. In the first place I wanted to present to the modern scholar the growth of dialectics in orthodox Vedānta with all its strength and purity and in the second place I was apprehensive that to make an attempt to present the arguments of these old dialecticians in the current philosophical terminology might serve to give a wrong version of our ancient thought. The temptation of using the terminology of European Philosophy was too great for me; but I mustered courage enough to shun the risk of presenting a distorted account. I preferred to leave the old philosophers speak for themselves in their own forceful diction with all their terminological resources and I could not dare to put a modern garb on them, because I do not possess the skill and art which will make our ancient thinkers appear in a modern role. It is too much to expect that highly technical works like those I have followed as my model can be made easily intelligible and popular. These speculations have got an appeal and interest for the select few and I shall deem my labours amply rewarded if the present endeavour serves to create an interest in the Indian philosophical speculations in circles of scholars whose knowledge of Sanskrit is not equal to tackling the original texts. I had all along counted on the indulgence of my prospective readers and I appeal to them to tread the tangled path of ancient dialectics with me with patience and sympathy and to treat with indulgence and charity of heart the deficiencies and drawbacks which are inevitable in a pioneer attempt.

The branch of study, which forms the subject-matter of the present volume, has not as yet received any clear and systematic exposition on the lines attempted here. Post-Śaṁkara dialectic as exemplified by Madhusūdana, Śrīharṣa and Citsukha, it is suggested, will not compare unfavourably with the best products of the Western thought as represented by Kant's Critique of Pure Reason, Fichte's Theory of Knowledge and Hegel's Logic. Without any claim to completeness and comprehensiveness of discussion the humble writer has only made an attempt to throw some light and focus attention on a subject so vast and complex. The hope, however, is entertained that in future, labour of competent scholars will serve to complete the edifice the foundation of which is sought to be laid here—a long-felt desideratum of Vedāntic epistemology.

I shall be failing in my duty if I do not take this opportunity to place on record my deep sense of gratitude to Raja Prafullanath

Tagore of Pathuriaghata, the enlightened Zemindar of Idilpur Pergana, my native place, and Babu Rukmininath Dutt Chaudhury, Zemindar of the Hatkhola Dutt family, Calcutta, but for whose munificence and ungrudging financial help I could not dream of completing my University education. Mr. Dutt has all along been an elder brother to me and I am not paying a conventional compliment to him in saying that without his encouragement and exhortation I would not have thought of carrying researches in Indian Philosophy and if there is even the slightest merit in my researches the credit belongs entirely to him as my patron, friend, philosopher and guide. I must offer my sincerest thanks to my esteemed friends and colleagues, Prof. Gopalchandra Bhattacharjee, M.A., Professor of Philosophy, B. M. College, Barisal, and Dr. Satkari Mookerjee, M.A., Ph.D., Lecturer, Calcutta University, for their ungrudging help and co-operation and valuable suggestions for the improvement of both language and thought of my present work in the manuscript.

I take this opportunity to express my sincere gratitude to my Professor, Dr. M. N. Sarkar, M.A., Ph.D., now Professor of Philosophy, Presidency College, for the encouragement and helpful suggestions he so affectionately extended to me in connection with my researches. I must also record my sense of obligation to Prof. Sir S. Radhakṛṣnan, Kt., M.A., D.Litt., Vice-Chancellor, Andhra University, for his kind patronage and encouragement. Finally, I am highly indebted to Dr. S. N. Dasgupta, M.A., Ph.D., I.E.S., Principal, Sanskrit College, for his loving encouragement and sympathy and for the opportunity he gave me to discuss with him my difficulties and problems and his weighty suggestions for the improvement of the work.

ABBREVIATIONS

Ad. S.	...	Advaītasiddhi
A. C. K.	...	Advaitacintākaustubha
Bh.	...	Bhāmatī
Bh. P.	...	Bhāṣā-pariccheda
Br.	...	Bṛhadāraṇyakopaniṣat
Cha.	...	Chāndogyopaniṣat
G\Cit.	...	Citsukhī
G. B.	...	Gauḍabrahmānandī
H. I. Ph.	...	History of Indian Philosophy—Vols. I and II.
I. Ph.	...	Indian Philosophy—Vols. I and II.
I. L. A.	...	Indian Logic and Atomism
Kh. Kh.	...	Khaṇḍanakhaṇḍakhādya
Kir.	...	Kiraṇāvalī
M. K.	...	Māṇḍūkyakārikā
N.Mr.	...	Nyāyāmṛta
N. Mr. P.	...	Nyāyāmṛtaprakāśa
N. Mr. T.	...	Nyāyāmṛtataraṅgiṇī
N. Pr.	...	Nayanaprasādinī
Ny. K.	...	Nyāyakandalī
Ny. m.	...	Nyāyamañjarī
Ny. mk.	...	Nyāyamakaranda
Ny. P.	...	Nyāyapariśuddhi
N. Bh.	....	Nyāya-Bhāṣya
N. V.	...	Nyāya-Vārttika
N. V. T. T.	...	Nyāya-Vārttika-Tātparya-Ṭīkā
P. D.	...	Pañcadaśī
P. P.	...	Pañcapādikā

P. V.	...	Pañcapādikā-Vivaraṇa
Pr. M.	...	Pramāṇamālā
Pr. K. M.	...	Prameyakamalamārtaṇda
Pr. P.	...	Prakaraṇapañcikā
P. Bh.	...	Praśastapāda-Bhāṣya
P.O.	...	Puṇyarāja's Commentary on the Vākyapadīya
R. Bh.	...	Rāmānuja-Bhāṣya
R. P.	...	Ratna-Prabhā
S. B.	...	Śaṁkara-Bhāṣya
S. D.	...	Śāstradīpikā
S. C.	...	Siddhānta-Candrikā
S. L.	...	Siddhāntaleśa
S. V.	...	Ślokavārttika
S. T. R.	...	Sattattvaratnamālā
S. M.	...	Siddhāntamuktāvalī
S. S.	...	Saṅkṣepa-śārīraka
S. S. S. S.	...	Sarvavedāntasiddhānta-sārasaṁgraha
T. C.	...	Tattvacintāmaṇi
T. C. R.	...	Tattvacintāmaṇi-Rahasya
T. S.	...	Tarkasaṁgraha
T. S. D.	...	Tarkasaṁgraha-Dīpikā
Ta. S.	...	Tattvasaṁgraha
Ta. S. P.	...	Tattvasaṁgrahapañjikā
Tat.	...	Tattvoddyota
Tarka.	...	Tarkatāṇḍava
T. M. K.	...	Tattvamuktākalāpa
V. P.	...	Vedāntaparibhāṣā
Vāk.	...	Vākyapadīya
V. K.	...	Vedāntakalpataru
V. K. P.	...	Vedāntakalpataru-parimala
Viṭṭha.	...	Viṭṭhaleśopādhyāyī

EPISTEMOLOGY

CHAPTER 1

NATURE OF KNOWLEDGE

Śaṁkara, Hegel and Bergson—Tendencies of Realism and Idealism in Śaṁkara's Episemology.

In the philosophy of Śaṁkara two lines of thought run parallel to each other, the one is epistemological and the other is metaphysical. In Śaṁkara epistemology has been distinct from the transcendental metaphysics, for by the very nature of his philosophy the theory of knowledge has been distinguished from the conception of being. No doubt, in Śaṁkara being is intuition, but that is in a transcendental sense. The theory of knowledge is a theory of empiric cognition. Although the Hegelian dictum,' 'whatever is, is consciousness' is accepted by Śaṁkara in entirety, yet Śaṁkara differs from Hegel when he comes to conceive the process of the concrete expression of being. To Hegel there is a constant tendency in being to overcome its bare potentiality and to express itself in dialectic concreteness and dynamic fulness. Hegel's Absolute is here pure logical reason, and the dialectic of reason in human mind, therefore, is only the reproduction of the dialectic expression of being and is the key to its knowledge. Bergson differs from Hegel in conceiving intuition to be the faculty of apprehending reality. But the *elan vital* of Bergson or his eternal duration appears to be an a-logical reality. Śaṁkara differs from Hegel in conceiving being to transcend logical reason and as complete in itself and not going through a dialectic expression to reach its fulness. Śaṁkara is emphatic that the process of dialectic expression is concretisation of being and does not express its absolute character. Absoluteness and concrete expressions are not compatible. Being is an ever-accomplished fact and not an accomplishing process and it is at the same time transcendental intuition shining by itself without implying any process of knowledge. Intuition in Bergson is akin to instinct. Bergson sees the limitation of conceptual thinking and how it fails to penetrate the heart of reality. He has, therefore, made a clear distinction between intuitive insight and conceptual thinking. But intuition in Bergson is apparently a psychological process and hardly approaches the transcendental intuition of Śaṁkara. Bergson has in him a touch of dualism inasmuch as he draws a distinction between intuition and reality. But Śaṁkara's system does not suffer from such a dualism. In him intuition is identical with reality and is not a process of apprehending it. Śaṁkara, therefore, differs from Hegel in characterising reality as super-logical and from Bergson in characterising reality as ultimately intuition and throwing away all distinctions between reality and intuition. Intuition is not only the faculty of the soul, but the transcendental truth. In Śaṁkara psychology and metaphysics have met together in affirming intuition as the ultimate truth. Psychology realises this in its highest flight of consciousness and metaphysics accepts it as the ultimate affirmation of knowledge and the highest pitch of being. The two fundamental faculties of apprehending truth, *viz.*, intuition and reason, accept being as unmodified, ever-accomplished fact, which is also consciousness. Psychology accepts this as a fact of direct experience. Reason accepts this as a fact implied in its own revelation. Sense-activity and reflective understanding are no doubt faculties of the mind. The one is directed to receive affections of sensibility, and the other, to understand the world of relations. The one belongs to the fringe of subjective consciousness and the other to the relational and objective consciousness. The one receives impressions, the other finds out their implications. But sense-impressions or the implications of reason are not illuminated in themselves. They are illuminated by the ever-accomplished fact of consciousness. Each of them, therefore, presupposes something which they cannot reveal, far less establish. In fact, the senses and reason are faculties directed towards the reception and examination of experience but not competent to establish truth. Śaṁkara, has, no doubt, found a place for enlightened reason,[1] for logic according to him has a negative result, and reason in its ordinary implications is involved in antinomies, though the transcendental culture in the Advaita-Vedānta generates a fitness in reason to approach reality if not to apprehend it. The negative dialectic of Vedānta is helpful in a way, for reason becomes free from the natural demands of life and breaks the realistic adaptations of knowledge and life. This goes a great way to foster the idealistic or transcendental attitude. No doubt it is clear that reason is never competent to establish transcendental truth or to reveal it. Advaitism makes a distinction between enlightened and unenlightened reason. Unenlightened reason does not see, far less apprehend, the oneness of being.

The enlightened reason of Philosophy gives the weight of its authority to this existence of the accomplished fact of intuition. In Advaita- Vedānta, therefore epistemology runs on two lines: (*a*) on the realistic line and (*b*) the idealistic line, Śaṁkara' s philosophy has in it an element which will give support to naive realism. Advaitism contains in it the antinomies which reason naturally meets with in the effort of knowing the ultimate reality. Though Śaṁkara has not made a clear distinction between sensibility and reason, still the functions of sensibility and reason can be distinguished in his philosophy and this distinction leads us to his theory of truth of appearance and of error. Sensibility in its immediate effect makes us believe in the reality of objects. It affirms the existence of the object and accepts its truth. This affirmation is 'naive.' The report of sensibility is often negated and in sense-affections no distinctions can be possibly drawn between false and true knowledge. Empiricism, therefore, dogmatically accepts the affirmation of the senses. Sense-knowledge cannot transcend this and the subject-object relations underlie empiric consciousness. But even in these implications reason soon finds by the constant changes and denials that the reports of the senses are not convincing. Nor do they present reality. Reality in Śaṁkara is not consistent with the constant shiftings of phenomena, for, the succession of presentations and their denials naturally impresses one with their transitory character. Truth, if it is anything, must be abiding. The constant changes of phenomena cannot establish their reality. Śaṁkara, so far as his epistemology is concerned, is eloquent on the thesis that the subject-object implications of knowledge cannot establish or reveal truth, for the constant shiftings or changes of phenomena at once stamp them with a degree of unreality. Empirical knowledge by its own denial establishes its own falsity. It is a common experience that perception is denied by perception, perception by inference, inference by authority and so on.[2] In this way a knowledge by experience is not a reliable source, for we shall see later on that all phases of experience are constantly changing and none, therefore, can be true in the metaphysical sense. Experience is always related to certain conditions and if these conditions change the experience can be sublated. Reason cannot, therefore, accept the verdict of experience. No doubt there is seeming uniformity in our perception, but these uniformities obtain under some conditions and do not obtain under others. Truth of experience then is subject to certain collocations. These collocations are of space, time and causality and sense-conditions. What Śaṁkara seems anxious to point out is the untrustworthy nature of empirical knowledge which cannot therefore be regarded as a fit instrument for the understanding of truth. This criticism applies even to all finer forms of perception whether of religion, art, morality or lower form of mysticism, for they are also intuitions of developed senses, moral, aesthetic or religious, and their impress carries with them a sort of conviction. They are the empiric intuitions of this state of consciousness, but the criticism which Śaṁkara applies to knowledge by experience can also tell upon them. The relative consciousness, through which our experience moves, can never be a source of higher wisdom, since everything in it is constantly changing and it is true only in its own universe. Its truth or falsity is always related to certain conditions. It is true in one way and false in another. Truth and falsity seem to be inherent in its nature. Śaṁkara, therefore, characterises every fact of experience as relatively true and relatively false. Apart from the ontological implications every fact is epistemologically also true and false, under different conditions. Throughout the whole course of experience appearance is simultaneously turning out true or false, true in one set of relations and false in another set of relations. Understanding of falsity is an exercise of reason. In this understanding, reason and judgment play an important part. When an appearance is negated leaving behind it another appearance, the denial is the part of judgment, though the latter appearance is a fact of experience. Facts are presented in experience and then denied. This is the nature of empiric illusion.

Nature of Falsity in Vedānt and an analysis of Empiric Illusion

By the complete analysis of an empiric illusion we get three elements, (1) the presentation of the locus; (2) the appearance of the illusory percept and (3) the negation of illusion. Even in empiric knowledge the percept is illusory, but its illusory character is not understood so long as the locus is not perceived. This is no doubt true of empirical illusions; it is true no less of empirical experiences. But the empirical intuition is not denied so long as consciousness dwells on the relative basis. Still, the relative character of empiric knowledge cannot be doubted. And this relative character is enough to indicate its illusoriness though it cannot completely establish it.[3]

Negative dialectic of Śaṁkara and its importance in the theory of knowledge

These three elements are more or less presented before consciousness. The first one is not completely presented and here arises the possibility of illusion. The second one is completely presented and the third one too. Between the presentation of the second element and that of the third two more intervening stages may be conceived:—1. a negative judgment that the presentation is not the locus, 2.before the locus can be presented, the negation of the illusory percept can be presented.

The mind passes through a negative judgment and consciousness still works in relativity. This relativity consists in this is not this, but this.' Knowledge still moves in the sphere of judgment and reason is here at work. Immediately after this stage as the effect of judgment, comes the immediate consciousnes of negation. This negation is really identical with the locus.[4] Before the locus, as it is, is perceived, such a negation being identical, with position, becomes the natural implication of knowledge. In fact, the Advaita-Vedānta does not draw any distinction between the negation of the false percept and the locus.

What we should like to point out is that reason has got a function and that function, as will appear from the above, is essentially negative. The function of reason is to judge the truth of relations in empirical presentations. Śaṁkara, like Kant, does not trace out the constitutive and integrative function of reason and understanding. The clear analysis of the untrustworthy character of empiric knowledge exhibits this negative function of reason. Śaṁkara has demonstrated this in refuting relational consciousness. Judgment construes relations and Śaṁkara points out that this is more or less the necessity of pragmatic consciousness. They are, therefore, constructions of a realistic will, but these relations cannot be established. The logical reason ultimately finds its own barrenness in not being able to establish an order of relations and in giving always a negative result. The logical consciousness stands revealed as self-contradictory. The self-contradiction is the only verdict that reason passes upon its own formation. Śaṁkara does not deny the inherent tendency of unilluminated reason to build up an order of relations, but when reason proceeds to examine its own affirmations, it is involved in contradictions and fallacies.

In the theory of empirical knowledge Śaṁkara has, therefore, accepted the contributions of sensibility and reason. The knowledge through sensibility is accepted as true so long as it is not denied by another presentation. Truth and falsity are to Śaṁkara matters of presentation and not of judgment, be it empiric or transcendental. Reason plays the subordinate function of negating the concepts of relations. Knowledge, therefore, proceeds from presentation to presentation until the relative presentations are ultimately denied in the absolute presentation. This absolute presentation is pure consciousness and transcendental knowledge.

Nature of knowledge. Is knowledge concrete or abstract

The important problem of epistemology faces us here. 'Is knowledge concrete or abstract?' Self-conscious evidence speaks for the concrete as well as the abstract aspect of knowledge, but is more in favour of the concrete aspect. Indian epistemology has faced this problem boldly. The distinction of *Nirvikalpa* and *Savikalpa* has found a place in the Naiyāyika, Bauddha, Sāṁkhya, Mīmāṁsā and the Vedānta systems. In fact, it is an all-absorbing topic in Indian Philosophy and the main tendency has been amongst a class of philosophers to lend their support to abstract knowledge. That knowledge has got a concrete expression is accepted by everybody, but when we come to logically examine the concrete aspect of knowledge we meet with certain difficulties. We have seen that Śaṁkara has accepted the concrete stage of knowledge and has not categorically denied it. Such has been the case also with other forms of transcendental philosophy. Psychologically, both the forms of knowledge are facts of consciousness and cannot be denied. But the Rāmānujists, Mādhvites and some others have noticed only the concrete expression of knowledge and have denied the constant tendency of cognitive experience to pass from the abstract to the concrete stage. Hence knowledge is a definite form of consciousness. Definiteness strictly is the differential of knowledge and so long as knowledge has not this character, it is not knowledge but simple apprehension. Apprehension and judgment are the two psychological stages of knowledge. Psychologically we cannot deny any one of them, though there has been an attempt in Rāmānuja not to call apprehension knowledge.

Logically there has been a difference among philosophers on the issue of denying one and retaining the other. The theists identify knowledge with judgment and Śaṁkara, with apprehension. Śaṁkara does not deny that relative consciousness is a matter of judgment and he lends his support to such knowledge in certain stages of consciousness. What he denies is its metaphysical character. Śaṁkara criticises this concrete knowledge (1) in its logical character and (2) in its epistemological import. Logically he is anxious to establish the point that knowledge as judgment is involved in fallacies. Judgment is relational consciousness and this relation is two-fold : (1) relation of subject and object and (2) relation of subject and predicate. These are the most potent forms of relations. Among systems of different relations epistemologically the first one is more important. The relation of subject and object is the essence of empiric epistemology and the ground of concrete knowledge.

The Advaita-Vedānta and subject-object reference in knowledge

Let us examine the nature of these relations. Epistemology here assumes rather than tries to prove the relations. There is no proof here other than the evidence of consciousness, but the evidence of consciousness is not always true, specially in empiric knowledge. The supposed relation may be nothing more than an appearance and a false creation of the pragmatic consciousness. Logically it involves us in difficulties. The subject is subject, and the object is object. How the object is related to the subject is not explained.[5] The relation is a term between the subject and object. It has a meaning to the subject, but not the object. Meaning is a psychological implication and the relation is relation to the subject. But the relations are true to the subject and they are of the subject. But on what assumption do we accept the object to be a term of relation? Even if it is accepted that the subject-object relation is inherent in knowledge, it is still in knowledge and expresses its concrete character; but still it does not establish a reference to anything besides knowledge and its own element. In fact, it is somewhat difficult to establish the objective reference of knowledge by starting from knowledge. How knowledge passes from abstract to concrete is what logical intellect cannot fully apprehend.

This is an epistemlogical implication of the Māyā doctrine of Śaṁkara. This aspect has been more fully developed in Śaṁkarites than in Śaṁkara.

The Necessity of later Vedāntic development

The presentation of the object to the subject is dogmatically accepted by naïve realism. Śāṁkarites do not deny the presentation, but the disappearance of the presentation of false percept makes them seriously think upon the issue. Is the presentation real? This is the most important question in the doctrine of perception. Śaṁkara has no doubt accepted the reality of presentation as has been made clear in his refutation of Vijñānavāda. He appears there as a realist. He is eloquent that perception gives us simultaneously the knowledge of self and not-self. This must have been a psychological admission. But the constantly shifting character of our perception, specially of false perception, makes us seriously ponder over the question: what do we actually perceive? Do we perceive appearance or reality? Do we percieve an appearance that presents reality for the time being? In false perception Śaṁkarites point out, that the appearance is real and unreal both, but in reference to different universes of thought. It is real, because it is presented; it is false, because it is denied. Śaṁkarites are anxious to avoid the complete unreality and illusoriness of a false presentation. In this sense, there is an element of realism in their system. But since, the presentation is denied, it is not real in a metaphysical sense. Śaṁkarites accept, therefore, the psychological realism and the metaphysical idealism in their theory of perception. This dual character of the presentation is what differentiates their theory of false perception from other theories. In Śaṁkara philosophy there is a constant change of outlook from psychological to metaphysical point of view. The objectivity of reference in perception is not denied by the Śaṁkarites, but how an appearance is objectified, is what passes comprehension. The objectivity and subjectivity of reference in false knowledge succeed one another; what appears as an object is, after a moment, denied as an object and is interpreted as a subjective creation or projection. This is clear in false perception. This projection and the supposed objectivity of the presentation are surely a creation of Avidyā, for no other factor can be logically conceived for such presentations. If this is true of empiric illusions, it is also true of empiric perceptions, though these have a more durable character and have, therefore, the mark of objectivity which cannot be reduced to subjective impression. This is the point on which Śaṁkara differs from the Vijñānavādi Bauddha and this has been the main foundation for the development of exoteric life and consciousness. The relative character of our perception as true or false corresponding to different universes of thought has all along been pursued in Vedānta metaphysics and so long as the transcendental intuition does not dawn upon us, the comparatively realistic consciousness dogs us to the last. Even in this realistic presentation, the relative character is apparent and therefore, it gives us the impression that it is real so far as consciousness dwells on the empiric basis. But its denial in transcendental intuition puts it into the category of false presentation. The only difference is that the one continuously hangs on empiric intuition, and that the other is denied there. This continuity lends unto it a touch of realism. This has been the ground of distinction between empiric illusion and empiric truth.

Though there has been a tendency among a class of Śaṁkarites to dispense with the distinction of empiric illusion and empiric truth on the ground that this distinction is more pragmatic than epistemological,[6] still, such has not been the view of the more prominent Śaṁkarites, and they still maintain a realistic element in knowledge and objectivity of reference in perception. This has been Vācaspati's position. The objectivity of reference, therefore, retains the distinction between *Jīvapratyakṣa* and *Īśvara-pratyakṣa.* But although the teachers accept as an implication a realistic consciousness, they cannot explain the relation of the subject to the object, which, still, is a perplexity of metaphysical consciousness. The truth seems to be that in the history of Indian thought the Naiyāyika conception of the subject-object relation has been unhesitatingly accepted. Later Vedāntism points out that this relation can be accepted only on the psychological ground.

The Predicative theory of Propositions

We come now to the consideration of the predicative theory of propositions. It is a general supposition that knowledge is a unit of judgment and even at perceptual level knowledge becomes definite in this that it expresses a judgment. Knowledge, in its clear concrete form, is a system of relations and it is identified with the system. The unit of knowledge is the unit of a system. And a system implies two or more terms in relation.

Here arises the great divergence between the theistic and non-theistic Vedāntists. That knowledge has an empiric basis is a position which has not been denied by Śaṁkara and his followers. But Śaṁkara is not ready to accept that the relational system represents the true being of knowledge. Śaṁkara can lend his support to the predicative view of propositions generally and he has actually done this by refuting the Naiyāyika conception of *Samavāya*. Vedāntists of all schools agree in refuting this relation, for *Samavāya,* according to Naiyāyikas, is a relation obtaining in substance and attribute, generality and individuality, etc. This conception of *Samavāya* has been refuted on the ground that it leads to an infinite regress, for the terms and the relation require the assistance of other relations to be related to one another and these others and so on.[7]

The Vedāntists in the place of *Samavāya* institute the relation of *Tādātmya* or *Svarūpa.* In other words, they maintain that the predicate is the concrete expression of the subject. It helps to draw out the connotation of the subject term or in other words, an abstract notion makes itself concrete through the concrete expression of a predicate. A judgment is, therefore, a subject fully developed and this development is an inner growth and an inherent necessity. Knowledge is dynamic; it has a constant tendency to fully affirm its concreteness through all the qualities it possesses. Knowledge is essentially then judgment. This is the decided opinion of Rāmānuja and other theistic teachers.

Śaṁkara and Śaṁkarites differ here. They may accept this predicative view in the sphere of relative knowledge but their tendency essentially lies in denying all relations between subject and predicate. They interpret the relational consciousness as the working of ignorance which impresses the empirical mind. Here again the logic of Śaṁkara has been essentially negative in the sense that the relation between subject and predicate cannot be established. Herein they point out the application of the same fallacy, *viz.*, the endless multiplication of relations. If relation is true, it must be conceived between two terms, since relation is not possible of a thing which stands by itself. Hence relational consciousness presupposes a differential consciousness too. The difficulty arises, how things in their nature different can be related to one another; and again how we can conceive of identity as synchronous. If there is identity there can be no relations, and if there is relation there must be some difference and unity cannot be established. The conception of unity embracing difference seems to be a hopeless one. In unity either there is difference or there is no difference. If there is difference there can be no unity and if there is no difference there can be no relation. The conception of unity does not admit of a relation without difference.

Even if a relation be conceived between the subject and predicate there arises the possibility of begging the question. A subject is subject in reference to predicate and a predicate is the predicate of the subject. There is a mutuality of reference. As such they are interdependent, and the conception of one is not clear apart from the other. Logically this position is not above criticism, for a definition of the subject term or of the predicate term should be sought independently of one another; otherwise the implications of the subject and the predicate are not independently clear. This mutuality of reference is an accepted fallacy in Indian Logic.[8]

So long we have a long story of the negative dialectic of Śaṁkara which shakes the foundation of all empirical knowledge and epistemology. These negative dialectics have a threefold importance : (1) they demonstrate the futility of thinking to know the ultimate truth; (2) they demonstrate the self-contradictions involved in the nature of thoughts; (3) indirectly they stress the value of the other methods of approach. In Śaṁkara the utter failure of logical thinking as regards the ultimate question has accentuated the importance of intuition as the means of apprehending truth and reality.

The truth which Bergson has only recently preached and the tendency which is becoming every day clearer in modern philosophy, that reason is not the final arbiter of truth, that it can only touch the shadow or fringe of existence, that there is a super-logical way of apprehending truth, were long felt and recognised in Indian philosophy, the more so in Śaṁkara. The service which Advaita-Vedāntism has rendered to philosophy is the propounding of the great truth that truth can be seen or intuited but not understood. Intuition and reason are therefore distinctive faculties and the function of one cannot be appropriated by the other. So long as consciousness moves with reason and categories of relations it becomes busily occupied in an attempt to construct a world of relations, but it is not absolute truth, for reason itself cannot accept the absolute to be a system of relations. A system is more a creation of reason than a reality, for a system has no meaning and cannot exist without the implication of relations, and relations have meaning to an interpretative consciousness. But where the system is called subjective or objective, it is clear that it cannot be truth, for truth denies relations. We cannot understand any necessity of truth entering into a system of relations. This necessity can be either internal or external. If it is external, it implies the existence of something besides the absolute truth. If it is internal, absolute becomes a system. But the absolute and system are two incompatible concepts.

Reason ultimately in this way comes to conceive the inherent impossibility of its knowing truth. And when the attempts of reason thus fail, we seek the other organ of intuition to apprehend reality. Intuition thus gives us what reason cannot. This difference between intuition and reason has been the fruitful source of conceiving truth in two different ways in the philosophy of Śaṁkara. The senses and reason are affected by the impressions of object and they are therefore ready to accept the affections of sensibility as pragmatic if not metaphysical truth, Śaṁkara feels and feels truly that so long as we are thus affected, we cannot deny their causes and our mind is forced to accept their objectivity somehow or other.

Hence the sense-objects, which offer pragmatic satisfaction, have not been denied existence but are said to be true in some sense. These are called *Vyavahārika* or empiric or pragmatic truths. They are true because they appear and affect our volitional and emotional being, they are the affirmations of practical reason. We cannot deny their certitude in certain phases of life and consciousness.

Śaṁkara is thus ready to accept the truth of becoming and he does so accept it so long as the soul has not the illuminated vision of the transcendental being.

So long as man has not the enlightened vision, he necessarily accepts the world of becoming as real presentation and seeks an explanation of its origin. This necessity is of reason and led by this necessity reason builds up an exoteric theory of creation or evolution and accepts the implications of practical reason, God, Soul, and Freedom. In the evolution of pragmatic consciousness Śaṁkara has retained the possibility of finer revelations and the onward progress of the soul. He has offered a theory of epistemology which can support the implications of life, of subtle realizations and finer consciousness. In this way religion, arts and ethics have been made possible in the philosophy of Śaṁkara. He has not gone to the extreme of immediately denying the intuitions of practical reason, the hopes of religion and the promise of immortality. In fact the Upaniṣads and Śaṁkara as the interpreter of the Upaniṣads have perceived the subtler move of life and consciousness in the yearning of the human soul to catch the divine spirit through the majesty of nature. And in the depths of human heart the finer urges clearly indicate the wonderful possibilities and the amazing revelations of the religious consciousness The Advaita-Vedānta is not irresponsive to the dawn of a new life and it has accepted the subtler causes of realization of a concrete spiritual life.

The spiritual life is essentially acquainted with the cosmic consciousness. And what Śaṁkara and the Śaṁkarites are anxious to affirm and point out is that cosmic consciousness has a partial expression. However fine and lofty the expressions may be, they are still expressions and they cannot be expected to express the absolute consciousness fully. But the concentration of the cosmic consciousness is only apparently real which Śaṁkara cannot deny, for the transcendental vision sees the infinite in every centre of existence or more properly the infinite is the only centre which has neither circumference nor radii. So long as truth of such an absolute is not before us, our finite consciousness can feel the expansive urges of spiritual life and call it truth. But as soon as the transcendental vision dawns upon us, the thread of divided life is cut and therefore the continuity between religious life and transcendental vision breaks up. In the transcendental vision, the soul becomes acquainted with such a reality before which the value-consciousness of arts, religion, poetry and philosophy dies out, for they are always expressions in concrete life and cannot feel the depth of joy and transcendence.

In this transcendental attitude Śaṁkara has denied all the implications of the immanent consciousness, be it of religion or of ethics. The denial is natural and spontaneous, for the soul now becomes deeply convinced of transcendence and becomes acquainted with a reality before which everything vanishes as relative and partial. The partial truth appears as truth so long as truth is not perceived in its entirety. But the vision of fuller truth frees us from the implications of partial life. Śaṁkara thinks that freedom goes with realization of fulness of being. There is a constant tendency in Śaṁkara towards the constant change of the presentations and their meanings according as consciousness feels the finer and finer urges of life, and in the life of expression there is nothing which does not change its character and meaning, according to the attitude of the percipient. In relative consciousness the object has only reference to the subject and its nature and meaning are more or less constructions of the subject according as the subject is affected. There is thus variability of opinion of relative existence inasmuch as the subject is affected differently. A presentation, therefore, which has meaning to one subject might have no meaning or a different meaning to another subject. What is truth, therefore, to one may be falsity for the other. But such cannot be the case when truth and falsity are not matters of judgment but indications of existences.

Criterion of truth

Śaṁkara perceives this and comes to the conclusion that degrees of existences are relative to the meaning of a conscious subject.[9] A *prātibhāsika* truth is supposed to be truth when it has a meaning to the subject, but when it is denied practically it ceases to have any meaning. Similarly, *Vyavahārika* truth is always related to a conscious subject and has a meaning for him and even here the meaning has a reference to a particular universe of thought. If the universe of thought is changed, the meaning certainly is gone, though the thing may exist as practically meaningless for the subject. But a truth which is thus related to its subject and has a meaning for it cannot be metaphysical truth according to Śaṁkara, for truth is abiding, eternal and non-contradictory and it is naturally hoped and maintained that it is what it is and it should have no reference to any conscious subject.[10] It exists whether a meaning is seen in it or not. Truth is truth. The rendering of a meaning is a necessity of the finite intellect, but whether the finite intellect sees or does not see any meaning, does not affect in the least the nature of truth. Truth does not enter into the time process, nor does it enter into the conditions of thinking and as such it is completely transcendental. In other words, it can be never put into the grasp of reason and its categorical setting.

The metaphysics of Śaṁkara cannot see its way to synthesise the transcendental truth and the relative truths, as the relative truths are sublated in the transcendental height of existence.

Śaṁkara does not find any continuity between higher and lower truths and in reference to the higher he cannot call the lower existence a truth. When the philosophic consciousness is transcendent, the seeming truth of divided life completely vanishes and, therefore, the transcendental truth does not stand in any relation to the order of appearances. From this level of existence they are not only practically but also theoretically non-existent. The transcendental truth of Śaṁkara is not only transcendental in the sense that it stands above the immanent order of space and time, but the immanent order does not really exist; in other words, the transcendent appears as the immanent under the sway of ignorance. How it so appears is another story and is not relevant to our topic. But what we want to impress is that reality according to Śaṁkara is one undivided being and the panorama of existence dwindles into nothing as soon as we cross the line of divided vision. This division of existence in different grades corresponds to different forms of knowledge. The same existence appears as different according to different organs of apprehension, though reality is the same. That it appears so is explained in the doctrine of Māyā. Whatever the implication of Māyā may be, it is no doubt certain that the existence is only one, it is all-pervasive though it appears as many. Śaṁkara's philosophy is finally an attempt to overthrow the divisions of existences and their empirical truths and to establish the transcendence of being. The conclusion at which philosophy arrives is that the absolute is the locus of existence and it does not admit the partiality of division. The truth is a complete being and is the absolute. Error is to be distinguished from nothingness which exists nowhere. But error has a seeming reality. It is error because it is only partial vision and not fulness of being. Śaṁkara has not attempted the synthesis of the partial presentations of appearance and being, for partiality is the mark which distinguishes error from truth. How the error arises in finite mind may be a psychological or logical question but not a metaphysical one. This partiality of vision is, in the Advaita-Vedānta, the mark of error and in our epistemological search the complete being is never presented. Knowledge therefore moves with the partial expression of being and can never transcend the division and apprehend the absolute truth. Truth is the absolute existence, error is the divided vision. With this standard of truth it is easy for Śaṁkara to deny all partiality of knowledge and being in the absolute, which, therefore, is not the synthesis of all partial truths but the complete denial of them. The synthesis of them cannot present the reality. The absolute is not a synthesis; it is identity.

Exactly at this point the theistic presentation of knowledge and truth differs from the monistic presentation. The theistic attempt is essentially synthetic. It does not see the sectional presentations of reality or the complete transcendence of it. The theistic reality is all-inclusive embracing as it does all phases of being. The theists argue that reality must be complete and all-pervasive. The seeming appearance, because it is seeming, has a reality and cannot be completely denied. The seeming presentation has to be explained. To say that it is presented and then denied is no explanation of its presentation. Finally, the complete denial is never a fact experienced by any one.

The theists do not see any distinction between being and presentation. Presentation only reports the being and as such there can be no complete division eternally obtaining in it, and anybody who denies it must make all knowledge impossible. Rāmānuja is emphatic in pointing out this gap in Śaṁkara's philosophy—the gap between knowledge and reality, for what is real is never an object of knowledge with Śaṁkara. Such a reality even if it exists for ever remains beyond human knowledge. But the greatest difficulty which arises in this forced division between truth and knowledge is the falsity and illusoriness of self-conscious evidence and of all other forms of knowledge. In fact our knowledge instead of serving us would do us positive disservice and in the words of Martineau, reason, the highest faculty given unto man, instead of being a faculty of apprehending reality will be a faculty of disproving it. This stricture of Martineau against Kant can be equally applied against Śaṁkara. His philosophy in this sense defeats its own purpose and declares the problem insoluble and all knowledge fallacious.

The least separation between knowledge and reality, originates almost insoluble problems in philosophy. The evidence of self-consciousness is the only trustworthy evidence and if it is denied nothing remains to hold to. Rāmānuja therefore accepts the evidence of self-consciousness and that which knowledge reports is unhesitatingly accepted as true. Self-conscious presentation is the test of truth. Here is the divergence between Rāmānuja and Śaṁkara. Śaṁkara led by transcendental instinct cannot accept the evidence of self-consciousness as truth, for self-conscionsness to him is relative consciousness. He calls nothing truth which has the least possibility of denial. Self-consciousness is also actually denied. Rāmānuja dissents strongly from this position. He claims that self-consciousness is never denied and as such it is the only source by which we can appraise truth or falsity. Our knowledge is always concrete and concrete knowledge has always a reference to being. Knowledge and being are supposed in each other. Knowledge is impossible when it is not expressive. And when it is expressive it is expressive of truth be it phenomenal or transcendental. Expressive consciousness can never be false, although it might express truth immanent or truth transcendent.

But a question may arise that this also is an extreme position and cannot be logically supported. If all experience is truth then the distinction between error and truth will disappear from human experience, but such is not the case. Rāmānuja replies that it is so. Error is not a logical fact. Whatever appears in knowledge is truth. Even in false perception there is an element of truth in the object though this element is practically not useful.[11] Falsity is therefore more pragmatic "than real, so far as knowledge is concerned. It is not false nor is the object which it reports. Falsity lies in respect of its practical value. Such a conclusion leads us to accept the truth of all forms of knowledge, and knowledge under any condition can never be conceived to be false. Knowledge of course is here concrete and its tendency is to reveal itself in its complete nature, as something that expresses its own object. Knowledge has always a reference to an object and is never free from it. If this be the ultimate character of knowledge, it can never be conceived as transcending relations. Knowledge is easentially relational consciousness and this relational consciousness can never be false. Knowledge is then always epistemological and logical, and since there is no distinction between truth and knowledge, truth ultimately becomes a logical reality. It can never transcend its logical nature it can never be super-logical.

Rāṅanuja's viewpoint

The first point that strikes us in the philosophy of Rāmānuja is his attitude and method of approach; and herein arises the fundamental difference between Śaṁkara and Rāmānuja. Rāmānuja's attitude has been essentially logical and though he claims the revelation of truth still his attempt has been essentially to bear out the intuitions by logical reason and to show the correspondence between intuition and reason. In Rāmānuja the apparent discord between reason and intuition has been set aside and it has been possible for him to show that intuition and reason give us the same truth. The fundamental points of difference between Śaṁkara and Rāmānuja arise out of the relation between reason and intuition. Rāmānuja does not find any conflict between the two, for in his case reason and intuition function in the same way: they are relational consciousness. Reason conceives, intuition perceives. Reason conceives relations, intuition perceives them. Both of them work in the same way. We may go far and say that intuition is a form of judgment, since intuition intuits.

The fundamental difference between Śaṁkara and Rāmānuja lies in their conception of intuition. In Śaṁkara intuition cannot be intuited, in Rāmānuja it can. Intuition is an accomplished fact in both Śaṁkara and Rāmānuja, for none can establish it. But in Rāmānuja this intuition is a unity and not an identity of consciousness and since it is unity, it is a fact involving a process within itself. A process implies a reference, intuition refers to itself and becomes self-intuitive.

This difference in the character of intuition has made the position of Rāmānuja fundamentally different from Śaṁkara. His position, therefore, has been more logical than psychological, for he cannot conceive of any state of consciou-sness where the logical self dies out in transcendental intuition. Knowledge is essentially judgment in any stage of consciousness. It does not matter whether the reference in judgment is self or something besides self.

Epistemology and metaphysics

The unique feature of Rāmānuja's system is his identification of the theory of knowledge with the theory of Being. Rāmānuja does not deviate from the chief Vedāntic principle that "whatever is, is consciousness." But he differs from Śaṁkara in conceiving of a dialectic necessity of expression in the metaphysical reality as well as in epistemological knowledge. Knowledge develops through a dialectic and it never denies a dialectic expression, be it finite knowledge or infinite knowledge. The more we understand our self-conscious life the more we approach towards the understanding of the infinite life and purpose, for between the finite and infinite there is no difference in nature although there may be difference in powers. Rāmānuja's is a completely logical principle and he in this respect is quite like Hegel and poles asunder from Bergson. The ultimate reality can be called energising reason, as distinguished from the a-logical principle of Bergson. And therefore there can be no gap between our epistemological thinking and metaphysical reality. For, if thinking has a law of its own in order to develop and build up a system of knowledge, this law cannot be essentially different from the way in which being expresses itself.

Epistemology therefore has greater importance in Rāmānuja than in Śaṁkara; for through it we can understand not only the inward nature of our self-conscious being but also the inward nature of the divine being. A clear understanding how knowledge does develop will throw a flood of light upon metaphysics.

The distinction of relative and absolute knowledge has not found a place in Rāmānuja in the sense of Śaṁkara. Śaṁkara has not been able to synthesise absolute knowledge with relative knowledge and he has therefore been led to deny relative truth and knowledge in the absolute. Such has not been the case with Rāmānuja. Rāmānuja has drawn no distinction between absolute and relative truth and absolute and relative knowledge in the sense in which Śaṁkara does. No doubt he accepts the distinction in another way, and calls knowledge relative when it is not seen in its full development and concreteness. An aspect of reality is no doubt relative if it is not seen in its place in the totality. Relative knowledge and truth therefore are partial and imperfect visions. They are partial and relative because the fuller vision and fuller appreciation of reality are still wanting. Popular knowledge is thus relative and imperfect, and so is scientific knowledge. But philosophic knowledge gives us the absolute truth and knowledge; for all the relations which knowledge implies are now seen in a completely unified system. Unity is truth. Presentations of diversity are imperfect presentations of truth. In Rāmānuja there is a persistent demand of thought developing this all-comprehensive unity and so long as it is done our knowledge may be relative or scientific but not philosophic or absolute.

Epistemology in Rāmānuja has philosophic significance and has not confined itself to popular realism or subjective idealism. It has not the tendency of denying the implication of subject and object nor of confining knowledge to this implication alone. It takes from realism the clear implication of the presentation of the object to the subject, and at the same time it moves towards a higher synthesis of the unity of subject and object in the same being, Śaṁkara, as has been already shown, has denied this unity of subject and object in a synthesis.

The epistemology of Śaṁkara, therefore, is true of relative consciousness; in Rāmānuja the epistemology is true of absolute consciousness. The difference between Śaṁkara and Rāmānuja arises from the nature of thinking. Rāmānuja agrees with Śaṁkara in accepting that the principal law of thinking is identity. Thought is anxious to establish identity though it may pass through distinctions and contradictions. Thought appears to contradict itself in order to make itself definite but this movement of thought is only temporary. The mere positing of a thing or an idea is a bare abstraction and thought is under a dialectic necessity to come out of this position and affirm an antithesis. This antithesis is a distinction which thought draws out in order to make the original position concrete and clear. But thought also cannot long remain in this attitude of keeping up distinctions without synthesising them in a higher integrity. It therefore by itself moves to a unity in which the distinctions of thesis and antithesis are assimilated.

Epistemology must take into consideration the principle according to which thought moves. The tendency of thought is to pass from abstract to concrete and make the bare notion of an indeterminate cognition definite and concrete. In Rāmānuja the tendency of thought is always to build up a concrete world of knowledge in which all the parts are unified in a system. But even in affirming this tendency of thought Rāmānuja has not lost sight of the importance of identity and has not recognised contradiction as a law of thought. Thought thinks in distinctions but never in contradictions. The distinctions which are apparently implicit are made explicit in the process and the whole which appears as a notion comes out as an idea. The necessity of thought is to build up a unity of system in which the parts are seen in the whole in their identity and distinctions. Rāmānuja thinks that when we perceive the whole we perceive a synthesised identity of existence. He differs from Śaṁkara in affirming that thought never embraces abstract identity; it only embraces a concrete identity. This dialectic of thinking is not present in Śaṁkara, inasmuch as he thinks that thought can think of identity but not of differences. The differences are illusive; and whenever logic wants to determine them they seem to involve contradictions and antinomies.

True to his epistemological theory Rāmānuja defines truth as that which appears in knowledge. Anything appearing before consciousness impresses it with its own existence and knowledge can hardly deny it. It is truth because it is a fact of experience.[12] Rāmānuja has offered a theory of error not from the epistemological standpoint but from a pragmatic standpoint. In this he seems to have drawn a distinction between reality and *actuality* and he thinks that all things are real which are objects of knowledge though all things are not *actual*. The falsity lies in *actuality* but not in reality. As a thing the false appearance is not false, for it has a theoretic existence but no practical usefulness. Here lies its falsity. It appears from this that according to Rāmānuja the ideal of truth lies in the unity of reality and actuality, for the ideal seems to be the complete agreement of knowledge and practice. Since this agreement is not to be found in all objects of experience, some are called true and some are called false. Error is, therefore, not logical for the correspondence of ideas to facts always remains, and is never violated. This correspondence is what marks out Rāmānuja' s theory of error from Śaṁkara's theory. According to Śaṁkara this correspondence is not always a fact, and therefore logical error is possible and is often the case. In Rāmānuja such possibility does not arise.

But purely from theoretical and epistemological standpoint, truth is, in Rāmānuja, a complete system, for knowledge is relational, and so long as knowledge does not develop the complete system within itself, it suffers from a limitation. Psychologically or logically a fact is true because it appears or there is a correspondence between our idea and a fact. We do not press the psychological or logical test further. But metaphysics cannot remain satisfied with this. It is anxious to see the whole network of knowledge spread out in a system and to apprehend the parts in the synthesis of the whole, and so long as this is not done it can hardly remain satisfied. Metaphysics, therefore, spins out a relational scheme of all forms of knowledge and tends to transcend division and partial presentations in a complete unity. From this standpoint we are forced to conceive even in Rāmānuja the distinction of truth and falsity. Truth is the full presentation of reality and falsity a partial presentation. The former is the function of philosophy, the latter of psychological knowledge. Epistemology, therefore, has an inherent urge to build up the whole system of knowledge and not to be satisfied with the psychological implication of the mutuality of subject and object. Since in Rāmāṇuja being is consciousness, the metaphysical theory is identical with epistemology, and epistemology must present the complete development of knowledge in a unified system, and must not be satisfied with the presentation of a partial aspect.

Determinate and indeterminate knowledge of Rāmānuja

Rāmānuja admits two forms of knowledge, *viz.*, *Nirvikalpa* and *Savikalpa,* indeterminate and determinate. But his theory of knowledge does not deny the subject-object reference in knowledge. Rāmānuja has no doubt drawn a distinction between indefinite and definite knowledge, but his indefinite cognition is not the bare sameness of consciousness apart from all distinctions.[13] Knowledge, to be knowledge', must possess a concreteness and definiteness. Indeterminate perception is the apprehension of an object as divested of certain forms of difference but not of all difference.[14] An object fully divested of all difference is impossible and cannot consequently be ever perceived. Consciousness takes notice of an object when the object is marked with certain characteristics, *i.e.*, apprehension becomes possible in and through certain points of distinction or difference. The true distinction between indeterminate and determinate perception is that the former is the apprehension of the first individual among a number of things belonging to the same class, while the latter is the apprehension of a second and a third individual and so on. On the perception of the first cow, for example, the perceiver is not conscious of the fact that the generic character of the class 'cow' extends also to this particular cow under investigation. The perception of the first cow therefore constitutes *Nirvikalpa* or indeterminate knowledge while the perception of the second or the third cow illustrates *Savikalpa* or determinate knowledge as in this case a comparison is made among cows. In the case of the second, and third individual, we apprehend, in addition to the thing possessing structure and to the structure itself, the special attribute of the persistence of the generic character, and hence the perception is determinate. From all this it follows that perception has never for its object that which is devoid of all difference.[15]

Nyāyapariśuddhi and *Tattvamuktākalāpa* of the *Viśiṣṭ ādvaita* School develop the idea more fully. They take the facts of experience and prove by an analysis of these facts that knowledge in its very first moment is also determinate. They use the term *Nirvikalpa* and interpret it in a more clear light. Whenever one perceives an object, the characteristics of the object flash out in the perceiver. He knows a cow and he is also conscious of the cowhood in the cow. This is *Nirvikalpa* knowledge. *Savikalpa* knowledge is the result of comparison and contrast and one is conscious only of cowhood in the cow and knows at the same time that there does not exist non-cowhood, *i.e.,* horsehood etc., in the cow.[16]

Knowledge of the first moment too cannot but be determinate and relational. The knowledge which forms a potent factor in our life is always characterised by some notions or previous ideas, and never transcends the subject-object reference.

Rāmānuja has an elaborate dialectic against Śaṁkara's conception of indeterminate cognition.

Rāmānuja's dialectic against Śaṁkara's non-differentiated indeterminate knowledge

According to Rāmānuja, there is no proof of non-differentiated consciousness. To enter into details, those who maintain the doctrine of one substance devoid of all difference have no right to assert that this or that is a proof of such a substance; for knowledge has for its object things affected with difference.[17] It is argued by the Śaṁkarites that such knowledge does not depend on proof but is due to one's own consciousness. This contention Rāmānuja holds to be unsatisfactory. All consciousness becomes possible only in and through distinction. All states of consciousness have for their object something that must be characterised by some point of difference. It is equally illustrated in the case of a judgment as well. For example, I form the judgment 'I see this pot.' The pot which stands as the object of judgment' is not devoid of all difference, on the other hand, it is perceived as having an individuality of its own when we say 'this.' The pot has not got mere being, but it has got certain characteristics of its own by virtue of which it becomes the object of apprehension. It is devoid of some points of difference in the sense that it is not perceived as belonging to a class nor does the knowledge of the pot result from comparison and contrast with other objects. In the very inception of the knowledge of the pot it is perceived in and through its own individual nature which stands as the mark that makes it conceivable. Hence this knowledge of the pot is not indeterminate but only devoid of some differences. Moreover, you yourself admit that to consciousness there actually belong different attributes such as permanency, oneness, self-luminousness, etc., and of these it cannot be shown that they are only being in general. And even if the latter point were admitted, we observe that there takes place a discussion of different views, and you yourself attempt to prove your theory by means of the differences between those views and your own. It must, therefore, be admitted that reality is affected with difference well established by valid means of proof.[18]

Śaṁkara holds that in the act of perception, we apprehend merely the being of objects *(sanmātragrāhi)* and not the different characteristics of the object that are due to recognition and inference. Difference is not the result of perception.

Rāmānuja points out the absurdity of this assertion. In perception, things are distinguished by their generic character. Generic character expresses its own nature as well as the object in which it inheres. Śaṁkarites also admit this characteristic of the relative terms. Knowledge reveals itself as well as its object simultaneously. Colour expresses its own nature and at the same time manifests the nature of the object in which it inheres. Similarly, difference, being a relative term, manifests itself as well as the thing that differs instantaneously. Even when perception takes place momentarily we apprehend within that very moment the generic character which constitutes on the one hand the difference of the thing in respect of others and on the other the particular characteristics of the thing itself. If perception reveals being only, then the particular judgments would be emptied of all meaning, *e.g.*, a man searching for a horse would be satisfied by finding a buffalo.[19]

Śaṁkara holds that consciousness is self-luminous but devoid of relations to objects. But Rāmānuja lays down that to think of consciousness as unrelated to objects is inconceivable. Such consciousness cannot be proved in any way. Moreover, consciousness is proved as self-luminous on the ground of its essential nature which consists in revealing its objects. If we deny this characteristic, we are bound to deny at the same time that consciousness is self-luminous. Therefore, consciousness has its meaning in and through the object which is revealed by consciousness. Again, if it be held that consciousness does not depend on its object for its apprehension, but is revealed by another consciousness, then we commit the fallacy of infinite regress and knowledge itself loses its own nature in so far as it fails to illuminate itself. Thus when we judge from our experience, we find that consciousness without its object can never be cognised. That consciousness in the state of deep sleep is without its object, is not experienced. That the knowledge in deep sleep is determinate is proved by a definite remembrance of experience in sleep, otherwise such knowledge as "I had a happy sleep" is impossible in the waking state.

Mādhva Epistemology

Mādhvites agree with Rāmānuja as regards the nature of knowledge. Both have held the synthetic and dynamic character of knowledge. This character of knowledge is revealed as a reality through differences subsisting between the subject and object which knowledge, as a synthetic activity, brings into unity. According to the Mādhvites knowledge is always relative. Even in its final stage, the stage of salvation or mukti, it is relative and never becomes absolute.[20]

Rāmānuja, Mādhva and the Grammarian Schools

It may be interesting to observe that the denial of indeterminate, non-relational knowledge on the part and the Grammarian of Rāmānuja and Mādhva is not altogether an original theory of their own. The Grammarian School long ago refuted the possibility of indeterminate cognition. Bhartṛhari in his monumental work, the Vākyapadīya, has taken elaborate pains to prove that knowledge is possible only through the use of words—nay, that word and knowledge are identical. This is but a logical consequence of the metaphysical doctrine that the whole universe is but a development from the eternal principle, *Śabdabrahman,* the eternal word which is the final reality.[21] Word and consciousness are the same thing, consciousness minus word is comparable to light without its illumination and since word refers to something beyond its own self and is thus by its constitution relational, all knowledge is therefore relational and determinate.[22] Even the primal cognition is a judgment and associated with verbal expression, though the verbal reference may be of a very general kind. Thus, though the particular verbal expression may not be known, the perceived object will at least be referred to in its most generic verbal character—*e.g.,* 'it is a substance or so.' But the full individuality is revealed when the specific word presents itself.[23]

Gaṅgeśa's viewpoint and his dialectic against those who deny indeterminate cognition

Gaṅgeśa, the founder of the Modern Bengal School of Logic, has entered into an elaborate polemic against those philosophers who deny the possibility of indeterminate apprehension *(nirvikalpakajñāna).* Gaṅgeśa divides perceptual knowledge into two categories,—indeterminate and determinate. He defines this indeterminate perception as a cognition which is devoid of association with name, class-concept, etc., and is thus unmodalised and incognisant of relation.[24] Gaṅgeśa, however, finds no evidence in favour of this cognition in empirical experience, nor in practical conduct, which is made possible by determinate experience alone.[25] But he contends that relational experience presupposes the previous knowledge of the terms out of relation, otherwise a determinate cognition cannot come into being.[26] Now a determinate cognition of cow is not cognisant of the individual alone, but is qualified and determined by the class-character, cowhood *(gotva).* This is a complex judgment constituted by three factors, the class-character *(gotva),* the individual cow and the relation *(vaiśiṣ ṭya)* which unifies the two into a judgment-whole. This complex judgment can be possible if there is a previous simple apprehension of the constituent terms out of relation. The contention of the theistic schools that all knowledge, the primal sensuous experience not excepted, is determinate and relational, is absurd, as it will inevitably lead to a *regressus ad infinitum.* For, a relational knowledge presupposes an independent knowledge of the *relata* and if this previous cognition is again determinate, that will require another determinate cognition and so on to infinity. So one has to postulate the existence of a previous non-relational, indeterminate cognition as the condition and *raison detre* of the determinate experience as a matter of logical necessity.[27] It is however worthy of remark that Gaṅgeśa is in full agreement with the theistic schools that there is no psychological evidence in favour of indeterminate experience, it being supra-sensuous and supra-mental *(atīndriya).* But he rightly insists that the existence of such knowledge is undeniable in deference to logical necessity—a position which is ignored or slurred over by the theistic philosophers to their cost. All other schools of philosophy, so far as our knowledge goes, have unanimously admitted the existence of indeterminate experience. The Buddhist and the Śaṁkarites emphatically hold that such experience is felt as much as determinate experience and so both psychological and logical evidence alike indubitably point to the existence of such experience. The denial of indeterminate experience by the schools of Rāmānuja and Mādhva is inspired by the metaphysical and religious doctrines to which they are committed. They deny the existence of simple, nonrelational and abstract being and this metaphysical commitment necessitates the denial of simple experience, which might prove the existence of a simple reality. The grammarians, who hold that word is the essence of consciousness, cannot but regard all knowledge as determinate and relational, being in separately mixed up with word-elements, which have invariably a reference to an *other.* We have seen that psychological evidence is not a strong point with them and logical evidence is decidedly against their epistemological position. Epistemological estimation should be based upon the testimony of psychology and logic and it is bound to err when metaphysical preconceptions are allowed to warp the epistemological vision.

Gaṅgeśa, after proving the necessity of a previous non-relational knowledge as the pre-condition of relational knowledge, proceeds to refute the possibility of this simple knowledge being supplied by means of sources of knowledge other than perception. Now, the primal determinate perception of the cow cannot be supposed to have been occasioned by a memory of the class-character 'cowhood,' which is found to enter into the composition of the determinate experience. Memory is possible if there is a previous perceptual experience at its back. But it being the first determinate experience and there being no previous perception of cowhood *(gotva)* memory has no *raison d'étre* of its own. Nor can it be supposed that this previous knowledge of cowhood was engendered in a past life and so memory takes place in the present life. Because such supposition has no logical necessity. Again, there is no possible stimulant for the memory-impression in question. To appeal to unseen destiny is a desperate attempt. If sense-contact with cowhood, which is admitted by the Naiyāyika as the cause of indeterminate perception of cowhood, be supposed to operate as the stimulant *(udbodhaka)* of the memory-impression, the *Naiyāyika* would urge that it is more logical to suppose that the knowledge of cowhood is caused by sense-object contact, which is admittedly the cause of perceptual knowledge in other cases, *e.g.*, of the individual cow. Because it is admitted on all hands that when the cause of perceptual knowledge and the cause of memory are identical, the resultant knowledge is perception and not memory.[28] If this dictum is not admitted, then the knowledge of eternal verities would always be memory and not perceptual experience, which is absurd.[29] In the case of eternal verities like Space and Time and the like we are acquainted with them every day and if memory would have precedence over perception, the knowledge of those categories would be memory alone. But this is opposed to experience. So memory cannot be requisitioned by the opponent as an explanation of the idea of cowhood. Moreover it is obvious that this shifting back to the past life for the explanation of common experience in this is neither sane nor helpful. Because, the difficulty is only pushed back and not solved by this subterfuge. It may be legitimately questioned whether the previous knowledge of cowhood in the past life is memory or simple experience *(anubhava)*. If the former is the case, then the difficulty remains as it is, or it will lead to the vicious infinite. If the latter alternative is conceded, we do not see any earthly reason why the possibility of such simple experience in this life should be denied. Gaṅgeśa however does not urge this objection perhaps because he thought it to be too obvious or that he thought that the opponent would regard this infinite regression as innocent like the infinite series of seed and sprout *(bījāṅkuranyāya)*. But Gaṅgeśa has emphatically pointed out that there is no logical ground for such unwarranted supposition, which rather complicates a simple issue.

To bring this discussion within the focus of Western thought, we find the same fierce controversy about the distinction of knowledge into Indeterminate and Determinate and the problems raised by it is a striking parallelism of thought between the Eastern and Western philosophers. That there is some form of indeterminate knowledge has been granted by Western thinkers under various names. James speaks of 'pure sensation,' Hobhouse of' a bare apprehension of the present, 'Kant expatiates on a 'pure manifold' and Lossky in his *Intuitive Basis of Knowledge* elaborates the conception of 'immediate experience or consciousness prior to the exercise of any discriminative activity.' Against this Prof. Dawes Hicks and others strongly maintain that "not even the crudest, vaguest consciousness of a content can be accounted for either psychologically or epistemologically without calling to our aid in the exposition the notion of a discriminative activity." According to Bradley also we have in the sensation of the blue colour a *that* which is actually present and a *what* or the peculiar quality by which it is distinguished and in *immediate apprehension* we are not conscious of the distinction between the two aspects. The Advaitins and Buddhists agree with Kant in holding the indeterminate state to be a pure manifold. The determinations *(vikalpas)* are extraneous and the manifold when schematised gives only phenomena. If according to Kant the manifold of sense arises as a result of the action of the things-in-themselves (Dinge an sich) which are different from the principle of consciousness, to the *Advaitins* the manifold is a determination in consciousness *(caitanyam)* due to *Adhyāsa* or illusory super-imposition conditioned by *Māyā*. Rāmānuja and the *Naiyāyikas* agree on the other hand with Hegel and his followers such as Bradley, Bosanquet, etc., in holding that in determinate perception there emerges nothing extraneous or adventitious except what has a prior implicit existence in the indeterminate state. If the indeterminate is something of which we are not directly conscious, it is a logical *prius* or indispensable background of determinate perception. While from the Hegelian standpoint this passage from the implicit to the explicit is itself something necessitated by the nature of the content, *i.e.*, the inner dialectic of the Idea, the *Naiyāyikas* hold that it is the relating activity of the thinker that makes this transition possible. Rāmānuja however differs from both in holding that this passage from the implicit to the explicit stage is due neither to the inner necessity of the content nor to the activity of the thinker but to the mediation of experience. The real difficulty about the existence of the indeterminate is that we cannot catch hold of it in a pure state. As Bradley points it, "the dilemma is that so far as I know of immediate experience, it does not exist, and that hence, whether it exists or not I could in neither case know of it." This is really what has induced Rāmānuja and others to deny it. But the fact remains to quote Bradley again that "there is an immediate feeling, a knowing and being in one, with which knowledge begins; and, though this in a manner is transcended, it nevertheless remains throughout as a present foundation of my known world." "If we have certainty anywhere," says Bradley, "this seems obvious we have certainty in feeling. Whatever else may be doubted, at least we know what we feel." This is why we also find Śaṁkara insisting on *anubhūti* as the highest court of appeal in our search for truth.

To sum up : The epistemological discussion so far has centred in the theories of knowledge as advanced by the Vedāntic teachers,

Śaṁkara, Rāmānuja and Mādhva. We have seen the fundamental differences between them. Rāmānuja and Mādhva have both denied indeterminateness in cognition, Śaṁkara has emphasised indeterminateness in cognition, though he has not gone like the Buddhists to the extreme of reducing all relations of subject and object to nothing. Śaṁkara has in transcendental intuition the denial of the subject and object theory of knowledge.

None will quarrel with Rāmānuja and Mādhva with their affirmation of subject-object theory, for it is a direct fact in experience and Śaṁkara will not differ from them in the characterisation of knowledge as involving the mutuality of subject and object. In this all teachers agree and cannot but agree, for a judgment is always an affirmation or negation of relation and cannot be non-relational.

The difference begins when the teachers come to determine the initial fact of knowledge, in other words, the minimum of knowledge or pure cognition. Śaṁkara holds that in this minimum the relational consciousness is neither explicit nor implicit. The datum of experience or judgment is not in the least affected by the subsequent judgment-construction, though the construction is made upon it. In other words Śaṁkara makes a distinction between the expression of Intuition and judgment-construction and does not find the link between them. To Śaṁkara the judgment-construction is more or less a demand of the empiric and pragmatic consciousness and here knowledge is not seen apart from its applicability to the practical affairs of life. Śaṁkara has had therefore to distinguish clearly between these constructions and intuition.

Rāmānuja and Mādhva identify knowledge with judgment-constructions and have not conceived knowledge independently of these constructions. Their position therefore appears more logical and with logical consistency they have made demands for the mutuality of subject and object and for a differentiating consciousness. No doubt they maintain stages where these are implicit and not explicit and knowledge appears as indeterminate.

But it is not really indeterminate. It is, in Hegelian term, notion. But a notion, however indeterminate it may appear, is always a differentiating factor. Rāmānuja and Mādhva have therefore identified the initial knowledge with perceptual synthesis. The absolute sameness of sensation is not to them knowledge, for they will ignore such an existence as not obtaining in concrete consciousness and characterise it as epistemologically non-existent.

The difference then between Śaṁkara and Rāmānuja and Mādhva begins here and this difference has caused the great divergence in their views and conception of life and experience. And, therefore, we must examine their contentions critically before we can pass an opinion on their theories.

A relational consciousness implies two terms and a relation. The knowledge of the relation is no doubt determinate, but the terms in their first apprehension cannot be held to be determinate, for determinateness is a characterisation and a comparison and these, are not possible in the inception of sense-perception. A concrete consciousness may be the demand of life, but this does not dispose of the existence of the initial cognition. Apprehension simple and pure is pre-supposed in thought-construction, as its datum. Now this apprehension, so long as it is an apprehension, cannot but be indeterminate. The criticism of Mādhva that the characterisation of undividedness and homogeneity will make knowledge determinate is not to the point, for this characterisation is also a judgment-construction which only attempts at a clear conception of the apprehensions, but is no differentiation of it. It is also an approach to it in the form of negative judgments, as an indication in concrete consciousness, but not a characterisation of the simple apprehension.

Śaṁkara has drawn a distinction between apprehension and knowledge, and so far as knowledge is concerned he does not differ much from the theistic teachers. Therefore we find in his system implications of relative consciousness and of the value and progress of such a life. This is more or less a pragmatic demand and satisfaction which requires a pragmatic theory of knowledge.

Śaṁkara appears to have held that the entire judgment construction is the demand of life and the fallacies and antinomies of relative consciousness are not detected so long as consciousness is dominated by pragmatic demands and thought unceasingly creates concrete universes to satisfy the demand of the divided life and consciousness. Thought is an instrument of divided consciousness and cannot conceive its own destruction by accepting the indeterminate consciousness. So long therefore as the empiric consciousness dominates us, the assertion of Śaṁkara of an indeterminate Being and knowledge seems to be an idle assertion. But the fact remains that simple apprehension is not thought activity nor a judgment, construction, and this cannot be explained away. This psychological minimum is a puzzle to Rāmānuja and Mādhva. In denying it they do not explain the problem, but rather take protection in subterfuges which have no clear meaning. And the fact should not be ignored that Śaṁkara in denying the empirical duality is conscious of a transcendence in intuition and knowledge which does not come under the ordinary logic. Śaṁkara's logic has two forms : *(i)* empirical and *(ii)* transcendental. When the transcendental consciousness dawns upon us the reality of empiric consciousness assumes an ideal character. The construction which appears so long as real now appears as ideal. This transcendental intuition modifies the logic of realistic consciousness by the higher logic, the organon of super-consciousness. Philosophy in its final judgment must abide by the intuition of transcendent consciousness.

REFERENECES

1. Sāvadyatarka-parityāgena niravadyastarkaḥ pratipattavyo bhavati.
—S. B., 2. 1. 11.

2. (a) Aparīkṣita-pratyakṣaṁ hi parikṣitānumānāpekṣayā durbalam. nīlaṁ nabha iti pratyakṣamiva nabho nīrūpatvānumānāpekṣayā.—Ad. S., pp. 369-70 (Bombay Edition).

   (b) Pratyakṣāderhi parīkṣayā vyavahārika-prāmāṇyamātraṁ sidhyati, tacca nādvaitāgamena bādhyate, bādhyate tu tāttvikaṁ prāmāṇyam.
—*Ibid,* p. 374.

   (c) Tātparyavatī śrutiḥ pratyakṣād balavatī.—Bh., 1.1.1.

3. *Vide* Ad. S., pp. 652-684 (Bombay Edition).

Ibid, pp. 648-51.

4. Nābhāvo nāma bhāvādanyaḥ kaścidasti, api tu bhāva eva bhāvāntarātmanā abhāvaḥ svarūpeṇa tu bhāvaḥ; yathāhuḥ "Bhāvāntaramabhāvo hi kayācittu vyapekṣayā" iti.

—Bh., p. 22 (Bombay Edition).

5. (a) Nahi jñānaṁ jñeyasaṁbaddhameva prakāśakam atiprasaṅgāt, nāpi svasaṁbaddham, ātmasvarūpasya tadguṇasya vā jñānasya jñeyena saṁbandhasyābhāvāt.

—Ad. S., pp. 453-64.

(*b*) *Vide* S. B., p. 6

(*c*) *Vide* P. D., sls. I. 50, 52.

6. This is the position of Prakāśānanda Sarasvatī.
7. The method of refutation of Samavāya relation will be fully (shown later on. *Cp.* Bradley, Appearance and Reality, pp. 28-32.
8. (a) Yugapad-grahaṇāyogādanavasthā-prasaṅgataḥ
Parasparāśrayatvācca dharmabhede'pi nākṣadhīḥ.

—Cit., p. 168 (Bombay Edition).

(*b*) *Vide* P. D., sl. I. 52.

9. *Cp.* Kant's famous distinction between phenomenal and noumenal knowledge (Critique of Pure Reason).
10. (a) Satyatvaṁ bādharāhityam.—P. D. 3.29.

(b) Anadhigatābādhitārthaviṣayaka-jñānatvaṁ pramātvam.

— V. P., p. 15 (C. U. Edn.).

(c) Abādhitā svayaṁprakāśitaiva sattā, sā ca svarūpameva cidātmanaḥ.—Bh., p. 25 (Bom. Edn.).

(*d*) *Vide* Ad. S., p. 193 (Bombay Edition).

11. (a) Tāsāṁ trivṛtamekaikāmiti śrutyaiva coditaṁ Śrutyaiva darśitā tasmāt sarve sarvatra saṁgatāḥ.

-R. Bh., p. 183 (Bombay Edition).

(6) Marīcikā-jalajñāne tejaḥ-pṛthivyorapyambuno vidyamānatvād indriyadoṣ eṇaṁ tejaḥ-pṛthivyoragrahaṇād adṛṣṭavaśāccāmbuno grahaṇād yathārthatvam. *Ibid,* p. 187.

This problem is fully discussed the "Epistemology of Illusion."

12. R. Bh., pp. 83-86 (Narasiṁhācārya's Edition).
13. Nirvikalpakamapi saviśeṣaviṣayameva, savikalpake svasminnanu bhūtapadārtha-pratisamdhānahetutvāt.

—B. Bh., p. 73, Bombay Edn.

14. Nirvikalpakam nāma kenacid viśeṣeṇa viyuktasya grahaṇaṁ na sarvaviśeṣ arahitasya; tathābhūtasya kādācidapi grahaṇādarśanād anupapatteśca.

—B. Bh., p. 73, Bombay Edition.

15. *Ibid,* p. 73.
16. Ny. P., p. 82; T. M. K., p. 53.
17. Nirviśeṣavastuvādibhiḥ nirviśeṣe vastuni idaṁ pratmāṇamiti na śakyate vaktum; saviśeṣavastuviṣayatvāt sarvapramāṇānām.

—R. Bh., p, 70, Bombay, Edition.

18. Svābhyupagatāśca nityatvādayo hyanekaviśeṣāh santyeva, te ca na vastumātramiti śakyopapādanāḥ; vastumātrābhyupagame satyapi vidhā-

bhedavivādadarśanāt; ataḥ prāmāṇikaviśeṣaih viśiṣṭameva vastviti vaktavyam.

—R. Bh., pp. 71-72, Bombay Edn.

19. R. Bh., p. 74.
20. Na ca jñātṛjñeyarahitaṁ jñānaṁ kvāpi dṛṣṭam.

—Viṣṇutattvanirṇaya.

Madhva epistemology is a chapter by itself, and a detailed discussion is impossible within these limits. We notice here only its agreement with the school of Rāmānuja as regards the subject-object reference in knowledge.

21. Anādinidhanaṁ Brahma śabdatattvaṅ yadakṣaram,
Vivartate'rtha bhāvena prakriyā jagato yataḥ.

—Vāk. P., Ch. 1. 1.

22. Vāgrūpatā cedutkrāmed avabodhasya śāśvatī,
Na prakāśaḥ prakāśeta sā hi pratyavamarśinī.

—*Ibid, 1,* 1. 125.

23. Yo'pi prathamanipātī bāhyeṣvartheṣu prakāśo viśeṣa nimittāparigrahe 'pi vastumātra idaṁ taditi pratyavabhāsayati vāgrūpatāyāñca satyam utpanno'pi prakāśo viśeṣavāgrūpam asvīkurvan prakāśakriyāsādhanatāyāṁ na vyavatiṣ ṭhate.

—P,C. on the Vākyapadīya, 1. 1. 12.

An elaborate discussion of the *Śabdabrahma-theory* of the grammarian school will not be relevant in the present context. The philosophy of Bhartṛhari however is remarkable for its originality and boldness. The gentle reader who may be interested to know further details, is referred to the original work, specially the first chapter entitled Brahmakāṇḍa of the Vākyapadīya and Puṇyarāja's Commentary, the Prakāśa thereon.

24. Tacca pratyakṣaṁ dvividhaṁ, nirvikalpakaṁ savikalpakaṁ ceti, tatra nāmajātyādiyojanārahitaṁ vaiśiṣṭyānavagāhi niṣprakārakaṁ nirvikalpakam

—Nirvikalpavāda.—T. C., p. 809, Bibliotheca Indica Series.

25. Na pratyakṣam asiddheḥ, atīndriyatvābhyupagamāc ca, na ca vyavahāraḥ, tasya savikalpasādhyatvāt.

— T,C., p, 809.

26. Gaur iti pratyakṣaṁ jñānaṁ janyaviśeṣaṇajñāna-janyaṁ janya-viśiṣṭajñānatvāt.

—T. C., p. 817.

27. Na ca tad viśiṣṭajñānam eva, tatrāpi viśeṣaṇajñānāpekṣāyām anavas thāpatter ity ālocanasiddhiḥ.

—T. C., p. 814.

Gaṅgeśa here remarkably anticipates modern neo-realistic thought in the West as exemplified in Russell, Perry, and others.

28. Ya eva gotvendriyasannikarṣastava nirvikalpake hetuḥ sa eva saṁskārodbodhaka iti cet, tarhi atra kḷptakāraṇa-bhāvād gotvendriyasannikarṣād gotvānubhava eva syāt, smaraṇasāmagrīto nubhavasāmagryā balavattvāt.

—T. C., p. 819.

29. Yadi cānubhavasāmagrītaḥ smaraṇaṁ, tadā nityānām vaidikārthā nāñ ca smaraṇam syān na tu anubhavaḥ.

—T. C., p. 819.

CHAPTER 2

SELF-LUMINOSITY OF KNOWLEDGE

Knowledge in the Advaita-Vedānta is held to be self-luminous and self-valid. Knowledge is self-luminous because it reveals its own existence as soon as it is born. Had it been otherwise there would be a doubt, or error or certitude of its non-existence. But even to an inquisitive mind such things are not seen to happen. Nobody doubts whether he has a particular knowledge or not when that knowledge originates. In the case of such objects of knowledge as pot and the like the fact of their existence is liable to doubt or misconception. So the absence of this contingency puts knowledge in an altogether different category from these material objects which depend for the revelation of their existence upon their relevant knowledge.[1] Our very experience, therefore, carries indisputable proof of the self-luminosity of knowledge.[2] The Naiyāyikas, however, have sought to explain the absence of doubt and error with reference to the existence of knowledge on the ground that knowledge, whenever it is born, is cognised by an act of introspection *(anuvyavasāya)* which certifies its existence.[3] But this only shifts the difficulty to this introspection itself. Well, the question arises, whether this introspection certifies its own existence or requires another introspection for this? If the former alternative is conceded the Naiyāyika gives up his own position. The Naiyāyika maintains that all existents are objects of knowledge and as such their existence is proved by knowledge only. Knowledge too being an existent fact has also got to have its existence certified by another knowledge. But if introspective knowledge is believed to be self-certified then the above position is surrendered and there is nothing to prevent the extension of this self-evident character to any and every instance of knowledge. So it must be held by the Naiyāyika that introspective knowledge is incompetent to prove its own existence. And in the absence of such proof existence is liable to doubt and error. Such being the case, how can you put absolute reliance on introspection as proof of knowledge when the former's own existence is open to doubt. The consequence would be that knowledge, too, for the proof of whose existence introspection was called into requisition, would become equally liable to doubt or error. And this contingency cannot be avoided even if three or four steps in the process of introspection are admitted, because in the case of the last introspection again the same difficulty would arise.[4] None of these difficulties arises if knowledge is regarded as self-illuminative, that is to say, if its own existence is believed to be self-evident. If, on the contrary, knowledge is not believed to be capable of revealing its own existence and if it is thought to be dependent on another distinct knowledge for the revelation of its existence, the consequence will be a vicious infinite series and so no knowledge would be possible. The existence of a thing is revealed by knowledge and if this knowledge again is unrevealed and so would have a doubtful existence, it cannot be conceived how this knowledge would serve as proof of the existence of the object. The proof of any thing must not be liable to doubt, otherwise its probative value would be doubtful. Thus knowledge being the proof of an object's existence must be free from doubt and error. And this can be possible if knowledge is believed to be self-evident. The multiplication of instances of knowledge would serve only to add to our embarrassment if each and every instance of knowledge is believed to be incompetent to prove its own existence and thus be made dependent on another.[5]

The Naiyāyikas here argue that the entire charge of the Advaitins, that the vicious infinite would be inevitable if knowledge is made dependent on another knowledge, is without foundation. If we (Naiyāyikas) held that all knowledge must be cognised by a subsequent knowledge then the charge could be brought home against our position. But such is not believed to be the case. We maintain that the cognition may remain uncognised and still reveals its object. The revelation of an object is not dependent upon the revelation of the knowledge which is assumed by the Advaitins without any reason. It may be urged that knowledge must be cognised by an introspection as the causal factors necessary for such introspection are present intact. Well, the Naiyāyikas postulate that the cause of introspection is the contact of the mind with the soul in which the particular knowledge inheres. Now this condition is present in full and there is nothing to prevent the introspection *(anuvyavasāya)* from coming into being. But this objection, the Naiyāyikas rejoin, is futile. Because the presence of the causal factor does not guarantee the emergence of the effect. The cause becomes operative only when there is no obstructive element *(pratibandhaka)* to frustrate the causal operation. In the case of prospective knowledge of introspection there it may be an obstruction from other factors, for instance, there may be presentation of a new perceptual datum or the rise of pleasure or pain which would divert the mind from its original objective. So there is no restriction that knowledge must necessarily be cognised as we have proved that knowledge may function even remaining itself uncognised. What is wanted for the revelation of the object is the mere existence of the knowledge concerned and not the cognition of the knowledge as well.[6]

The Advaitins urge in reply that this assertion of an unproved knowledge is only an *ipse dixit* which cannot be accepted unless independent proofs are advanced in its favour. In the absence of such proofs the existence of such knowledge is a matter of doubt, and it can be asserted, on the contrary, that such knowledge does not exist. The existence of an entity is attested by an independent proof and when such proofs are lacking and the existence is only dogmatically asserted the opponent can equally assert its non-existence. Likewise the existence of the knowledge at issue has got to be proved on the evidence of another knowledge and this would necessitate a *regressus ad infinitum.* If the existence of a proof could be accepted without regard to its own proof then the existence of a pot also could be asserted with equal disregard of all proofs.[7] The result will be that logical procedure will be rendered absolutely futile and nugatory. No evidence can therefore be advanced for the existence of an unknown knowledge which is made the corner-stone of the Nyāya epistemology. It has been argued by the Naiyāyikas that general evidence is not lacking though specific evidence in all cases of knowledge is not sought after. The existence of knowledge is revealed to us when there is an enquiry about it. The existence of the knowledge before the enquiry is made, remains unknown and unattested. On the analogy of such unattested knowledge the existence of other cases of unattested knowledge is inferred. And this inference by reason of its universal reference carries its own proof also. But this contention of the Naiyāyika is opposed to the testimony of experience. We could admit the validity of such inferences if we had even a single experience of a series of knowledge-instances in which each succeeding knowledge would have for its content all previous instances of knowledges with their respective contents. As a matter of fact our experiences are of the form 'this is a pot' and I know this pot, and no further knowledge is known by us which could be pressed by the Naiyāyikas as evidence of the aforesaid experiences. And even if it had been possible this would inevitably give rise to an infinite series. The contention of the Naiyāyikas, that the presence of other perceptual data cuts short this process, is equally hollow and unsubstantial; because the mind could not be diverted from this process of infinite knowledge making for the attestation of the previous knowledges. The Naiyāyikas however have urged that this contingency would occur in the case of any and every instance of cause and effect. The effect must have its cause and this cause again would have a further cause and that again another and so without end. This sort of infinite regression is not a fault, because it could arise only if there be such a series of enquiries which however are absolutely redundant. The Advaitins point out that the analogy here is not on all fours. The infinite series of enquiries about the cause and effect does not arise because there is no doubt about this causal relation ever coming to a cessation. If this break in the causal series could be possible the effect in question would have been uncaused and so would have been either eternally present or eternally non-existent. But no such *a priori* absurdity affects the question of infinite series in regard to knowledge. The series of knowledge instances is certainly causally determined and if it breaks down at any particular instance of knowledge then the last knowledge would become impossible without its cause, so retrospectively it would entail the absurdity of all previous instances. If to avoid this contingency it is presumed that a particular knowledge is cognisant of all knowledge-instances in general we, the Advaitins, would ask, is this knowledge cognisant of its own self? If so, it would become self-luminous which is our position. If it is believed to be cognised by another it would lead to the vicious infinite, and if it is held to be uncognised and unattested it would fail to serve as evidence of the previous series.

Moreover the contention of the Naiyāyikas, that knowledge is cognised by another knowledge when there is an enquiry about it, is an assumption which does not save it from the charge of the vicious infinite. Enquiry about anything is possible only if there is a previous knowledge of it. But how could this previous knowledge be possible if the knowledge in question is not believed to be self-evident. If this previous knowledge is held to be caused by another knowledge this would cause a rearward infinite series. If the knowledge about a knowledge is held to be caused by the influence of the latter without there being an enquiry this would lead to an infinite regress in the forward order,[8] All these contingencies however are avoided if knowledge is believed to be self-luminous and self-evident as held by the monistic teachers.

The monistic conception of self-illumination has been challenged by the Naiyāyikas on the ground that a logical determination of self-luminosity *(svaprakāśatva)* is an impossibility because, as they contend, the concept cannot give us any definite idea. The author of the *Tattvapradīpikā* has set forth a number of definitions of the concept of self-luminosity *(svaprakāśatva)* which, in our judgment, seem to be different landmarks in the history of the evolution of the concept. These definitions are not to be regarded as mere scholastic elaborations having little philosophical interest. There is good reason, on the other hand, to believe that these definitions, despite their scholastic appearance, really represent the development of the dialectic movement of philosophical thought in course of which the status and function of consciousness in relation to the objective reality were brought to a focus. The problem is one of absorbing interest and has a profound value in its bearing on the philosophical issues. We propose to examine the different conceptions that have been discussed by Citsukhācārya, one of the greatest dialecticians in the Śaṁkara-Vedānta, and shall assess their philosophical value.

Self-luminosity defined

Now what is the import of the concept of self-luminosity? It may be conceived to consist in the union of existence and illumination. In other words, we shall regard a thing to be self-luminous if we have reason to believe that illumination constitutes its very being and nature.[9] Objects of our empiric knowledge have existence of their own, but as they lack the character of illumination they cannot be thought to be self-luminous or *svaprakāśaḥ*. Knowledge, on the other hand, combining in itself both existence and illumination thus alone becomes fit to be characterised as self-luminous. This conception of self-luminosity however would be futile. For the Naiyāyikas to whom knowledge is cognised by introspection *(anuvyavasāya),* do not deny the fact that knowledge has its own existence as well as illumination though not caused by itself. And the definition would obliterate the line of demarcation between the concept of *auto-illumination (svapra-kāśatva)* as held by the Vedāntists and that of *alter-illumination (para-prakāśatva)* as maintained by the Naiyāyikas.

Now this conception of self-luminosity may be so modified as to avoid this absurd issue and this can be done if the illumination in question is regarded as caused by its own self. To be explicit, we should regard that alone to be self-luminous, the illumination of which is caused by its own self and not by an *alter.*[10] But even this modification would not make the concept of self-luminosity free from objections, because it makes consciousness both its subject and its object—both cogniser and the cognised—which is evidently absurd, as the same thing cannot be regarded as the subject and the object in the same reference. The subject *(kartṛ)* is what exercises a function and the object is that on which an effect is produced by the operation of the subject. The operation must exist in a thing which is distinct from the object operated upon. The carpenter converts a piece of timber into a table by exercising an operation, which is found in the carpenter and not in the timber which is operated upon, nor in the table which is the resultant product. The timber is the object because the effect, namely, a transformation of the shape, is induced on it by virtue of an operation which inheres in another distinct entity, *viz.*, the carpenter.[11] So to make the same thing the subject and object is logically absurd because it splits up an identity into two opposed factors, which is against the law of identity.

This absurdity has been sought to be avoided by a further amendment. Knowledge, it is contended, is self-luminous because it is not lighted up by any homogeneous illuminating factor.[12] Thus a lamp might be called *svaprakāśaḥ* or self-luminous because it is not illuminated by any other illuminating factor which may form the same class with the lamp. Cognition too is self-luminous, because according to the theory of the monists cognition is cognised neither by its own self nor by any after-cognition or *anuvyavasāya*.

The qualifying adjunct *sajātīya* (homogeneous) is of vital importance as it serves to make the definition precise and definite, excluding the possibility of extending its application to the Naiyāyika view of cognition, for *prakaśa* without *sajātīya* may mean both material and intellectual illumination. If the former sense is accepted, the Naiyāyika cognition revealed by the after-cognition and not-by any material illumination would come under the definition.

Criticism

This definition has been seriously challenged by the critics who argue that this very adjunct would prove suicidal, for the definition would then apply to the lamp, etc., which is admittedly not self-luminous according to the Advaitin. The lamp is revealed by knowledge which is not homogeneous with the inert lamp. If, however, the definition were without the adjunct there would be no question of extension to the lamp because *prakāśa* then might mean intellectual illumination by which it is revealed. Thus the Advaitin is in a logical seesaw, the definition with or without the adjunct *sajātīya* being absurd.

These difficulties led the Advaitins to further modify their conception of self-luminosity and the result was a new formulation. Knowledge is called self-luminous because, when it arises, it never remains unmanifested.[13] According to Advaitins knowledge is called *jñātasattāka* or something whose existence is always known and never remains unknown. That knowledge exists but remains unmanifested, is a position which has been denied by the Advaitins. It is also a common experience that knowledge reveals itself to its knower at the very moment it originates. No sane knower argues that he has knowledge but it is not manifested to him.

This new formulation however is also faulty for it is applicable to pleasure, pain and other feelings which never remain unmanifested to the persons who feel them.

This difficulty is sought to be avoided thus. "What does not form the object of knowledge is called self-luminous."[14] Pleasure, pain, similar other feelings and the lamp, the sun, and all other physical illuminations being objects of empiric knowledge cannot be characterised as *jñānāviṣaya* and claimed to be self-luminous.

It might however be argued that in avoiding the defects of the previous formulations which it successfully does to a great extent this new formulation creates an impossible position for the Advaitins as it takes away the only ground from under their feet. How could knowledge be *aviṣaya* or incapable of being an object of knowledge, seeing that this very thesis has to be established by inference and authority, etc., thereby making it at least the subject (object) of such discussion?

To obviate such an obvious criticism, a little modification might be introduced by saying that self-luminous character may be ascribed to "what is subject to *vyavahāra* or empiric usage while at the same time is not an object of knowledge."[15]

The latter part of the definition as already explained simply means that knowledge itself is not an object of knowledge like other ordinary objects such as the pot, cloth, etc. And by the first part '*vyavahāra-viṣayatvam*' it is merely implied that the logical judgment in the form "knowledge is self-luminous" is capable of being logically proved, *i.e.*, subject to inference and other proofs like other logical judgments.

This however affords no real escape from the difficulties of the position, for the admission of its being subject to logical criticism means no more than that it is subject to inference and other proofs which are not other than knowledge.

Again, this position is suicidal, because it is inapplicable to the case of Brahman, the Highest Consciousness, which being beyond all logical determinations cannot be characterised by *vyavahāra-viṣayatva* or subject to the usages. For all usages cease and limitations are negated, reasonings or *tarka* are denied at the dawn of super-consciousness.

The final solution

In order to meet the criticisms that have been levelled by the Naiyāyikas, the Advaita-Vedānta defines finally the self-illuminative character of knowledge as follows :

"Though incapable of being an object of knowledge, yet possessing competence for perceptual use."[16]

Even this elaboration of the concept might be made the target of criticism. For this would be inapplicable to Brahman, the final consciousness, which is beyond all determination and therefore also all usage. To avoid this, the Advaitin has to take a roundabout course in order to explain the definition so as to make it applicable also to Final Consciousness. Following the well-known Nyāya method of explanation by negations, he takes the phrase *aparo-*

kṣavyavahārayogyatvam or 'capability of perceptual usage' not in its apparent ordinary positive sense but in a technical sense to imply or connote "what would be the non-receptacle *(anadhi-karaṇa)* of eternal and absolute negation *(atyantābhāva)* of the capability of perceptual usage."[17] Thus by use of two negations the Advaitin seeks to apply it to both empirical and transcendental or absolute consciousness. It is of course clear that empiric knowledge has capability of perceptual usage, but can the same thing be said of transcendental consciousness? Evidently it cannot be said that absolute knowledge has this capacity as empiric knowledge has it. Now if 'capability of perceptual usage' be absent in Final Consciousness, it logically follows that the absolute negation *(atyantābhāva)* of the' capability of perceptual usage' would be there and the critic's charge of a 'too narrow' definition would stand unassailable. But 'absolute negation' truly construed means that it is eternal *(nitya)* and therefore it can never reside in any locus where its counterpart or *pratiyogi* can be found at any stage or in any form. The Naiyāyika vindication of the definition of Substance or *dravya* as essentially a seat of qualities *(guṇavatva)* illustrates it. The Naiyāyikas define the substance as the seat of properties, but they admit that at the time of origination, there is no quality or property attached to substance; and the definition would become 'too narrow' as it would not cover the case of substance at the time of origination. To avoid this difficulty, they too have to maintain that 'the seat of property,' the essential mark of substance, implies the "non-location of the absolute negation of the seat of properties,"[18] thereby making the definition applicable to substance both at the time of origination and thereafter : for though at the time of origination there was no quality in a substance, its absolute negation was not also there; since absolute negation means eternal negation in the locus of its counterpart, and eternality or absoluteness attributed to negation means that its counterpart or *pratiyogi* is to be found in the locus at no time or stage.[19] For example, there is absolute negation of form in the air because at no time and under no circumstances, is there any form in air, *i.e.*, air is eternally formless.

The expression *avedyatva* or unknowability has been introduced as a qualifying epithet to the second condition to exclude pot and such other things which may form the objects of perceptual usages. They being the objects of our empiric cognitions cannot come within the scope of *avedyatva.* Now the critic may return to the charge and say how it is possible to speak of Super-consciousness as *avedya?* For in the admission of the Advaita-Vedānta the self-luminous knowledge forms the object of authority or verbal cognition. *Āgama* or scriptural testimony is the only source to realise the true nature of the Absolute, Pure Being-Bliss-Consciousness. The highest being or Brahman has been characterised as *aupaniṣada, i.e.,* the reality cognisable through the *Upaniṣad* texts which only can vouchsafe unto us the truths of revelation. And no knowledge in Vedānta, empiric or intuitional, can be marked as self-luminous or *svaprakāśa,* as all forms of knowledge came under the scope of *vedya* or knowable. Hence to avoid the suicidal character of the definition the expression *avedyatva* should be taken in a technical sense. It means *phalavyapyatvābhāna,*. *Phala* implies the result of the definite functioning of the psychosis or mental process in the immediate cognition; and the mental process functions in revealing objects of cognition in its due vividness. *Phalavyāpyatvābhāva* is a negative mark which denies the determinate or definite mental functioning necessitated in the immediate cognitive process. Psychosis or *vṛtti* in the Advaita-Vedānta works definitely and indefinitely. In the case of concrete objects it is definite and determinate but in the case of the Absolute it is undefined and indeterminate. The former called *phalavyāpya* and the latter is called *vṛttivyāpya* in the is Vedāntic terminology, or, in other words, a concrete object is characterised as *phalavyāpya* and Brahman is known as *vṛttivyāpya.*

To put it more clearly, a perceptual process in the Advaita-Vedānta implies the identity of the percipient-consciousness *(pramātṛcaitanya)* with the object-consciousness *(viṣayacaitanya).* The object-consciousness is the locus of the object and directly reveals it. The immediate knowledge of the object to the subject supposes that the percipient-consciousness must acquire an identity with the object-consciousness.

"The external perception is marked by the *antaḥkaraṇa* going out through the senses. The outgoing *antaḥkaraṇa* soon gets the form cf the object. This transformation is called *vṛtti*. *Vṛtti* is a psychosis which acquires a definiteness due to the functioning of mental consciousness according to a mould and form. Consciousness in that determinate form removes the ignorance and establishes the identity of the percipient and object consciousness." It is called *phala* in the determinate perceptual process. Advaita-Vedānta recognises three aspects of consciousness and their identity in perception. *Pramātṛcaitanya* is the subject-consciousness, *Viṣayacaitanya* is the object-consciousness and *Vṛtticaitanya* is the consciousness immanent in the psychological process. "*Antaḥkaraṇa* is a dynamic entity and is unceasingly active in receiving the forms of objects. It goes out through the sense channels and is engrafted on a thing and takes impression of the object. "Revelation of objects to the percipient subject is called *phalavyāpyatva* in the Advaita-Vedānta. The negation of such a *phalavyāpyatva* is evident enough in the case of objects of past and future and of unperceivable things, *e.g.*, merits, demerits, etc., as in those cases the outgoing of *antaḥkaraṇa* through the sense channels is not possible because all those objects lie beyond the range of our senses; and identity of the three aspects of consciousness is also impossible. As a result the definition of self luminous knowledge characterised by *phalavyāpyatvābhāva* connoted by the expression *avedyatva* in no way extends to the objects beyond the class defined.

The Advaitins further observe that the self-luminous character of knowledge is a logically valid concept which might also be established by proofs *(pramāṇas)*. And what is established by proofs must have some essential characteristics which are set forth in the definition. The function of definition is to point out the essential features of the things defined and to classify them on the basis of their essentials. It is therefore clear that if the Advaitic category under discussion is established by proofs *(pramāṇas)* it can also be logically defined. But the proofs advanced by the monistic teachers, have strongly been criticised by the Naiyāyikas. To appraise the value of their arguments we should give an account of the dialectics used by the rival schools of philosophy.

Advaitin's inference to prove self-luminosity

The Advaitins advance the following syllogism in their favour. "Consciousness is self-luminous because it possesses the characteristic '*anubhūtitva.*' And what does not possess this characteristic '*anubhūtitva*' is not characterised as self-luminous or *'svaprakāśa,' e g.,* the pot.[20] Or in other words :

(A) all self-luminous things are possessing the characteristic *anubhūtitva.*

(E) No pots are possessing the characteristic *anubhūtitva.*

(E) No pots are self-luminous.

The syllogism may be explained thus : (1) *pratijñā* or proposition or the thesis to be established is : consciousness is self-luminous, (2) *hetu* or the reason is : because it possesses the characteristic "*anubhūtitva,*" (3) *udāharaṇa* or explanatory example is the pot *(yathā ghaṭaḥ).* Examples may be homogeneous or affirmative or '*sādharmya*' where the property to be proved and the ground *(hetu)* are present, and heterogeneous or negative *(vaidharmya)* where the property to be proved and the ground are both absent. In the syllogism under discussion all positive instances come under the scope of the minor or '*pakṣa*' and this is why there is no concrete positive illustration to be cited to prove the co-presence of the major or the property to be proved and the middle or the ground. As the syllogism is purely negative in its character only the negative instance is shown to prove the co-presence of the *'hetu'* and '*sādhya'* on the basis of the negative dialectic patent enough in the proposition *'yannaivaṁ tannaivam'* or whatever does not possess the characteristic '*anubhūtitva*' is not to be called '*svaprakāśa*' or self-luminous, (4) *Upanaya* or application: It asserts the presence or absence of the ground in the *'paksa'* or minor. In the former case it is affirmative and in the latter it is negative, '*upanaya*' or application is evident in the judgment '*tathā ceyam*' or so is this consciousness. Because consciousness possesses the characteristic '*anubhūtitva*' it is self-luminous. (5) The statement of conclusion is called *nigamana*. *Nigamana* restates the proposition as grounded. What is tentatively put forth in the proposition or '*pratijñā*' (the first member of the syllogism) is established in the conclusion.

The Naiyāyikas' objections

This syllogistic argument, the Naiyāyikas point out, is vitiated by a number of fallacies. The syllogism involves a dilemma whose two horns or poles are rendered faulty by the two fallacies—*siddhasādhanatā* and *sādhyāprasiddhi*. The Naiyāyikas ask whether the prior conception of the major or *sādhya* is a necessary element in the Advaitic inference? If the monistic teachers are positive in their answer, the major or *sādhya* being an attribute in its nature cannot stand by itself; it must be located in a substance. Conception of an attribute without its substrate or location is an absurdity. To be logical one has to admit that the attribute *(dharma) (svayaṁprakāśatva)* or self-luminosity—the major of the Advaitic syllogism—resides in a capable *(yogya)* substratum which may be characterised by such an attribute. Consciousness or *anubhūti* is the only possible substratum where this attribute is ascertained *(niścita)*. As a result the existence of the major in the minor becomes a pre-admitted fact and the syllogism commits the fallacy of *siddhasādhanatā*.[21]

Again if the preconception of the major be an admitted fact, the purely negative character of the inference *(kevalavyatireki)*, as has been suggested by the Advaitins, is an illogical assumption. *Kevalavyatireki* or the purely negative character of the inference implies that the positive concomitance or *anvayavyāpti* of the middle and the major is an impossibility and the concomitance is apprehended only negatively. Now if the prior conception of the *sādhya* be accepted the positive concomitance is not an impossibility and the purely, negative character of the syllogism, as given by the monistic teachers, is illogical. If, to be consistent, the Advaitins adopt the negative course, or, in other words, if they deny the prior conception of the major they commit the fallacy of the unproved major or *sādhyāprasiddhi*.[22] The inferential judgment, that knowledge is self-luminous, is intended to prove that the subject or knowledge possesses the feature indicated in the predicate. Knowledge marked out by the predicative idea *(viśiṣṭabuddhi)* implies the previous notion of the property to be proved. Concrete conception depends upon the pre-notion of the property which makes it concretised. Predicative idea or *viśeṣaṇajñāna* stands as the causal factor of the concrete aspect of knowledge *viśiṣṭabuddhi*. As the judgment, 'a man characterised as the holder of the stick,' logically presupposes the notion of the stick, similarly, all concrete notions imply the pre-cognition of the property predicated of the subject. Hence the particular judgment construction of the Advaitins 'consciousness is self-luminous,' to be logically valid, must presuppose the predicate which is to be proved in knowledge by means of inference. And though the syllogistic argument might avoid the fallacy of *sādhyāprasiddhi* it would be vitiated by the fallacy of *siddhasādhanatā* or proving the proved.

Advaitins' reply

To repudiate the charge of *sādhyāprasiddhi* and *siddhasādhanatā* which represent the two poles of the Naiyāyika dilemma, the Advaitins argue that the *sādhya* or the major of the syllogism is not an unknown factor. The major or *sādhya* has its pre-cognition in a general way on the basis of an inference known as *sāmānyato-dṛṣṭa* in the Naiyāyika terminology. When we see a horned animal and infer that it has a tail, we have a case of *sāmānyatodṛṣṭa* inference. It is based on general observation and on the uniformity of experience. Experience teaches us that self-luminosity or *svaprakāśatva* is not an absurdity. It is an attribute located in a substrate. But the special features of the substrate are not known to us and we cannot characterise the substrate with its particular name and form and other essential natures.

The charge of *sādhyāprasiddhi* does not arise

To establish the prior conception of the major, the Advaitins observe that all *dharmas* because they are *dharmas*, are subject to eternal negation or *atyantābhāva* in a particular substrate, *e.g.*, '*śuklatva*' or whiteness.[23] Whiteness which serves as an attribute to a white pot, is denied in a black pot. And on the basis of such an explanatory instance it is inferred that all attributes are absolutely negated somewhere because they are the property of a particular substance only. *Vedyatva* or knowability is a property; it is therefore subject to absolute negation in a particular substrate. In this way *avedyatva* or negation of *vedyatva* in a substrate being logically established, it implies the *svayaṁprakāśatva* or self-luminosity — the major *(sādhya)* of the syllogism under discussion. *Svayaṁprakāśatva,* as is understood by the Advaitins, rests on the absolute negation of *vedyatva* or knowability. What does not form the object of cognition is called *svayaṁprakāśa*. *Avedyatva* thus is the essential characteristic of *svayaṁprakāśatva* as we have studied before. Now the major or *sādhya* being thus a logically established factor, the syllogism cannot be vitiated by the fallacy of *sādhyāprasiddhi* as pointed out by the Naiyāyikas.

Question of siddha-sādhanatā against the Advaitins

The argument, on the other hand, cannot also be rendered faulty by the fallacy of *siddhasādhanatā* because the given syllogistic argument based on general obsertation or uniformity of experience may indeed indicate the necessity of a substrate, for a property without a substrate cannot be conceived. But the substrate with its particular name and form and other essential features which may characterise or individualise it as such and such a thing, may yet remain totally unknown and unapprehended by the suggested inference. And it is now individualised with all its special features, if there be any, as consciousness by the suggested syllogistic arguments. And the question of *siddhasādhanatā* cannot be urged here because the substrate of self-luminosity with all its essential marks was not pre-established. It is however to be noticed in this conncetion that the *sādhya* or the major of the Advaitin's inference is known not in its positive phase but only negatively through the negation of *vedyatva*. *Vedyatvābhāva* is only one of the negative essentials of self-luminosity. Self-luminosity has been defined by its two essential marks *avedyatva* as well as *aparokṣavyavahārayogyatva* or capability of its direct or immediate apprehension. And hence the negation of *vedyatva* is not sufficient ground to establish self-luminosity, the major of the Advaitic syllogism. The question of *sādhyāprasiddhi* still vitiates the whole circle of argument. In refuting the objection the Advaitins argue that the capability of immediate perception or *aparokṣavyavahārayogyatva* as a characteristic mark receives support even in the Nyāya-theory of knowledge. Negation of *vedyatva* is therefore the only other essential mark which has evoked criticism from the Nyāya standpoint. But *avedyatva* in knowledge having been established on the basis of inference, the *sādhya* or the major with all its essentials is proved and the objection of *aprasiddhaviśeṣaṇata* or unproved probendum falls to the ground.

The charge against the purely negative character of the inference cannot stand

We have already seen the reason why the Advaitic syllogism does not commit the fallacy of *siddhasādhanatā* though the major or *sadhya* has its preestablished character. The real nature of the substrate with all its special features being unknown and unestablished, the co-presence of the *hetu* and *sādhya* in their positive concomitance cannot be logically urged. And the coexistence or the positive co-ncomitance of the middle and the major is to be explained only through the negative dialectic. Negativity is therefore the only mark which will explain the *vyāpti* or concomitance of the middle *(hetu)* and the major *(sādhya)*. The negation of the major *(sādhya)* implies the negation of the middle *(hetu)*. It is therefore that form of inference wherein the middle and the major do nowhere co-exist except in the particular locus and the concomitance being merely negative, the inference is known as *kevalavyatireki*. The objection, based on the negative character of the inference, can in no way stand.

We have already seen that the major of the Advaitic syllogism is not an unestablished factor and the Naiyāyika objection of the *aprasiddhaviśeṣaṇatā* or unproved major is based on the misapprehension of the Advaitic position. It is now to be examined whether the *pakṣa* or the minor and the *hetu* or the middle can be logically determined.

As regards the minor, Naiyāyikas contend that consciousness, which according to the thesis of the monistic philosophy is one and absolute without any characteristic of its own, escapes all logical determinations and cannot therefore be styled a valid category to form the minor of a sound syllogistic reasoning. Again a thing is characterised by its essentials and an entity without any essential feature and characteristic of its own can in no way be logically defined and determined. *Anubhūtitva,* which serves the function of the middle, must subsist in the minor as is demanded in a valid syllogistic argument. Presence of the middle in the minor is an absolutely necessary condition of syllogistic reasoning and *anubhūtitva,* the middle, has thus to be assigned to consciousness, the minor term. This is fatal to the fundamental principles of absolute monism. Again *anubhūtitva* itself which is the determining feature *(pakṣatāvacchedaka)* of consciousness, the minor term, cannot be logically categorised. It exists in one absolute consciousness and cannot therefore be styled '*jāti*' or generality which resides in many things and not in one thing and helps us, in a way, in grouping together the things which possess the same features. Oneness of object is held by Udayana as one of the six causes which prevent common characteristic becoming a true generality or class concept.[24] Categorical determination being thus impossible, *anubhūtitva* cannot be styled a logically valid concept. And its validity or reality being thus questioned it lays itself open to the fallacy of *svarūpāsiddhi* in the Advaitic syllogism.

The Nyāya charge of *Svarāpāsiddha*

Svarūpāsiddha or unreal in itself is that type of reason which does not exist in the subject and therefore cannot afford the basis for any reasoning, as in the proposition, "the lake is a substance, because it has smoke."[25] Unreality attributed to the middle *(hetu)* vitiates the whole system of inferential argument. It affects the subject, and the relation of the middle term to the subject, and the relation of the middle and the major terms.

The Nyāya charge of *Āśrayāsiddhi*

When the subject itself is an unreality the syllogism suffers from the fallacy of *āśrayāsiddha* or unreal as regards substratum. The subject or *āśraya* or the minor term may be unreal in two ways : it may be a wholly imaginary thing as in the case of reasoning, 'The sky-lotus is fragrant, because it is a lotus; where the unreality of the subject renders the conclusion impossible.[26] Or the subject may be deprived of the essential characteristic which makes it fit to be a subject of a syllogism. "In either case the reflection or *parāmarśa* on the elements of the syllogism is impossible, since unreal things—things imaginary or devoid of categorically definable essentials cannot be made the objects of such reflection or *parāmarśa* "Hence this species ranks as 'unreal as regards the substratum' *(svarūpāsiddha).*" The Advaitic syllogism under discussion comes within the scope of the latter division. For the reason or *'hetu'* or the middle term being unreal in itself *(svarūpāsiddha)* and non-existent in the subject cannot be counted as the essential mark of the subject, and the subject is left without any logically valid essential.

The charge of *Vyāpyatvāsiddhi*

As regards the concomitance or *(vyāpti)* of the middle and the major the Advaitins' syllogism commits the fallacy of *vyāpyatvāsiddhi*. The reason, which is unreal in regard to the concomitance between the middle term and the consequence, and does not present itself as inevitable and invariable, is called *vyāpyatvāsiddha*.

There are two forms of this class : in the first, the concomitance simply does not exist; in the second, there is concomitance but only a conditional *(aupādhika)* one, which is of no value for inference. In the first case, we have such inference as "The mountain has fire because it has golden smoke."[27] For the addition of the 'golden' destroys the concomitance since golden smoke does not, in the Indian view, exist. "The conditional concomitance is illustrated by such a case as the argument,' the mountain has smoke, because it has fire.' The proposition is conditioned by the fact that there is no universal concomitance between fire and smoke, but only between fire produced from wet fuel and smoke."[28] This is the real essence of the Nyāya charge of *vyāpyatvāsiddhi* or the reason which is unreal in regard to the concomitance. It is assigned to the Advaita-syllogism on the ground that for want of proofs or *pramāṇas* there is no concomitance possible between the major and the middle of the syllogism under discussion.

Concomitance or *vyāpti* being thus questioned for want of proofs, it is obvious that its very existence as well as its universal character is challenged.

Advaitin's reply

In order to repudiate the charge of *asiddhi* or unreality of reason in its three different aspects, *viz., (a) svarūpāsiddha* or unreal in itself, *(b) āśrayāsiddha* or unreal as regards the substratum, *(c) vyāpyatvāsiddha* or unreal in regard to concomitance, the Advaitins observe that the Nyāya charges are groundless and based only on the misapprehension of the monistic position. As regards the objection of *svarūpāsiddha* or the unreal in itself the monistic philosophers argue that though consciousness or 'cit' in its finality is purely absolute and featureless and all ideas of empirical duality die out at the dawn of supreme Reality yet they do not deny the fact that so long as empiricism exists and consciousness is dominated by the pragmatic demands, concrete and relative ideas and thought constructions possess validity of their own and are not called erroneous. Logic has its value in its own province. The generic character, representing the middle or hetu of the Advaita-syllogism, is attributed to consciousness or to the subject. Generic character implies its own nature as well as the characteristic of the object in which it inheres. Consciousness characterised by its generality is no doubt opposed to the spirit of absolute monism, but it cannot be denied so long as the Advaita-Vedānta is studied as a science of reasoning.

Though the charge of *svarūpāsiddha* may be disposed of in this manner, the objection of *āśrayāsiddhi* still vitiates the argument. The charge of *āśrayāsiddhi* is founded upon the falsity of the essential characteristic of the subject or pakṣa of the proposition. It is contended by the Naiyāyikas that *anubhūtitva* or essential mark of the subject (pakṣatāvacchedaka) being posited in one unitary consciousness, cannot be logically categorised. To judge the question from the standpoint of the monistic teacher it appears as an absurdity. Plurality of consciousness due to different conditions and limitations is not denied in the Advaita-Vedānta. Knowledge transcends all limitations only when it reaches its finality and empiric logic dies out. The Nyāya objection arises from the failure to distinguish between two forms of knowledge, *viz., (a)* empirical, and *(b)* transcendental. Advaitism is very eloquent on the fact that plurality in consciousness is conditional or rather superimposed *(kalpita),* consciousness is one and unitary in its reality. But this superimposed nature of plurality will not affect the notion of generality residing in consciousness though one as an inherent essential. For the Naiyāyikas on their own admission accept moonhood or *candratva* as a genus or 'jāti' on the ground that the moon, though one, appears as many when reflected in water. And it is on the basis of these plural appearances that moonhood is categorised as genus or *jāti*. An estimation of the Nyāya position will clearly explain the fact that *anubhūtitva* or the essential nature of consciousness or the subject or *pakṣatāvacchedaka* is not *non est;* it can be logically categorised as genus existing in the apparent plurality of consciousness due to super-imposition just like moonhood residing in many moons due to reflection in water. And the charges of *svarūpāsiddhi* or the unreality in itself and of *āśrayāsiddhi* or unreality as regards the substratum fall to the ground.

As regards the objection of *vyāpyatvāsiddhi* or the unreality with regard to the concomitance, the Advaitin's argue that the opponents, in assigning this objection, question the inevitable and invariable nature of concomitance between the middle term and the consequence. And their objection is valid only in the case wherein the concomitance cannot invariably and unconditionally be proved. To establish the logical validity of concomitance

Gaṅgeśa argues that the *hetu* is that which immediately and always precedes the effect. The essence of inference lies in the invariable concomitance *(vyāpti)* between the middle *(hetu)* or *vyāpya* and the resultant or the major or *vyāpaka*. How is the invariable concomitance known? Simple observation or concomitance in a particular case or a few cases is not enough for the logical validity of inference. To attain certainty the notion of concomitance must be examined by the method of positive and negative instances. If a discrepancy occurs 'then it must either be shown to be an apparent exception, or the doctrine of concomitance must be admitted to be conditional *(aupādhika)* and therefore useless for logic.' The concomitance can be either positive-negative *(anvayavyatireki)* or an agreement in presence and absence between the *hetu* and *sādhya;* or an agreement in presence only *(kevalānvayi)* or there can be a negative concomitance only *(kevalavyatireki)*. In the proposition 'Living organisms have souls, since they possess animal functions' there can be a negative concomitance only *(kevalavyatireki),* since the proposition 'What has no soul has no animal functions' can be illustrated by the case of the pot, but the positive proposition 'that which has animal functions has a soul' cannot be illustrated since the conclusion has precisely the same extension as the subject and cannot therefore be found anywhere outside it.[29]

If this form of syllogism which is based on the explanatory instance, heterogeneous with the proven *(vipaksa),* and is not supported by a similar case or (*sapakṣa*)—which is an impossibility in the case of negative concomitance—is taken by the Naiyāyikas as the logically valid form of inference, their charge of *vyāpyatvā-siddhi* urged against the negative syllogism of the Advaitins is not to the point. The Advaitins reject both the forms of inference *kevalānvayi* and *kevalavyatireki*. The former because the *kevalānvayi* inference rests upon the invariable and undeniable concomitance between the *hetu* and *sādhya*—a concomitance which excludes proof of negative examples. In the Advaita-Vedānta all things are negated in Brahman and therefore the negative concomitance is not an impossible one. *Kevalavyatireki,* being founded upon negative concomitance only, comes under the scope of *Arthāpatti* where we proceed from the effect to the cause.[30] Advaitins accept the inference known as *anvayi* or agreement based on concomitance invariable but not undeniable. It is only on the admission of the Nyāya-view that the Advaitins put forward the purely negative form of inference to establish the self-luminosity of knowledge. This being the position of the Advaita-Vedānta, the Naiyāyikas' attempt to criticise the purely negative concomitance of the Advaita-syllogism is to assail their own position.

Again the condition or *upādhi,* as its definition indicates, cannot be urged in the purely negative form of inference. For the Naiyāyikas define condition or *upādhi* as what covers the major but not the middle or in other words, what invariably co-exists with the major but not with the middle.[31] This being the essential characteristics of condition or *upādhi,* the conditional concomitance, to prove its invariable existence in the major, requires an explanatory example. Now the question arises whether this explanatory instance proves the invariable and universal co-presence of the major and the condition or *upādhi* in the suggested minor *(pakṣa)* or elsewhere. If it is to be proved elsewhere, a *sapakṣa* or an instance homogeneous with the proven is absolutely required to satisfy the first condition of the conditional concomitance or to prove the universal co-presence of the major and the suggested condition. But this inference being purely negative in its character it becomes an impossibility to adduce any similar example or *sapakṣa;* co-presence of the condition and *sādhya* may, therefore, be proved only in the suggested minor *(pakṣa)* of the inference. But the existence of the major in the minor is a matter of doubt in any syllogistic reasoning and requires to be proved by inference founded on these premises. If the presence of the major in the minor is pre-ascertained, the necessity of inference as well as supposition of condition become futile.

Condition or *upādhi* makes the inference impossible. It vitiates the invariable concomitance or *vyāpti,* the true foundation of inference, and thereby renders the inference faulty. Now if the existence of the major in the minor be pre-accepted, inference, as a valid source of proof, becomes useless and naturally the question of condition vitiating the true foundation of *vyāpti* bears no utility of its own. Hence to prove the validity of inferential proof the presence of the major in the minor is to be everywhere doubted and to be established by the syllogistic reasoning. Again if *sādhyavyāpakatva* or the co-existence of the major with the condition or *upādhi* is proved in the suggested minor or *pakṣa,* it becomes an admitted fact that the condition exists in the minor and as a result the co-existence of the condition with the middle is also established as the presence of the middle in the minor *(hetoḥ pakṣadharmatā)* is an absolutely necessary condition of the inference. And in this way the condition becomes a part and parcel of the syllogism and its own conditional character rendering the inference faulty, is denied.[32] Hence the question of *vyāpyatvāsiddhi* or unreality of concomitance cannot arise in the purely negative form of inference. To estimate the correctness of the middle *(hetu)* it is also further observed that the middle term is not subject to any other form of fallacies which invalidate the inferential judgment.

The reason or *hetu* advanced by the Advaitins is not a contrary one

The reason or "*hetu*' advanced by the Advaitins cannot be called a contrary *(viruddha)* one. The contrary reason is what goes to prove exactly the opposite of the thesis it is adduced to establish. It is defined in the Nyāya literature as *sādhyābhāva-vyāpyahetu* or the middle which exists only wherein the major is wanting. The *viruddha hetu* therefore does not exist in the positive instance *(sapakṣa)* but does exist in counter-examples *(vipakṣa)*. 'The lake is fiery because it has water' *(hrado vahnimān jalāt)*. In this inferential judgment it may be observed that where there is water there is no fire. Or, in other words, where water representing the *hetu* exists, *e.g.*, in the pond, the negation of fire or *sādhyābhāva* is apprehended. And again wherein fire or the major is cognised, *e.g.*, in a kitchen, the *hetu* or water does not exist. This form of reasoning is styled *viruddha* or contradictory. The Advaita syllogism escapes this contradiction because knowability or *vedyatva,* which represents' *sādhyābhāva*' or the negation of self-luminosity, the major of the monistic inferential judgment, may exist in the pot and such other concrete objects but *anubhūtitva* or the 'hetu' of the syllogism, which, as an essential nature, inheres in consciousness, where in the existence of the major is only a matter of doubt, cannot reside in the knowable. The middle term therefore cannot be characterised as *sādhyābhāvavyāpyahetu* or the cause existing only where there is the negation of *sādhya;* and it does in no way violate the conditions of valid inference or go to prove the opposite thesis and cannot be called a contrary one.

The Advaitic middle is not inconclusive

It is also not inconclusive or discrepant or *anaikāntika* in its character. *Anaikāntika* or inconclusive. reasoning leads to more conclusions than one; the conclusion ceases to possess any certainty and remains therefore as an object of doubt. "From the ground of intangibility we may conclude either the eternality or the non-eternality of sound, since both eternal atoms and non-eternal cognitions are intangible. The middle term is not pervaded by the major. As the middle term is not uniformly concomitant with any one alternative, it is called *anaikāntika* in later logic. Three subdivisions of these are admitted, namely, *(a) sādhāraṇa* or common, where the middle term is too wide, *(b) asādhārāṇa* or the uncommon, where the middle term is too narrow, *(c) anupasaṁhārin* or the indefinite, where the middle term cannnot be verified." None of the three divisions of the *anaikāntika* fallacy can find its way to vitiate the Advaita syllogism.

The middle term is not too wide

Sādhāraṇa anaikāntika has been defined by the Naiyāyikas as *sādhyābhāvavadvṛttihetu* or a type of inference in which the middle term co-exists even with the negation of the major term, *e.g.*, 'the hill is smoky because it is fiery.' In this inferential judgment the middle term fire exists even in the overheated iron ball *(ayogolaka)* wherein the major, smoke, is wanting and the middle term being too wide in its nature the inference is called *sādhāraṇa anaikāntika* or the common inconclusive. But in the Advaita syllogism under discussion *svayaṁprakāśatva* or self-luminosity, the major term, is negated in the knowable, *e.g.*, the pot, etc., but the middle term cannot be predicated of it because consciousness does not exist in the pot or such other inert substances; and the middle term is not too wide or *sādhāraṇa anaikāntika* and is therefore distinct from the common inconclusive.

The middle term is not too narrow

The middle or 'hetu' is also not too narrow and the charge of *asādhāraṇa anaikāntika* cannot be urged in the Advaita syllogism. For the too restricted reason *(asādhāraṇa)* occurs nowhere outside the subject itself. Its absence from the opposite instances or counter-examples tends to establish the validity of the conclusion, but its absence from the similar instances or examples tends to invalidate the result which remains therefore a matter of doubt. "Sound is eternal because it is audible" is the standing example of *asādhāraṇa anaikāntika* fallacy. As we have seen the fallacy is distinguished in the modern school from the purely negative inference by the reason that in the fallacy the major term has greater extension than the other terms, while in the inference which is valid all three terms have the like extension." Now in the given inference audibility or the *hetu* does neither exist in a similar instance or in an instance homogeneous with the proven, *e.g.*, the sky, nor in the counter-example or example heterogeneous with the proven, *e.g.*, the pot, etc.; it exists only in the subject or the minor and the reason becomes too narrow or *asādhāraṇa* in its character. The question of too restricted reason cannot invalidate the Advaita inference because the inference being purely negative in its nature has no similar instance or *sapakṣa* to prove the negation of its middle term in homogeneous cases.

The charge of indefinite reasoning cannot stand

Again the charge of indefinite reasoning or the reasoning in which the middle term escapes verification cannot also be brought against the Advaita syllogism. "The reason which does not subsume *(anupasaṁhārin)* is that which is alleged of a subject which is so extensive as to permit neither of examples or counter-examples, as in "All is eternal, because it can be known." The nature of all forbids the possibility of any universal concomitance. Or equally well the opposite argument can be used "All is transitory, because it can be known." It is therefore a doubt which makes valid inference an impossibility. The existence of the middle in the instance heterogeneous with the proven or *'vipakṣa'* or in the instance in which the negation of the major is doubted, though not ascertained, invalidates the syllogistic argument. And to prove the validity of inference, the possibility of such an existence of the middle should be denied by the help of *"bādhakatarka"* or contradictory reasoning. If there is no counter-reasoning or *bādhakatarka* to prevent the existence of the middle in the counter-example or the example in which the major term is doubted, the reason cannot lead to a valid inference. In the Advaita syllogism, the Naiyāyikas contend, consciousness is the minor term and *svayaṁprakāśatva* or self-luminosity major term is doubted in the minor, for otherwise the inference commits the fallacy of *siddhasādhanatā* and the presence of the middle in the minor *(hetoḥ pakṣadharmatā)* being one of the conditions of the inferential judgment the *hetu* or the middle term invariably exists in the minor. Now doubt as a logical category implies two poles—(a) position and (b) negation; and *svayaṁprakāśatva* or the major term in the Advaita-inference being doubted in the minor, maybe negated in the said minor and the reason becomes an indefinite one.

To repudiate this charge of indefiniteness of the reason the Advaitins argue that the position taken up by the Naiyāyikas has been rendered faulty by infinite regress and cannot therefore be accepted. If knowability is urged in consciousness the first cognition forms the object of the second one and the second of the third and so on. The Nyāya theory, in this way, cannot escape the unending question of infinite regress. It is to be prevented by reasoning or *tarka* for such an endless regress will go to prove the non-existent character of consciousness. Hence the negation of self-luminosity cannot be urged in consciousness and the inconclusive or indefinite character of the *hetu* or reason on the basis of doubt cannot be logically put forward in the Advaita syllogism.. There are, rather, favourable arguments *(anukūla-tarka)* to posit the monistic view against the standpoint of the Naiyāyikas in which the question of unending regress makes knowledge itself an impossibility. Centra-arguments or *bādha-katarka* put forward by the Advaitins may refute the Nyāya standpoint but this does not establish their own theory. Arguments are therefore necessary in their favour to lead the Advaitins to a valid result. The Advaitins argue that there are two points which can be urged by the opponent school: *(i)* consciousness is not known at the time when it illumines its objects, or *(ii)* it is illumined by another consciousness. In the former case cognition remaining totally unknown and unobserved its validity might easily be questioned by an inquisitive mind. Knowledge lights up its objects and if it is not, later on, vitiated by falsity, doubt, imagination, etc., then it is an objectively valid cognition and is therefore capable enough to satisfy the demands of pragmatic life. Such an empiric knowledge not, later on, vitiated by falsity, doubt, etc., goes to prove the existence of its own self. It is a universally accepted principle that the want of the later idea of falsity doubt, etc., with regard to a thing originates its definite and empirically valid cognition which is styled *pramā* or true knowledge as distinguished from the faulty or doubtful notion. For example, if the definite knowledge of the pot is not proved false or doubtful in a later stage it is taken as definite and pragmatically valid *(pramā)* notion. When an inquisitive mind observes a thing and forms a judgment 'I have seen a thing,' the thing shines forth and knowledge also is apprehended at the time of the enlightening of objects. For otherwise there would arise the possibility of doubt or falsity as regards the knowledge which lights up the object. But a normal mind never suspects the definiteness of knowledge when the objects of knowledge satisfy the pragmatic demands of life. Want of falsity or doubt, etc., therefore, stamps knowledge with a degree of reality. As a source of pragmatic usage therefore it is also self-shining or self-illuminated.

Denial of illumination of knowledge at the time when it lights up its objects would invalidate its nature and would put a stop to all endeavours. It is rather an absurdity to suppose that knowledge whose only essential nature is illumination illumines or lights up things and it itself remains totally unnoticed and unobserved.[33] The second alternative which represents the viewpoint of the Nyāya can in no way escape the question of the unending regress. Hence the only way out is to accept the Advaita view of self-luminosity.

Vācaspati's view

Vācaspati in his *Bhāmatī* also establishes the *svayaṁprakāśatva* of knowledge by a different though very interesting piece of dialectic : what is the nature of the cognition in which the object *(artha)* and the self are revealed? he asks. Is it self-revealing *(svaprakāśa)* or other-revealed *(jaḍa)?* If it is taken as other-revealed *(jaḍa),* then the whole world would be steeped in darkness being without a revealer; for the object and the self being both taken as revealed are *jaḍa* and the cognition itself being now taken as other revealed also becomes *jaḍa* and there would be no revealer.[34] Now can it be held that the *saṁvit* or consciousness, though itself not self-revealing, reveals the objects and the self just as the eye though not seeing itself sees everything else; for what is meant by this revelation of objects is nothing but the production of their cognition or awareness *(jñānajanana)* and if the cognition is supposed to be not self-revealing, the knowledge of a thing becomes impossible. In short, revelation means nothing but the generation of a process of consciousness and if consciousness itself is not self-revealing, then the case for all revelation is lost. Hence Vācaspati urges that *saṁvit* must be regarded as depending not on anything else for its revelation.[35] But here a new difficulty crops up : Even supposing that *saṁvit* is self-revealed, how does this self-revealing character help the revelation of objects that are essentially *jaḍa?* These objects cannot be revealed simply because they are brought into relation with the self-revealing consciousness; for a *mere* relation with something self-revealed does not qualify the objects unrevealed for being revealed. To argue like this is the same as arguing that because the son is a learned man, therefore the father also is learned.[36] Mere relation is not enough; the relation has to be further determined; if it were so, the self-revealing consciousness would reveal everything at the same time which is as absurd as the above argument. If however it is argued that it is the nature of *saṁvit* that it reveals itself only in conjunction with the revelation of objects and the self and that there is no revelation of *saṁvit* where there is no revelation of objects and the self, the Vedāntist replies that if the revelation of objects and self is different from the *saṁvit,* then the self-revealing character of *saṁvit* also would disappear since it has to depend on something other than itself for its revelation. If however it is not different from *saṁvit,* then the revelation of objects and self being not different from *saṁvit* becomes identical with *saṁvit* and there is no force in the argument.[37] Besides, the consciousness of absent objects such as the past and the future cannot be simultaneous or in conjunction with the objects themselves. And what is more gross material things cannot be object of the self which is of the nature of pure consciousness—these material things being always perceived as external having extension and magnitude and pure consciousness being felt to be wholly internal having no extension and magnitudes. Hence the only right conclusion to be drawn is that the object as something different from self-revealing consciousness is indefinable in character.[38] This revelation or consciousness has no internal division of its own and the division of the object which is indefinable *(anirvācya)* cannot introduce any division into consciousness which is determinate and definable; for that would mean determination of the determinate by something indefinable which is an absurdity.[39] Hence the Vedānta concludes that there is no revelation of the conscious or the unconscious as such by another, that pure consciousness is self-revealing and the object becomes revealed only when it is in illusory identification *(tādātmyādhyāsa)* with pure consciousness.

Prakāśātman in his Vivaraṇa corroborates the same by saying that consciousness *(saṁvit)* is self-revealing and that its self-revelation is not due to any other self-revealing cause.[40] It is, on account of this natural self-revelation of consciousness, that its objects also appear as self-revealing.[41] Padmapāda also in his Pañcapādikā means the same thing when he states that the self is of the nature of pure self-revealing consciousness. When this consciousness appears in connection with other objects and manifests them it is called experience *(anubhava),* and when it is by itself it is called the self or *ātman.*[42]

Ānandabodha Bhaṭṭārakācārya further observes that if at the time when an object is known, knowledge itself were not revealed, then there might arise the doubt "Have I known or have I not?" "Did I see or did I not?" No one however has such a doubt. Thus it stands to reason that knowledge itself is revealed when an object is apprehended. Now admitted that knowledge is revealed, it may still be doubted whether it is revealed by *anuvyavasāya* or after-cognition as held by the Naiyāyikas or by *jñātatā* or cognisedness as held by Kumārila Bhaṭṭa or whether it is self-revealed. If knowledge is supposed to be revealed by another cognition then that cognition itself will require, for its revelation, another cognition and so there will be unending regress.[43] Even when it is said that knowledge is inferred from *jñānajanya-jñātatā,* the question arises: "Does *jñātatā* generate knowledge being itself unrevealed or does it generate knowledge being itself revealed simultaneously with it?" If *jñātatā* were unrevealed at the time of knowledge then there would arise the doubt, "Did I cognise the fact or did I not?" But no such doubt arises. And if cognisedness *(jñātatā)* is revealed simultaneously with knowledge, then the objection would be that simultaneity is not possible as one is the effect of the other. Cognisedness being the product of knowledge and knowledge being inferred from cognisedness, knowledge and cognisedness are not simultaneous; the one produces the other so that knowledge is inferred from cognisedness which again being produced by knowledge there would be the fallacy of *Itaretarāśraya* or mutual dependence. Again when an object is cognised, there is said to be produced in the object a peculiar property called cognisedness or *jñātatā,* and so when this cognisedness is known, there will be produced another cognisedness in that cognisedness, and so on *ad infinitum.* If, to avoid such an infinite regress, cognisedness be regarded as self-luminous it may as well be argued that the cognition itself is self-luminous.[44]

This self-luminous character of knowledge has also been advocated by the Jaina and Buddhist thinkers in their theory of knowledge.

Self-cognition or *svasaṁvedanam* of the Buddhists

Buddhist thinkers hold that all consciousness, cognition *(citta)* and feelings *(caitta)* are known by themselves; or in other words, they are self-transparent and self-luminous.[45] Consciousness is diametrically opposed to matter in this that it is of the nature of illumination like the luminary in the firmament, whereas matter is veiled and hidden by a constitutional darkness. The being of consciousness is its illumination, its luminosity and so it cannot be unknown. Consciousness thus differs from dead unfeeling and unthinking matter which has no light in itself. The immateriality of consciousness carries with it the prerogative of self-revelation and does not connote any subject-object relation in its constitution, which its very immateriality precludes. Matter alone can be divided and consciousness can be consciousness only if it refuses to be split up into compartments, which the subject-object relation involves.[46] So self-luminosity of consciousness does not connote a bifurcation of consciousness into a subject and object, which would be absurd in a single unit. Consciousness and self-consciousness, therefore, are interchangeable terms. The light of consciousness makes the dead matter shine and if the consciousness is supposed to be hidden and veiled in and by itself, there is no knowing how knowledge can arise at all. Dharmakīrti has very pertinently observed "perception of an object is impossible if perception itself is unperceived."[47] If cognition cannot shine in its own light but only in the borrowed light of another cognition, how can the second cognition, which equally lacks original light like the first, make it shine? Certainly there must be light somewhere and if it is supposed to belong to some remote cognition, what is the harm if it is be conceded to the first? If you deny original light to any cognition whatsoever, perception of objective reality will become impossible, as darkness cannot be removed by darkness. And the alternative of shining in borrowed light is exposed to the charge of *regressus ad infinitum*. The contention that a cognition reveals its object, though lying unknown by itself, like the sense-organ, has been proved to be a colossal hoax. A cognition reveals objects, which are foreign to it, only because it is self-revealing iike light. The subject-object relation does not exist and so there is no dichotomy in consciousness. It is immediate in all knowledge and is not known like an external object. Its nature is to be revealed and revealing. It shines, it sheds lustre and all things coming in contact with it are revealed. To say that I do not perceive consciousness in perceiving an object is tantamount to saying that I do not know if I have a tongue or not. Argument will be lost upon him—a human statue-in stone, who perceives an object but is not conscious that he perceives it.[48] To say, therefore, that the object is known and not the fact of knowledge is to talk nonsense. The contention, that awareness is only implicit in objective perception and so knowledge is not always of the form 'I know the object,' but it is simply of the object, does not prove that the knowledge is unknown. Implicit or explicit awareness is always self-awareness. The reference to the subject and the object in a judgment is a question of emphasis and is possible only if there is a recognition of the fact of knowledge. So the self transparency of knowledge is the presupposition of all knowledge and cannot be denied without denying the very possibility of knowledge.*

The Jaina position

Prabhācandra in his *prameyakamalamārtaṇḍa,* strongly criticises the Nyāya-Vaiśeṣika view that "cognition is manifested by another cognition since it is an object of knowledge like a cloth."[49] The argument that a cognition is cognised by another cognition is refuted by the fact that pleasure is self-cognised and also by the fact that the cognition of God though not cognised by another cognition is valid. If however, it be held that cognition of God is cognised by another cognition then that will involve unending regress.[50] If this infinite regress is sought to be avoided on the assumption that there are two cognitions in God, one cognises the universe and the other cognises that cognition, then the answer is that the assumption is absurd as two cognitions of the same nature and existing as long as the object endures are nowhere found. Even if the assumption be supposed possible in God, the question is "Is the second cognition perceived or not? if it be not perceived how then can it reveal the first cognition?" if it be held that even though itself unperceived it can cognise the first cognition then the first cognition though not perceived may also cognise the object; if it be held that the second cognition is perceived then the question arises "Is it perceived by itself or another?" If it be perceived by itself then this capacity may also be attributed to the first cognition. If it be perceived by another, *i. e.,* a third cognition, then there will be the fallacy of infinite regress. If the second cognition be perceived by the first and the first by the second then there will be the fallacy of mutual dependence *(anyonyāśrayatvam)*[51]. Moreover, does the second cognition arise when the first cognition exists or after its disappearance? In the first case there will be two simultaneous cognitions which is absurd. In the second case, what will the second cognition perceive? If it be said that the non-existent first cognition is perceived by the second cognition then the cognition becomes false as its object is non-existent. Similarly, in human consciousness, is the second cognition perceived or not? If perceived, is it perceived by itself or by another cognition? If it be perceived by itself then we may as well attribute the capacity of self-perception to the first cognition. If it be perceived by another it will lead to infinite regress. If it be not perceived then how can it perceive the first cognition? If it be said that unperceived second cognition perceives the first cognition as the sense organs though themselves unperceived, produce apprehension of objects, then why should not the first cognition though unperceived perceive the objects?[52] Thus the assumption of a second cognition is useless.

To obviate all difficulties, it must be held that consciousness is self-revealed. In the case of God his cognition in apprehending the universe apprehends itself. Self-revelation is inherent in the nature of consciousness as such, whether divine or human.[53]

REFERENCES

1. Ghaṭādivyavahāre jñānānvaya-vyatirekādastu tadapekṣā. —T.C., p. 784. Bib. Ind. Series.
2. (a) Vijñānaṁ tāvat svaprakāśaṁ svata evaṁsiddhasvarūpam, na khalu vijñāne sati jijñāsorapi kasyacit jānāmi na veti saṁśayah, na jānāmīti vā viparyayo vyatirekapramā vā. —Kh. Kb., p. 81.
3. Vyavasāyasya anuvyavasāyaniyamān na tatra saṁśayādi.—Kh. Kh., p.33.
4. Kh. Kh., pp. 83-85.
5. (a) Anubhūteranubhāvyatve' navasthāpātāt. —Cit., p. 15.
   (b) Yadi vijñānam parataḥ sidhyedanavasthā syāt.—Kh. Kh., p. 85.
   (c) Paraprakāśatve anavasthayā jñānāsiddhā vāśrayāsiddheḥ. —T.C., p, 791.
6. (*a*) Avaśyavedyatā vitternābhyupeyate, svārthovyavahārastu svarūpa-sattayā prasūyata iti kvānavasthā. —Kh. Kh., pp. 86-87.
   (*b*) Vitteravaśyavedyatvābhāvena anavasthā vigamāt. —T. C., p. 798.
7. Tathā ca pramāṇasattāpi tatpramāṇasattāmantareṇa na prāmāṇikasyāṅgīkārārhā..... yadi hi vinaiva pramāṇasattām pramāṇasattām paroṅgīkāryeta tadā ghaṭasattāmapi tathaivāṅgī kāryatāmiti ghaṭe'pi vṛthā pramāṇopanyāsāyāsaḥ. —Kh. Kh., p, 90.
8. Kh. Kh., p. 96.
9. Svaścāsau prakāśaśca svaprakāśaḥ. —Cit., p. 3.
10. Svasya svayam eva prakāśa iti vā.—Cit., p. 3.
11. *Cf.* Parasamaveta-kriyā phala-śālitvaṁ karmatvam.
12. Sajātīya-prakāśāprakāśyatvam.—Cit., p. 3.
13. Svasattāyām prakāśa-vyatireka-virahitatvam.—Cit., p. 4.
14. Jnānāviṣayatvaṁ svaprakāśatvam.—Cit., p. 5.
15. Vyavahāraviṣayatve sati jnānāviṣayatvam.—Cit., p, 5.
16. (a) Avedyatve sati aparokṣa-vyavahārayogyatvaṁ svaprākāśatvam. —Cit., p. 9.
    (b) Aparokṣa-vyavahṛteryogyasyādhīpadasya naḥ saṁbhave svaprakāśasya lakṣṇāsaṁbhavaḥkutaḥ.—*Ibid,* p. 9.
17. Aparokṣavyavahārayogyatvātyantābhāvānadhikaraṇatvam. *Vide* N. Pr., p.9.
18. Mokṣadaśāyāṁ ca vivakṣitadharmābhāve'pi kadācit sattvena tadatyantābhāvānadhikaraṇatvasya guṇāśrayo dravyamitivat siddheḥ. —Citsukhī, p. 9.
19. Na ca yogyatālakṣaṇa-dharmāṅgīkāre avyāptirmokṣṣadaśāyāṁ tadasambhavād apasiddhāntaśceti śaṅkanīyaṁ, yogyatvātyantābhāvādadhikaraṇatvasya tattvāt, guṇavattvātyantābhāvānadhikaraṇasya dravyatvavat, tena nāvyāptiḥ.—Citsukhī, p. 9. Cp. Advaitasiddhi, p. 768; Bombay, edition.

20. Anubhūtiṁ svayaṁprakāśā anubhūtitvāt yannaivaṁ tannaivaṁ yathā ghaṭaḥ ityanumānam.—Cit., p. 11.
21. The condition precedent of inference is the fact of *Pakṣatā,* which means in simple language the absence of previous proofs in favour of the probandum *(sādhakamānābhāva).* In other words, the probandum must not be known to have been established before. Inference in Indian logic aims at material truth and not formal consistency alone and the truth which is sought to be established must be such as constitutes a real advance in knowledge. So when a particular inference is found not to prove anything unknown before and as such only repeats a known fact and does not make any advance, it infringes the fundamental condition of inference and virtually forfeits its right to be regarded as an inference. This is technically called the fallacy of *Siddhasādhana* which is a purely Indian conception.
22. *Sādhyāprasiddhi.*—Another condition of inference is that there must be an invariable and universal concomitance *(vyāpti)* between the probans and the probandum without which no inference is possible. The universal proposition or the major premise in Aristotelian syllogism embodies this invariable concomitance. Now, the universal concomitance fails to materialize if either the probans or the probandum is an altogether unknown fact, because the relation between two unknown facts or of one unknown fact with another known cannot be conceived. If the probans is not known, it constitutes a case of fallacy called *Sādhanāprasiddha* and in the case of an unknown probandum, it becomes *sādhyāprasiddha.* The above fallacies also occur, when the probans or the probandum, though known to be existent facts, are qualified by an unknown and non-existent adjective in which case it gives rise to the fallacies of *vyarthaviśeṣaṇasādhana* and *vyarihaviśes aṇasādhya,* respectively.
23. Vedyatvaṁ kiñcinniṣṭhātyantābhāvapratiyogi dhatmatvāt śauklyavat.—Cit., p. 12.
24. (a) Vyakterabheda stulyatvam saṁkaro' thānavasthitiḥ
Rūpahānirasaṁbandho jātibādhakasaṁgrahaḥ.
—Kir., p. 33, Benares Edition.
(b) Anubhūtitvaṁ nāma na tāvajjātiḥ, anubhūterekatvāṅgīkāreṇa vyaktya-bhedasya jātibādhakatvāt.—N. Pr., p. 13.
25. Hrado dravyaṁ dhūmavatvādatrāsiddhirathāparā. —Bh. P. and S.M., sl. 76.
26. Gaganārabindaṁ surabhi, arabindatvāt sarojārabindavat, atra gaganārabindamā śrayaḥ sa eva nāsti. — T.S., p. 85, E. Ghosa's Edn.
27. Parvato vahnimān kāñcauamayadhūmāt.
28. I.L.A., pp. 148-49.
29. *Vide* I.L.A., p. 149.
30. *Vide* A.C.K., p. 26.
31. Sādhyasya vyāpako vastu hetoravyāpakastathā sa upādhiḥ—Bh. P. and S. M. S. 1. 80.
32. Na ca pakṣe sādhyena anvayaḥtatra sādhyasya adyāpi sandigdhatvāt niścaye ca siddhaṁ naḥ samīhitamiti kimupādhiḥ kariṣyati. pakṣe ca upādhivṛttau sādhanavyāpakatā ca durvārā, etc.—Cit., p. 14.

33. Some Western thinkers also advocate the similar view. *Cf.* Varisco : "That I may know, it is necessary that I should be conscious, that I should know that I know." It follows that the act of consciousness proves the reality of itself and of the thinking subject (Know Thyself, p. 5).

    Bonatelli the Italian philosopher observes that in the knowledge of any fact there are given together the knowledge of the fact and the fact of knowledge.

    Cf. Hamilton: "An act of knowledge may be expressed by the formula 'I know;' an act of consciousness by the formula 'I know that I know'; but, as it is impossible for us to know without at the same time knowing that I know, so it is impossible to know that we know without our actually knowing."

34. Bhāmatī, p. 35, Bombay Edition.

    Yo'yamarthaprakāśaḥ phalaṁ, yasminnarthaśca ātmā ca prathete, sa kim jaḍaḥ, svayaṁprakāśo vā, jaḍaścit viṣayātmanāvapi jaḍāviti kasmin kim prakāśeta aviśeṣāt, iti prāptamāndhyamaśeṣasya jagataḥ.

35. *Ibid,* p. 35:

    Na ca nilīnameva vijñānatnarthātmānau jñāpayati cakṣuradivaditi vācyam, jñāpanaṁ hi jñānajananam, janitañca jñānaṁ jaḍaṁ sat noktadūṣ aṇamativarteteti, evamuttarottarāṇyapi jñānāni jaḍānītyanavasthā tasmādaparādhīnaprakāśā saṁvit upetavyā.

36. Bhāmatī, p. 36:

    Tat kim putraḥ paṇḍita iti pitāpi paṇḍito'stu.

37. Bhāmatī, p. 36 :

    Sahārthātmaprakāśena saṁvit prakāśo na tu arthaprakāśaṁ vineti tasyāḥ svabhāva iti cet, tat kiṁ saṁvido bhinnau saṁvidātmaprakāśau? tathā ca na svayaṁprakāśā saṁvit, na ca saṁvidarthātmaprakāśa iti, atha saṁvidarthātmaprakāśau saṁvido na bhidyete, saṁvideva tau tathā ca na vivakṣitārthasiddhiḥ.

38. Bhāmatī, p. 37 : Tasmāt candre anubhūyamāna iva dvitīyaścandramāḥ svaprakāśādanyo 'rtho' nirvacanīya eveti yuktamutpaśyāmaḥ.

39. Bhāmatī, p. 37 : Na ca anirvācyārthabhedaḥ prakāśaṁ nirvācyaṁ bhettumarhati atiprasaṅgāt.

40. Saṁvedanaṁ tu svayaṁ-prakāśa eva na prakāśāntarahetuḥ. P.V., p. 52.

41. Tasmād anubhavaḥ sajātīyaprakāśāntaranirapekṣah prakāśamāna eva viṣaye prakāśādivya-vahāranimittam bhavitumarhati avyavadhānena viṣaye prakāśādivyavahāranimittatvāt.—*Ibid,* 52.

42. Tasmāt citsvabhāvā evātmā tena tena prameya-bhedena upādhī yamāno' nubhavābhidhānīyakam labhate avivakṣitopādhirātmādiśabdaiḥ. P.P., p. 19.

43. (a) Vijñānamarthaprakāśasamaye prakāśate tadupādhāvanantaraṁ sandehāyogyatvāt arthavat, prakāśamāuatābhyupagame tu yadi vijñānāntarādhīnamasya prakāśanaṁ tadaiva tatrāpi vijñānāntaramavaśyaṁbhūvītyanavasthā prasajyeta, na ca asti ekadaiva anantavijñānapratibhāsaḥ

    —Ny. M. K, pp. 138-139.

    (b) Adyasaṁvedanasya vedanāntaravedanīyatve anavasthāprasaṁgalakṣaṇatarkopakrtānulaṁbhādeva tasya abhavasiddhau pariśeṣāt svaprakāśatāsiddhiḥ, uktañca—Asaṁvittau vitterna khalu tadupādhivyavahṛtiḥ, pratītāvanyasyāṁ prasabhamanavasthā prasarati iti. —Pr. M., pp. 14-15.

Cf. Mind, 1908, p. 33: —

"To affirm that all cognition is mediate in this sense leads inevitably to a vicious circle. If mediate cognition could only be mediated by cognition which are themselves merely mediate, knowledge could never get a start. It is as if one should say that, in building a wall, every brick must be laid on the top of another brick and none directly on the ground."

44. Yathā ca arthe jñāyamāne jñātatā, tathā jñātatāyāmapi jñāyamānāyāṁ jñātatāntaramityanavasthā, atha iyaṁ svaprakāśā jñāne kaḥ pradveṣaḥ.—Ny. K. P., 97, Benares Edn.

45. Sarvaṁ citta-caīttā nāmātma-saṁvedanam.

46. *(a)* Vijñānaṁ jaḍarūpebhyo vyāvṛttam upajāyate
Idamevātmasaṁvittirasya yā'jaḍarūpatā,
Kriyākārakabhāvena na svasaṁvittirasyatu
Ekasyānaṁśarūpasya trairūpyānupapattitaḥ.—Ta. S., Sls. 2000-2001.

(b) Nahi grāhakabhāvena ātmasaṁvedanam abhipretam, kiṁ tarhi, svayaṅ prakṛtyā prakāśātmatayā nabhasthalavartyālokavat. —Ta. S. P., Sl. 2000.

47. Apratyakṣopalambhasya nārthadṛṣṭih prasidhyati.

48. (a) Bodhe'pyanubhavoyasya na kathañcana jāyate
taṁ kathaṁ bodhayet śāstraṁ loṣṭaṁnarasamākṛtim.

(b) Jihvā me'sti nave'tyuktir lajjāyai kevalaṁ yathā
na budhyate mayābodho boddhavya iti tādṛśī. *Cf.* Pañcadaśī, 111, 19-20.

49. Jñānam Jñānāntaravedyam prameyatvāt paṭavat.

50. *Vide* Pr. K. M., p. 34.

For the Buddhist exposition I am highly indebted to my friend and colleague Dr. Satkari Mukherjee, M.A., PH. D., Lecturer in Sanskrit and Buddhist Philosophy, Calcutta University.

51. *Vide* Pr. K. M., p. 34.

52. *Viāe* Pr. K. M., p. 34-37.

53. *N.B.*—In order to give an insight into the incisiveness and subtlety displayed by Indian thinkers, it was felt necessary to give this rather elaborate logical disputation about the nature of *svaprakāśatva* or self-revealing character of knowledge. Sometimes it does happen, as is natural, that in their enthusiasm to pick holes in the armour of the opponent, they lose sight of the main point and wander into byeways but on the whole the argument never misses or ignores the challenge but tries to meet it fairly and squarely.

CHAPTER 3

VALIDITY OF KNOWLEDGE

The most important question which demands our attention in the epistemological survey is the validity of knowledge. We derive knowledge every day from different sources, *e.g.*, perception, inference, authority, etc., but in every case validity constitutes the chief problem. The question invites keen interest of the epistemologists in the domain of Indian Philosophy because the teachers of Indian Philosophy I differ widely in recording how far the claim of epistemology is sustained and justified. Both as regards the nature, validity and sources of knowledge the opinion of the sister schools of Philosophy are divergent. Our task, in the present thesis, is to examine these different theories of knowledge and to estimate their respective position in the science of knowledge.

As regards the validity of knowledge there are chiefly two issues in Indian thought, (*i*) *svataḥ prāmāṇyavāda'* or the theory which advocates the truth or validity of knowledge as self-constituted and self-evident, and *(ii) 'parataḥ-prāmāṇya-vāda'*—a theory which maintains that the validity of knowledge is borrowed or imported from without. Knowledge does not carry with it its own conviction of proof. Its validity depends upon something else which does not itself constitute knowledge. The term '*vada'* means the bone of contention upon which the teachers of philosophy form divergent opinions and about which they are divided among themselves.

(1) The Sāṁkhya school maintains that both validity and non-validity, proof and disproof, are inherent in the cognition itself.
(2) Naiyāyikas hold that both are proved by something else, *i.e.,* by extraneous causes as inference, etc.
(3) The Buddhists are of opinion that invalidity inheres in all cognitions but validity is established by something else.
(4) Mīmāṁsists and Vedāntists believe that validity is self-evident and invalidity is determined by extraneous causes.[1]

Explanation of the theory

An elaborate treatment of the question requires a fuller account of *prāmāṇya* or validity as a philosophical concept. What 'prāmāṇya' connotes is a problem which faces us here. And divergent opinions which have been formed by the teachers of Indian Philosophy are mainly due to their different conceptions of *pramā* and *pramāṇa* in the theory of knowledge. To estimate the nature of validity as advocated by the teachers of Indian thought what demands our attention first is the nature of *pramā* or true knowledge to which *prāmāṇya* or validity is assigned as its essential nature or property. If the definitions advanced by the different schools of philosophy are critically viewed, two striking features are revealed. Knowledge which reveals the nature of things as they are *(yathābhūta)* and which is not sublated *(abādhita)* is called *pramā* or valid.[2] Revelation of objects in their true perspective and correspondence of ideas with objects are essential marks of valid apprehension. This correspondence of ideas to objects, the Naiyāyikas hold, cannot straightaway be known. One has to infer this correspondence from the capacity of knowledge to lead to successful action. Validity is determined by an appeal to facts. Knowledge is an incitement to action. It unfolds to us an object which may be desirable, or undesirable, or indifferent. The percipient subject is not a purely passive spectator interested in mere contemplation of things. He is eager to attain desirable objects and to avoid undesirable ones. The Naiyāyikas here agree with the modern pragmatists in their view that "Knowledge has its basis in the practical needs of human life and its validity lies in the practical results in which it issues." The study of the Nyāya theory of knowledge reveals the fact that truth of validity of knowledge depends upon its relation to facts it reveals, and the relation is one of agreement and correspondence inferred from the working of ideas, our knowledge leads us to action. When by acting according to it we attain the desired object we call it valid knowledge; when we fail to attain it we call it invalid knowledge. So from con-sequences we infer causes. Here we see that *parataḥ-prāmāṇya* of the Naiyāyikas is a logical necessity. Thus this successful issue of knowledge is the *ratio cognoscendi* that it is valid.

The question may be viewed from another standpoint: "Truth is prior to verification. A judgment is true, not because it is verified by an appeal to facts; but it is verified because it is true." When the problem of validity is tested from this standpoint, it is clear that the validity of knowledge as revealed by the inference from its pragmatic utility presupposes that the truth of knowledge was already pre-existing independently of such inference and it is in this sense that knowledge may be said to be self-valid. In other words, pragmatic utility merely reveals and confirms the pre-existent truth of knowledge. Hence as regards the *ratio-essendi* or origin, validity was already there in knowledge. The question whether such self-validity is due to the inherent elements of knowledge itself or is the result of extraneous elements is a different problem which requires separate treatment. Śavara, the great exponent of the Pūrva-Mīmāṁsā and his followers Prabhākara, Kumārila and teachers of the Vedānta, who advocate the self-established authority of the Vedas, maintain the self-evident character of knowledge as an imperative demand of logic. We shall try to give an account of their respective positions when we shall deal with their standpoints. It is here noted only by way of introduction how those two theories *svataḥ-prāmāṇya* and *parataḥ-prāmāṇya* came into being in the study of epistemology.[3]

This analysis of the problem of validity in Indian noetics rests on two well-known principles, *viz.*, (i) appeal to facts and correspondence on the one hand and *excessive belief in the maxim,* (ii) that 'a power by itself non-existent cannot be brought into existence by another,[4] on the other. It is further significant that Buddhists propounded their theory of validity on the basis of the first principle while the Sāṁkhyists take their stand on the more second in explaining their viewpoint.

Explanation of the Buddhist view

Thus Buddhist thinkers in explaining the valid nature of experience lay stress on correspondence, and workability is the only test of truth in their theory. Right knowledge is uncontradicted knowledge *(avisaṁvādijñāna)* which enables us to attain the knowledge.[5] Attainment of objects means successful activity in regard to the objects and implies understanding them in their true perspective.

Dharmottara thinks that the object attained is not identical with the object known, for the object attained is different from the object known, because the latter does not exist when the former is attained though they belong to the same stream or series.

The Buddhists and the Naiyāyikas agree in this that they accept practical efficiency or *"arthakriyākāritvam"* as the test of truth. The relation of facts and ideas of the Buddhists, however, differ from that advocated by the Naiyāyikas. It should be remembered that the Buddhists hold that invalidity inheres in all cognitions but validity is established by something extraneous; for, according to the metaphysics of the Buddhists, *śūnyam* or *Universal void* is the highest truth. And in order to establish this position, Nāgārjuna, the greatest Bauddha dialectician, has shown that everything is full of contradictions admitting of no logical scrutiny. Nāgārjuna thus assailing the realistic position, establishes the Bauddha theory that the inherent nature of knowledge is bound to be invalid and validity in any particular case can only be established as due to extraneous causes. In the Buddhist epistemology knowledge is studied from its two different aspects:

(i) knowledge transcendental, and
(ii) experience immanent.

Knowledge from the metaphysical standpoint is momentary, *svalakṣaṇa* and *nirvikalpa*. Experience, however, has some practical validity as it leads to the attainment of the object Dharmakīrti speaks of this kind of practical knowledge as *pramājñāna* or right knowledge. *Samyagjñāna* or true knowledge, Dharmakīrti observes, is the invariable antecedent to the attainment of all a man desires to have.[6]

When with the presentation of any knowledge we get the object presented by it, we may be said to have right knowledge. The process of knowledge starts with the perceptual presentation and ends with the attainment of objects represented by it and fulfilment of some practical need. There are five stages in the acquisition of experience.

(I) The presentation of the object, *i.e.*, pure sensations as "something" which causes these sensations of sight and touch, etc., by stimulating the appropriate nerves, *i.e.*, the book.

(II) Representation—In this stage ideas from memory due to past experiences are called up and associated with the pure sensations so as to make them intelligible by bringing them under different categories of genus, differentia, etc., such as this sensation-giving object belongs to the book class and so on.

(III) In the next stage, there is a consciousness that this object may serve some good purpose *(Iṣṭasādhanatājñānam)*.

(IV) In the fourth stage there is the prompting of desire in response to it.

(V) In the last stage there is an activity in accordance with the prompting to realise the object following the direction of knowledge.

It is this realisation which is called *arthakriyākāritvam* of knowledge and determines its validity from the practical standpoint. This *arthakriyākārirvam* is almost the same as the test of workability of the Western Pragmatists.[7] This, in its extreme form', implies that no perception or knowledge can be regarded as in any way valid unless it leads to the realisation of objects fulfilling the need which it was meant to fulfil. This however to be rather an extreme position even from the Buddhistic standpoint. For how could we then explain perception when it is not accompanied by the effort to test it by practical efficiency? If the knowledge of the object is not put to the test by practical effort are you to reject it as invalid? Obviously this cannot be so; for a very large number of perceptions is never put to such actual practical test. Therefore it would seem that all that the Buddhists mean to imply by this *arthakriyākāritvam* is that perception or knowledge gained thereby must be capable of being verified in some practical manner when occasion arises. It is this difficulty which leads Dharmottara to make a distinction between the right knowledge which is the immediate antecedent of attainment *(arthakriyānirbhāsam)* and that which leads to attainment through certain intermediate stages *(arthakriyāsamarthe ca pravartakam)*.

Thus though pure sensations are *nirvikalpa* still perceptions as they enter into our experience would seem to involve many notions which elaborate the sensations which we receive. But the question is : Are the notions to be regarded as real and empirically valid or are they to be looked upon as creation of mere imagination and therefore as utterly illusory?

Nature of notions which make knowledge concrete and determinate

An analysis of the perceptual process will reveal how the notions enter into our perception and make our knowledge concrete and determinate, Whenever anything is presented it excites and revives the memory of similar past impressions through spontaneous suggestive forces of the word implying the object *(śabda smṛti)*. As soon as these impressions are recalled they help to revive some non-sensuous elements such as the notion of substance,' universality and particularity, etc. The sensuous or presentative elements are then synthesised with these non-sensuous elements and the object is apprehended as a substance having attributes, as a particular belonging to a certain genus, and as a whole having parts and so on.

These non-sensuous elements being subjective con-tributions without any objective counterpart have not got that particular vividness and distinctness which is the distinguishing mark of the sensuous element *(viśadāvabhāsa)*. They, however, by virtue of their synthesis with the sensuous elements appear to be apprehended as equally vivid, distinct and objective and ordinary minds therefore fail to notice the distinction between sensuous and non-sensuous elements in perception and their notions of universality, etc., are regarded as extramental. Thus it is their association with sensuous elements which makes them appear as sensuous and objective. Non-sensuous elements therefore shine with a light not their own but borrowed from the sensuous ones. Perception involves both sensuous or presentative and non-sensuous or representative elements. The problem therefore arises—as to how are we to construe and explain the origin and nature of these non-sensuous notions?

Perception is the result of the conjunction of the organ of sense and the object. But neither the sense-organ nor the object has any capacity to act upon the non-sensuous elements by appealing through memory. For by the time the non-sensuous elements are revived and integrated with the sensuous ones, the operations of the organs of sense will have ceased. The subsequent apprehension of the revived elements cannot therefore be said to be due to those operations. The subject alone has the function and capacity to revive these elements through memory. Hence the so-called sensuous apprehensions of the universal, etc., by means of the senses is erroneous.[8]

If sensuous apprehension of the universals, etc., were at all possible, it must be due to the sense-organs acted upon by the object characterised by universality, etc., present in the object or by these revived notions *(smaraṇasahitendriyajam)* or by the object and the revived notions operating together. In the first case, the universal, etc., not being in touch with the sense-organ could not be sensuously apprehended, in the second case, they would be apprehended simultaneously with the sensuous processes waiting for the revival of the word images and the notions but that is absurd. In the third case, the resulting apprehension would not be sensuous but a combination of sensuous and non-sensuous elements.

Deeper metaphysical speculation shows that the so-called universality, substance, etc., do not exist as eternal self-existent realities and that these very notions of universality, substantiality, etc., involve antinomies and contradictions. Hence in the absence of such realities, any sensuous apprehension thereof, even though certified to be valid by sense-perception for the time being must be regarded as erroneous; for obviously what does not exist at all is unfit to occasion any sense-perception.[9]

Thus it is clear that what appears to be a substance having attribute, as a thing having parts and so on, is not an extra-mental fact, but something built up by the subject out of elements contributed from within.[10]

An analysis of the notions as involved in the mental processes reveals that there are some notions which have an objective basis and reference while there are others which are purely subjective being the products of imagination. Thus there are two distinct groups of notions, according to the author of Nyāya-mañjarī—one *idantāgrāhi* apprehended as implying an objective reference, the other *anidantāgrāhi* implying no such objective reference. The first group comprises notions of universality, substantiality, etc., for they are apprehended though erroneously as something sensuous and objective and implying extra-mental reality. The second group includes the processes which are purely subjective implying no objective validity *(chātramanoratha-viracita)*. The Buddhistic schools call both the kinds of notions, *vikalpas* or notions wrongly apprehended. This the Buddhistic schools maintain by showing how these notions enter into our knowledge though they have no metaphysical validity.[11]

This is what may be called the phenomenal aspect of knowledge or the aspect in which knowledge appears to us. Knowledge, in this sense, is dependent or *pratantra* and is the work of the understanding and its categories having validity only experience. Thus the phenomenal existence of the world with its distinctions of subject and object is accepted by the Buddhistic thinkers; and judgments are formed to explain the empiric experience which helps our life progress. When such experience answers the need of our practical life it is called valid, otherwise it is invalid, What is called valid or normal knowledge is, from the standpoint of the Buddhistic metaphysics, invalid as the categories themselves which form the so-called valid judgments are erroneous or false. Buddhists have emphasised the false character of all existence consistently with their views of non-validity of all knowledge *(svataḥprāmāṇya).*

Criticism of the Buddhist's validity of knowledge

In analysing the viewpoints of Dharmottara and Dharmakīrti it appears that the Buddhist thinkers take their stand only on the workability *(artha-kriyākāritvam)* of knowledge. Determinate knowledge or experience by itself is from the standpoint of the Bauddha metaphysics, erroneous and its erroneous character has been justified by their explanation of determinate factors of knowledge. But our experience of the pragmatic life, which enables us to attain the object and is therefore uncontradicted, is taken as valid. The only test of truth is its verification.[12]

Experience is verified because it is true. Verification is not the cause or guarantee of truth. In that case, some forms of valid experience themselves would be divorced from the category of validity. For example, the inferential knowledge which goes to establish the objects of past and future apprehension is to be taken as invalid in its nature as at the time of inference the verification of past and future objects becomes an impossibility. And again if such an inferential knowledge is denied validity, then the definition of validity based on verification becomes too narrow. The definition becomes also too wide as it will include *smṛti* or memory knowledge if memory-knowledge is to be excluded from the category of valid knowledge or *pramājñāna*—for in memory verification cannot be questioned. Uddyotakara thus says that practical efficiency is not, however, the sole test of truth. There is such a thing as inferential validity. The Naiyāyika definition of *pramājñānam* thus does not deny validity to past and future facts where the test of practical efficiency is inapplicable, nor does it include *smṛti-jñānaṁ* or memory-knowledge which is placed in a different category as *smṛtijñānam* is based on *saṁskāra* only *(saṁskāra-mātrajanyaṁ jñānaṁ smṛtiḥ)*. This will be made clearer when judging the Naiyāyika position.[13]

Sāṁkhya conception of Validity

The Sāṁkhya school advocates the doctrine *"exnihilo nihil fit"* the existent cannot come out of the non-existent nor can the non-existent come out of the existent. The effect persists in the cause in an unmanifested state. What is valid is always valid and what is invalid is always invalid. Validity inheres in valid knowledge and invalidity inheres in invalid knowledge. Validity and invalidity are therefore to be admitted in knowledge. Pre-existence of validity and invalidity before manifestation follows from the Sāṁkhya theory of causation or *Satkāryavādaḥ*.

Sāṁkhya explanation of the Validity of Knowledge

In every determinate cognition we have two elements in the Sāṁkhya epistemology, determination of *Buddhi* particularly modified and consciousness reflected in the modification. *Buddhi* works in determinating the nature of objects and the force of consciousness *(citiśakti)* works in reflecting itself in the modified Buddhi and imitating the modification. Question of doubt, invalidity, etc., cannot be urged in the pure consciousness; they are functions or modifications of *Buddhi*. Consciousness even in the determinate conscious process being only an aspect of pure eternal consciousness can in no way be called invalid in its nature. Invalidity may therefore be urged in the function of *Buddhi*. Truth of knowledge consists in recording the things as they are. When *Buddhi* determines the object in its true nature the experience is called valid, otherwise it is invalid. Through the mediation of *Buddhi* connection of the unattached *Puruṣa* with the object has been established and called knowledge, again the connection of *Puruṣa* with this definite knowledge resulting in the determination 'I know' is known as revelation of apprehension *(pramā-bodaḥ),*[14] Validity invalidity, proof and disproof are inherent in the nature of this apprehension of Puruṣa. It is proved and disproved by itself. All appearances forming the objects of knowledge "are valid entities.[15] As regards the validity of knowledge the *Sāṁkhyas* belong to the school of extreme realism. To them appearances have value and validity of their own. Even false appearances, because they are appearances, are not false, they are also valid entities implying objective reality.[16] What we call valid and invalid knowledge, the *Sāṁkhyas* hold, stand on the same footing. The facthood of theoretic assuredness of the false percepts is not denied in the *Sāṁkhya* system. In explaining the epistemology of illusion the *Sāṁkhyas* argue that in every case of perception, true or false, an object is actually perceived. Prabhācandra in his *Prameyakamalamārtaṇḍa* mentions *prasiddhārthakhyāti* as the view supported by Bhāskara and the followers of *Sāṁkhya.* According to this theory whatever appears, is; for, there can be no appearance of what never exists. Though what appears at one moment may not exist in the next moment, still it is at the moment when it appears. If non-existence at a subsequent moment be the ground of invalidity of knowledge, then existence will have to be denied to lightning which disappears immediately after it has flashed.[17]

Criticism of the *Śaṁkhya* theory

In criticising the view, Prabhācandra argues that this view is not at all satisfactory because it makes all cognitions valid and the distinction between truth and falsity of cognition is without any meaning, for all knowledge records the objects as they are.[18] This is an absurd position and involves contradiction. In the explanation of the *Sāṁkhya* theory of valid knowledge we have already noticed that in defining *Pramā* or valid knowledge the *Sāṁkhya* logicians take their stand on the record of things as they are *(yathārtha-paricchittiḥ).* The form *artha,* Vijñāna-bhikṣu observes, indicates its distinction from false knowledge.[19] And now if the Sāṁkhya teachers explain the object of illusory cognition as an established object *(Prasiddhārthakhyāti)* they cannot avoid self-contradiction. If falsity and truth of knowledge be self-constituted, then the contradictions in cognitions cannot be explained. The *Saṁkhya* maxim that *śakti* or capacity which is not existent by itself cannot be originated otherwise, is not enough to give the satisfactory explanation of the validity and invalidity of knowledge. When I cognise water as water we call it valid and when I mistake the rays of the sun as water it is called invalid. In both cases judgment has been formed 'I. see the water,' it is now therefore to be admitted by the advocates of the *prasiddhārthakhyāti* that the *śakti* or capacity of both validity and invalidity lies in the judgment construction 'I see the water.' But a question may be asked that if validity and invalidity, proof and disproof, are equally self-constituted, conformity and non-conformity would arise indiscriminately in cognition, as there is no law or limiting principle to guide conformity in the case when it is called valid and non-conformity in the case of invalidity and thereby to establish truth and falsity on the sound logical basis. To explain away the apparent contradiction if the *Sāṁkhya* logicians advance different sets (groups) of causal relations (elements) in the case of conformity and non-conformity with the objects in cognition, their own theory of self-dependence falls to the grounds; by introducing the extraneous causes to explain true knowledge they will have to admit the *Naiyāyika* theory of *parataḥ prāmāṇya* discarding their own theory.

The *Nyāya* theory of validity and invalidity of knowledge.

Pramā or valid knowledge has been defined by *Udayana* in his *Tātparyya-pariśuddhi* as 'Cognition of the realnatine of things.'[20] What constitutes the real nature of things? It is nothing else but being or existence in the case of that which is and non-being or non-existence in the case of that which is not. That is to say, when something that is. is apprehended as it really is *(tathā-bhūtam)* and not as something of a contrary nature *(aviparītam),* then that which is thus apprehended constitutes the true nature of the thing, and analogously when a non-entity is apprehended as such, *i.e.,* as what is not, as something of a contrary nature, then, that which is thus apprehended constitutes the frue nature, of the thing."[21] Knowledge advances with judgment construction. And a judgment consists of subject and the predicate linked together by a copula. Subject is something which is characterised by the predicate which characterises the nature of the subject. The subject gives us a glimpse of its existence, it is at first apprehended as "this" without any particular characteristics, and the predicate determines the nature of the given by specifying its properties. Where the determinateness agrees with the nature of the object, it is called valid or *Yathārtha,* and where it does not agree it is called invalid or *ayathārtha*. Valid knowledge, according to Nyāyā view, copies reality of things. Things are the grounds of logical truth. It is the external world existing apart from our knowledge that determines the true nature of our knowledge. Experience is the product or resultant of the causal action of the nut-sell on the self. The causal categories are called *pramāṇas* or sources of valid knowledge and the absolute and universal characteristic of valid knowledge is known as *pramāṇya* in the Nyāya epistemology. This explanation of valid experience is shortsighted. It cannot include God's eternal knowledge in its scope. The God of the *Naiyīyika* is the creator of this universe. He possesses existence, knowledge and bliss *(saccidānanda)*. He is endowed with such qualities as absence of demerit *(adharma),* wrong knowledge *(mithyājñāna),* and negligence *(pramāda),* and presence of merit, knowledge and equanimity *(dharmajñānasāmādhisampad)*. He is omnipotent in regard to his creation, though he is influenced by the results of acts done by the beings he creates. He is omniscient since he possesses right knowledge, which is an independent apprehension of reality. He has eternal intelligence and since his cognitions are everlasting there is no need for memory and inferential knowledge.

This eternal ever-valid consciousness of God cannot be styled the product or resultant of proofs *(pramāṇaphala)* and the suggested explanation of validity is not enough to prove the validity of God's supreme consciousness. The *Nyāya* explanation of *pramāṇa* as means of vahid knowledge, cannot be taken as all-comprehensive. Such an explanation only goes to prove the logical validity of empirical knowblge. Udayana in his Kusumāñjali explains the notions *pramā,* and *pramāṇa,* etc., in an all-comprehensive way which comprises both empirical knowledge as well as the eternal consciousness of God. Varadarāja in his *Tarkikarakṣa* follows the view-point of Udayana and gives twofoll explanations of the notions of *pramā* and *pramāṇa,* etc., from its eternal and non-eternal standpoint. This gives us a clue to understand the real nature of valid knowledge in the *Nyāya* epistemology. *Yathārthānubhava* or knowledge of things as they are, is the characteristic mark of valid knowledge and this special feature may be noticed both in the individual experience and in the eternal experience of God. But the notion of *pramāṇa* Varadarāja observes, differs in eternal and non-eternal knowledge. In the case of God's eternal consciousness, on account of its eternality, *pramāṇa* cannot be explained as means or source of knowledge, but it means the substratum *(āśraya)* of consciousness, while in the ordinary logical experience, *pramāṇa* is defined as *pramā-karaṇa* or means of valid knowledge.[22]

Prāmāṇya or the absolute characteristic of *pramā* or valid knowledge may thus be explained in two ways. In the case of valid logical experience it is valid because it is the result of the causal categories which bring forth the correspondence of ideas to objects. Experience belonging to God is taken as valid because God Himself who is endowed with the absence of false knowledge is the substratum of such experience. This explanation thus avoids the narrowness of the definition of *pramāṇa.*[23] Both God and individual beings are called knower in the Nyāya theory of knowledge. Here again the same question arises that knowership or *jñāna kartṛtva* implies activity on the part of the agent. And this explanation again fails to explain the knowership or *pramātṛtva* of God, the possessor of eternal consciousness; for any activity attributed to the knower to originate knowledge will negate the eternality of the divine experience. To explain away this difficulty Udayana in his Kusumañjali defines *pramātṛtva* or knowership as the basis of the absolute relation with pramā or valid knowledge. The nature of this relation may specifically be explained in different cases. In the finite exprience of the individual beings senses, mind, etc., are the apparatus which constitute means of their valid knowledge, and they prompt men to action, to examine the correspondence of ideas to outward objects and thereby to appraise the value of knowledge. In this way, in the cause of originated knowledge some form of activity is attributed to the knower or *pramātā* or one endowed with the action favourable to valid knowledge *(pramānukāla-kṛtimatvam)*. Each of the elements constituting the apparatus of knowledge has a function peculiar to itself. But that function depends on the activity of the percipient subject. No question on activity dependent or independent can be introduced in the eternal consciousness belonging to God. Notions of *prāmātṛtva* and *pramānatva* applied to God imply no idea of agency or instrumentality. What they connote is his inherent and absolute relation with *pramā* or valid knowledge.[24]

Validity and its origination in the Nyāya epistemology

Prāmāṇya or validity, which inheres in valid knowledge, is studied in the Nyāya-epistemology from two different standpoints : origination and apprehension *(utpatti* and *jñapti)*. The bone of contention regarding validity of knowledge centres round the causal elements which originate knowledge *(janaka-kāraṇa-viṣ ayaka)* and the factors that make knowledge intelligible *(jñāpaka kāraṇa-viṣayaka)*. Here the Nyāya explanation differs from that of the *Mīmāṁsists* who advocate self-validity of knowledge. According to the *Naiyāyikas* validity is established by *parataḥ* or something other than the constituents of knowledge. In support of their proposition regarding origination, the *Naiyāyikas* argue that *pramā* or right knowledge depends on some causes *(e.g.,* absence of defect, etc.) other than common constituents of knowledge and is an effect just as false or wrong knowledge is, by common admission, an effect originated by causes other than the elements giving rise to the cognition.[25] In explaining the position Udayana followed by Gaṅgeśa contends that if knowledge for its origination depends only upon the common constituents of knowledge themselves, there would be no generic distinction between right and wrong apprehension; for even in the case of invalid knowledge the presence of the common elements of knowledge cannot be denied.[26] If, however, it is contended that distinction would be there as invalid knowledge is due to certain particular defective elements *(doṣas),* it might be urged; that this does not much improve matters; since the distinctions then lie in certain special features superadded to the common elements. Since invalid knowledge is explicable by the introduction of certain defective elenents *(doṣas)* in addition to the common constituents, invalid knowledge would be only a particular form of *praṇā.* For it is a well-known truth that a particular form or variety of anything is constituted when the common essence works itself out in conjunction with special elements.[27] And if it be urged that the presence of the common elements or essence does not altogether obliterate the distinction between *pramā* and *apramā* or the analogy that inspite of the common essence between two pots *(ghaṭas)* or twins the difference between them is well-marked and cannot be mistaken, the *Naiyāyika* argues that the analogy is not applicable. For the distinction between one pot and another is a distinction between two objects belonging to the same genus and constituted by the particular elements forming the individuality of each pot, while the distinction between *pramā* and *apramā* is not one between two species of the same genus, as the two are contradictory terms forming two different classes. If, therefore, this generic difference is to be explained satisfactorily, it is inevitable that the reason must be sought for in the causal differences originating the two. For Gaṅgeśa in his *Tattvacintāmaṇi* says that it is a well-known principle and a fact of experience that whenever. there is a generic difference between two things, the reason for the difference must be in the causes giving rise to them. Thus the pot and the cloth belong to two different classes because their originating causes are different. Similarly, the knowledge of pot and the knowledge of cloth are two separate effects as their originating causes are distinct, the contact of the sense organ with the pot being the cause of the former while sense contact with the cloth is cause of the latter.[28] In the case of *pramā,* it is common ground to say that it arises as a result of certain defective elements *(doṣas)* as its cause and if we are to distinguish *pramā* as a separate genus, the inevitable demand of logic is that we must postulate some causal difference (such as *guṇa)* which is opposite or contradictory to that of *apramā* and since *doṣa* is, by common consent, the originating cause of *pramā, guṇa,* its contradictory, must be regarded as the differential originating cause of *pramā,* thus constituting the two as separate distinct categories.[29] By this dialeçtic the *Naiyāyika* shows how inevitably we are led to conclude that valid knowledge has causes other than those constituting common elements. For if we are to distinguish *pramā* from *apramā* which by common admission is *parataḥ,* we cannot help introducing other elements as the originating cause of *pramā* which therefore is also proved *parataḥ.*

Validity is not self-apprehended

As regards the cognoscibility of validity the *Naiyāyikas* argue that apprehension or cognition of validity is also not sell-evident.[30] If validity were self-apprehended, then there would be no doubt in regard to a cognition, for then cognition itself would imply or certify its own validity. If cognition itself does not assume the certainty of validity, then the inevitable implication is that validity is not self-apprehended.[31] This fact of doubt about the validity of knowledge leading to the inference that validity is not self-apprehended but other-apprehended may be put syllogistically thus : validity of the first cognition is not apprehended by the causal conditions of knowledge, it is apprehended by elements other than those causal conditions; since inspite of the presence of the causal conditions of knowledge, doubt about its validity rises at the next moment just as in the case of invalidity or *aprāmāṇya.*[32] Cognition is apprehended by sense perception but sense perception does not carry with it an assurance of its own validity. Validity is apprehended by the mediate process of reflection, or in other words, by means of *inference.* A man seeking water perceives water at a considerable distance and on the basis of his perception he attempts to have it. If the exertion he puts forth becomes fruitful the cognition is called valid; if again it is futile, cognition is invalid. Now from the fruitfulness of the cognition, validity of knowledge is inferred for that which is not valid does not give rise to fruitful exertion.[33] This is a purely negative form of inference *(kevala-*

vyatireki) based on the failure of one's attempt. There are other stages to be marked to prove validity of knowledge. First an indeterminate cognition of water arises and it becomes determinate as this is water, and then his desire for water springs forth and activity begins. And when the activity of the knower answers his need, the cognition is taken as valid by reason of his successful activity. The negative inference further implies that no positive instance is possible to prove the validity of a first case of cognition. In the first cognition of water *(anabhyāsadaśotpannajñāna)* validity cannot be established except by this purely negative inference.[34] In the second, third and subsequent cognitions the validity may be proved by the inference based on both positive and negative instances. The valid nature of the previous cognition serves as a positive instance and its invalidity as a negative one. The inference is thus called *anvayavyatireki* or positive-negative in its character and runs as follows : The second and third cognition of water is valid because it belongs to the same category in which the activity of the knower has been proved fruitful, *e.g.,* the first cognition of water.[35] Similarly, invalidity of cognition is also inferred in the Nyāya theory from the failure of the attempt of the knower.[36] In the pragmatic affairs of life some activities are fruitful and some are futile. The question may naturally arise—what are causes of success or failure in the activity of life? Perception themselves cannot explain the enigma. For it is obvious that the sense-perception cannot always unfold to us the true nature of objects. We perceive the sun moving and the earth steady but in reality the fact is quite otherwise. We see the moon having a particular size and shape but the moon is far bigger than what she appears. Hence perception itself is not the guarantee of its validity. To explain the success and failure of life and thus the validity and invalidity of knowledge we must endeavour to find out some extraneous causes which determine the true nature of cognitions. When our attempts fail we conclude that we are mistaken because some defects in addition to the common causes must have crept into the process of our cognitions and it is these defects which veil the real nature of objects from our sight and make them appear what they are really not. And again in cases where the objects of knowledge appear as they are and the exertion undertaken by the perceiver is fruitful, the cognition is regarded as valid and it is concluded that the causes which lead to unsuccessful activity are here absent and in addition to the common causes there are some extra qualities, vividness of objects, etc., as a result of which the objects flash out in their true perspective.[37] These defects or *doṣas* and *guṇas* or extra qualities are of various kinds in different types of cognition.[38] And absence of defects or presence of extra-qualities *(guṇas)* in addition to the common causes lead to the validity of cognition and thereby answer our need in the pragmatic life. Defects in addition to the common ground make our attempts vain and thereby invalidate our cognition.

Criticism against the *Nyāya* conception of *Pramā*

Śrīharṣa in his *Khaṇḍanakhaṇḍakhādya* proves the unsatisfactory character of *pramā* as defined by the *Naiyāyikas. Naiyāyikas* define *pramā* or valid knowledge as *tattvānubhūtiḥ* or cognition of a thing as it really is. Both the words *tattvam* and *anubhūtiḥ* are significant for *anubhūtiḥ* or apprehension cannot by itself constitute valid knowledge, for there may be wrong apprehension. Again, *tattvaṁ* alone cannot be *pramā,* for *tattvaṁ* means reality and may thus include objects of knowledge, *pramā* is however, subjective.[39]

Śrīharṣa says that this definition is fallacious; it will not bear scrutiny. In *tattvānubhūtiḥ,* there are two component terms *tattvam* and *anubhūtiḥ*. Now what do the Naiyāyikas mean by *tattvam?* It may have a derivative meaning *(yogārthaḥ)* or it may have an accepted meaning independent of its derivation *(rūdhārthaḥ)*. In the first alternative the term *tat* implies a previous reference and *tattvam* will then mean the essence or quiddity of the referred. In immediate knowledge the presented object will call up a memory image, and knowledge will result from a synthesis of the presented and represented elements, but the memory image called up may not correspond to the object presented and the synthesis will not result in valid knowledge. The term *tat* may refer only to the object of memory image which is representative of an object previously known, but the memory image may not unfold the reality of the presented object, and the definition of *tat* cannot stand on the basis of reference to objects previously known. Take the example of nacre mistaken for silver. The image of silver called up by nacre will make nacre appear as silver. If by *tattvam* the essence of the represented object is meant, then the *tattvam* will be *rajatatvam* and nacre appearing as silver will satisfy the condition of *tattvānubhūtiḥ* and will constitute valid knowledge.[40]

If by the term *tat* is meant the object called up only in cases where there is correspondence between the memory image and the object presented, then the definition will involve the charge of *ālmāśrayatvam* or *proving idem per idem.* Again, if *tattvam* is taken as *bhāvavāci* or in the abstract sense to mean only quiddity, then *tattvam* will not include concrete objects such as pot, cloth etc., and the knowledge of particular objects will not be *pramā* or valid and the definition becomes too narrow.

To avoid these difficulties if *tattvam* is taken in a technical sense as *svarūpam* (peculiar characteristics) even then the definition cannot steer clear of fallacies. If by *svarūpam* is understood a being not immanent in many but the special form of every individual object, the question arises : does *tattvam* connote all the peculiar forms of all individual objects combined or these forms separately? In the first case, all the forms are not to be found in any particular object and the definition becomes absurd. In the second case, one particular form, say of pot, is not to be found in another particular object, say cloth, and so the apprehension becomes invalid.[41]

Again, this definition of *tattvānubhūtiḥ* cannot bar wrong apprehension, though *tattvam* is taken to mean *svarūpam,* in the case of wrong apprehension such as the apprehension of silver in nacre cognition of *svarūpa* cannot be questioned. The judgment in wrong apprehension has three elements or component parts, namely, thisness *(idantā),* characteristic of silver *(rajatatvam)* and the relation *(saṁbandha)* existing between the two—there is *svarūpam* in all these elements. The *svarūpam* of 'this' *(idam)* cannot be denied nor can the *svarūpam* in *rajatatvam,* or the *svarūpam* of the relation of inherence *(samavāya saṁbandha)* be gainsaid. Therefore, even in wrong apprehension there is *svarūpānubhūti.* To avoid this charge the *Naiyāyikas* may argue that an inherent relation should not be taken in the sense of pure existence or existence as such, *i.e.,* as a mere abstraction free from the concrete components. But it should be taken in the sense of an inherent relation between the presentation and the representation. So the problem of validity turns really on the nature of inherence. The presentation *(idam)* appearing as silver presents a case of wrong inherence; there is nothing wrong in the presentation *(idam)* as such, nor is there anything wrong in the conception of silver as such, the wrongness is in the relation between the two, there being no correspondence between the presented *idam* and the represented element (silver). *Idam* not appearing as nacre which it really is, the falsity really lies not in the individual components, but in their mutual relation. This relation between the two components being false, it cannot be held that we have here a case of *svarūpa* of their inherent relation. The advaitins however contend that the relation of inherence itself is not thus invalidated though in this substratum it might be false and therefore the apprehension of its real character *(svarūpa)* is not an impossibility. As Śrīharṣa puts it, when it is said that *Devadatta* is not at home it does not mean that *Devadatta* is non-existent. The inherent relation though denied in a substrate has a *svarūpam,* and *svarūpānubhūti* will include a case of wrong inherence and therefore of wrong apprehension.[42]

As regards the definition of right cognition as the direct apprehension of the real nature of things, Śrīharṣa argues that such a definition is faulty, since, if one by accident hits rightly on certain things concealed under a cover and not perceived, or makes a right inference from faulty data or by fallacious methods, though the awareness may be right, it cannot be called right cognition. Cognition, to be valid, must be produced through unerring instruments ; here, however, in case of chance guesses it may sometimes be light without being produced by unerring sense instruments. Correspondence of the cognition with its object *(yathārthānubhavaḥ pramā)* cannot also be taken as a proper definition of right cognition. Such correspondence might mean either that which represents the reality of the object itself or similarity to the object.The real nature of an object is indeterminable, and so correspondence of awareness with the object may rather be defined as similarity of the former to the latter. If this similarity means that the awareness must have such a character as is possessed by the object *(jñānaviṣayīkṛtena rūpeṇa sādṛśyam),* then this is clearly impossible ; for qualities that belong to the object cannot belong to the awareness; there may be an awareness of two green pots, but the awareness is neither two, nor green.[43] It may be contended that the correspondence consists in this, that the greenness, etc., belong to the object as qualities possessed by it, whereas they belong to awareness as being qualities which it manifests.[44] But even this would not hold good in the case of illusory perception of silver in a conch-shell; the awareness of "before me" in the perception of 'before me the silver' has to be admitted as being a right cognition. If this is admitted to be a right cognition, then, it is meaningless to define right cognition as true correspondence. If, however, entire correspondence of awareness and its object be insisted on, then partial correspondence like the above can hardly be brought within the definition. But, if entire correspondence is considered indispensable, then the correctness of the partial correspondence has to be ignored. It is, however, conceded by the *Naiyāyika* that all cognitions are valid, so far as reference to an object is concerned, and only the nature of cognition may be doubted as right or wrong, when we are considering the correspondence between the nature of the object and the mental modification qualified by the awareness of the object. Moreover, the correspondence can refer only to the character, form or appearance of the thing as distinguished from the thing itself. Hence our affirmations regarding the objects as distinct from the characters and to which the characters are supposed to belong would be false.

Udayana's definition of right cognition as *samyak paricchittiḥ* or proper discernment is next taken up and Śrīharṣa says that the word *samyak* (proper) is meaningless; for if *samyak* means 'entire' then 'the definition is useless, since it is impossible to perceive all the visible and invisible constituent elements of a thing, and no one but an omniscient being could perceive a thing with all its characters, properties or qualities.[45] If right discernment means the discernment of an object with its special differentia, this again is untenable, for even in wrong cognition, say of conch-shell as silver, the perceiver seems to perceive the distinguishing marks of silver in the conch-shell. The real point centres in the difficulty of judging whether the distinguishing marks observed are real or not, and there is no way of determining this in the definition advanced. If, the distinguishing features be described as being those characteristics without the perception of which there can be no certain knowledge and the perception of which ensures right cognition, then it may well be said that it amounts to begging the question. Besides it is impossible to discover any feature of any cognition of which one can be positively sure that it is not wrong. A dreamer confuses all sorts of characters and appearances and yet perceives them all as right. It might be argued that in the case of right perception the object is perceived with its special distinguishing features, as in the case of the true perception of silver, whereas in the case of the false perception of silver in the conch-shell no such distinguishing features are observed. But even then the question is how to determine the essential nature of the distinguishing features; for if any kind of distinguishing feature would do, then in the case of the false perception of silver in the conch-shell the distinguishing feature of lying before the eyes is also possessed by the conch-shell. If all the particular distinguishing features are insisted on, then it is impracticable as an object has an almost infinite number of distinguishing features and it would be simply impossible to make the definition include them all.[46]

Finally taking the definition of right cognition as "apprehension which is not incorrect or not defective" *(avyabhicārī anubhavaḥ),* Srīharṣa contends that 'not incorrect' or 'not defective'..... cannot imply that *pramā* or valid cognition exists only when the object exists, for then inferential cognition, which often relates to past, distant and future things, would be false. It cannot further mean that the right cognition is similar to its object in all respects, since cognition is so different in nature from the object that it is not possible that there should be any case in which it would be similar in all respects. And, if it be maintained that awareness and its object are one and the same, then this would apply even to those cases where one object is wrongly perceived as another and hence the word *avyabhicārī* would not be able to distinguish right knowledge from wrong cognition. In other words, distinction between *pramā* and *apramā* would be obliterated.[47]

Criticism against the Nyāya explanation of the origination of validity

Now, if we examine the *Nyāya* syllogism advanced to explain the genesis of validity, we meet with a number of difficulties. In the first place, it might be asked in the given inference[48] what is the implication of the major term—"elements other than the common constituents of knowledge?" If knowledge in the major means all cognition, the major would imply' "generated by causal conditions other than the causal conditions of knowledge. In other words, the absence of elements generating knowledge would give rise to knowledge—which is an absurdity.[49] And the absurdity again would extend to the minor *(pakṣa)* and the middle. So far as the minor is concerned, the major as thus determined cannot reside in it; for *pramā* or validity, the minor term, having already been identified with knowledge, cannot be "generated by causal conditions which are not the causal conditions of knowledge." that is, there would be *bādha* or incompatibility between the minor and the major as "conditions of knowledge" and "conditions other than the conditions of knowledge" are incompatible.[50] Similarly, there would be contradiction between the middle *(hetu)* or the major *(sādhya);* for the middle being defined as "because it is originated knowledge" *(janya-jñānatvāt),* it cannot be related to the major which is characterised as "generated by conditions other than the conditions of knowledge" and the two are obviously contradictory. Moreover, the explanatory example *apramā* or invalidity suffers from the fallacy known as *sādhya vikala;* for *sādhya* or the major as thus defined, cannot be found in *apramā* or in the example as the latter is a particular form of knowledge and is, therefore, bound to be originated by conditions originating knowledge though, of course, with additional defects or *doṣas*. Hence the major is inconsistent with the example.[51] Again, the expression *jñāna* or knowledge in the major taken in the sense of cognition *in general,* would include God's knowledge which being eternal, is without any cause. Hence the said major would be impossible (or *aprasiddha)* since in the case of divine knowledge, which is without any cause, the question of there being elements other than those originating knowledge, seems to be absurd.[52]

If again, 'knowledge' in the major be taken to mean either any particular cognition, such as inference, perception, etc., or the collection of all particular cognitions *(i.e.,* if we take knowledge in its distributive or collective sense), there would arise the fallacy of *siddha sādhanatā* or proving the already proved on either supposition; as the *major, viz.,* "conditions other than those originating knowledge" would be found in the minor taken in either of the above senses. If taken in the former sense, the minor would include perception which has as its cause or *hetu,* the sense-organ which is something other than those elements, which constitute, say inference, a particular form of knowledge. If understood in the latter sense, the major "conditions other than those originating knowledge," would be already, proved in perception in as much as the sense-organ involved in perception would be an element or condition which is other than the conditions of all particular cognitions taken collectively. For the cause of one particular cognition is obviously different from the causes of all particular cognitions taken together.[53]

The middle term of the syllogism *(kāryatve sati tadviśeṣatvāt i.e.,* because of knowledge which is originated) is also not free from defect as it suffers from the defect of redundancy. The middle has two parts—a part qualifying and a part qualified. The first part *kāryatve sati* is the qualifying part and it has been introduced by the *Naiyāyika* to exclude God's knowledge which being eternal is not *kārya* or originated. But this is unnecessary, since it is not yet established and can be established only when the syllogism under discussion has been able to establish the validity of knowledge as originating from *guṇas* or certain additional or extra qualities.[54] Besides middle term would not be admitted by both parties *(ubhayavādisiddha)* as is required by logic, since the questioners cannot admit God's eternal knowledge in the same sense in which the *Naiyāyikas* understand it.

Lastly, the basic principle on which the *Naiyāyika* argument is founded is, as we have seen, that wherever there is difference in the effect, difference in the originating cause has to be postulated; as for example, the difference between the pot and the cloth can be explained only on the basis of difference in their originating causes. Now the question is, what is the meaning of this *vaijātya* or difference? Does it mean generic difference such as in the case of the pot and the cloth as so obviously intended by the *Naiyāyikas?* If so, this cannot apply to *pramā,* validity, and *apramā,* invalidity; for invalidity does not differ from *pramā* as the pot differs from the cloth, as both being forms of cognition. And this is further proved by the fact that even in the invalid cognition of the oyster, as silver, we have an element of *pramā* or validity so far as the perception of the *Idantā* or thisness is concerned.[55]

Moreover, the *vyāpti* or concomitance is not universal; for though as in the case of different pots we can mark the difference (or *vaijātya)* in forms and tastes resulting from the application of heat, the cause is the same, and the difference of the causal elements which explain the difference in the effect in the *Nyāya* exposition, is wanting here.[56]

The *Naiyāyika* syllogism is again sought to be counter-balanced by the advocates of the self-validity of knowledge by showing that with the same middle term a contradictory major may be established in the same minor, with equal logical cogency. The opponents argue that "right knowledge is not the result of any causal condition which is other than defects or *doṣas* and the common conditions of knowledge since it is knowledge as wrong knowledge itself is." They thus reason that because *apramā* or invalid knowledge is due to the presence of some defects or *doṣas* it does not necessarily follow that *pramā* or valid knowledge is due to the absence of *doṣa (doṣābhāva)*. On the contrary *dosābhāva* or absence of defects should logically be regarded as an obstacle to the presence of *apramā* and to attribute *doṣābhāva* as the cause of *pramā* is to accept an irrelevant antecedent *(anyathāsiddha)* in the causal conception of *pramā,* since *pramā* or valid knowledge may very well be explained as due to the causal conditions of knowledge *(jñānasāmagrījanya)* without the absence of defect or *doṣābhāva* having anything to do with it.[57]

Criticism against the Nyāya apprehension of validity

Now as regards the Nyāya theory of other-apprehendedness of validity *(parataḥñapti)* some severe criticisms might be offered. First of all, the Nyāya explanation suffers from the charge of *mutual dependence.* For validity of knowledge is first inferred from its pragmatic utility but does not the pragmatic endeavour imply a prior apprehension of validity leading to it?[58] If this defect of mutual dependence be avoided on the ground that knowledge of validity is not always a *sine qua non* of pragmatic effort, it might be pointed out that in all serious endeavours to achieve success, the prior cognition of validity is always present as an indispensable condition. Moreover if validity is to be inferred from this correspondence or agreement with pragmatic uses, it will lead to a twofold *regressus ad infinitum*—one by way of antecedents *(kāraṇamukhī)* and the other by way of consequence *(phala-mukhī).* Thus the real reason of the apprehension of validity, according to the *Naiyāyika* theory, resides in the conditions (such as minor, major and middle, etc.) of the inference about correspondence; and in order that the inference might be free from fallacies, the conditions themselves must be valid. This means that the validity of these conditions will have to be proved by another inference based on similar conditions and so on *adinfini-tum.* Again the resultant knowledge which certifies the validity of any particular cognition must depend on another valid inference based on correspondence to prove its own validity, and that again on a third and so on leading to another regressus.[59]

If to avoid this charge of infinite regress it is argued that this dependence of validity on correspondence is not always necessary, but required only where there is any suspicion of defect, the logical implication would be that this dependence on correspondence is only to avoid or get rid of the obstacle to *pramā* or validity and not to give rise to it. And this clearly establishes the fact of self-validity of knowledge.[60] Moreover to avoid the regress, the *Naiyāyika* will have to stop somewhere and say that this particular knowledge is self-valid. That being so, it stands to reason to argue that there is no harm in regarding the first cognition as self-valid. Lastly, doubt does not argue against self-validity; for doubt or *saṁśaya* is always the result of some defects or other and does not spring out of the causal conditions of cognition itself. The supporters of self-validity establish their own thesis by showing negatively that *paratahprāmāṇya* theory is not logically a sound doctrine and positively that the theory of self-validity can overcome all criticisms directed against it.

Mīmāṁsaka explanation of self-validity

It is necessary, therefore, to more clearly define the meaning of self-validity or *svataḥ prāmāṇya* in order to make it free from any vagueness; but as soon as the *Mīmāṁsists* and the *Vedāntins* proceed to define its meaning, the Naiyāyikas come forward pointing out defects and in this duel of logic the real meaning of self-validity. emerges ultimately. In refuting the self-constituted character of cognition, the *Naiyāyikas* ask what does this self-validity connote? "Is it *(a)* that the self-constituted character of knowledge springs from itself? or *(b)* that it springs from the right knowledge in which it resides? or *(c)* that it springs from the causal conditions which produce the right knowledge in which it resides? or *(d)* that it resides in a particular knowledge produced by the causal conditions which produced right knowledge? or *(e)* that it resides in a particular knowledge produced by the causal conditions only which produce the right knowledge?"

The first proposition is untenable because it implies a causal relation and wherever the relation of cause and effect is found there must exist a difference between the cause and effect in their particular essentials; and they being characterised by their distinctive nature cannot reside in the same subject or in other words validity cannot cause itself. The second alternative cannot be maintained because if cognition be taken as the inherent or intimate cause *(samavāyikāraṇa)* of its own validity, a property to be produced in knowledge by itself, cognition would no longer remain a quality, but being the cause of property, it would be classed with substances which only can cause properties or qualities.[61] Against the third it may be argued that validity according to the third explanation cannot be produced at all. For validity as a logical concept must be categorised as '*upādhi*' or general characteristic or '*jāti* or a 'genus.' But in either case, the question of origination seems to be an absurdity. For as a general characteristic or *upādhi* it may be defined as the absolute non-existence of any contradiction to a certain kind of knowledge which does not possess the nature of recollection. Now validity characterised by such an absolute negativity cannot be called 'originated.' As a genus or '*jāti*' also, eternality being its criterion, it escapes origination and the suggested definition becomes an impossibility.[62] The same objection may be urged against the first and second explanation of validity as well. The fourth interpretation is too wide as it extends to wrong knowledge; for wrong or invalid knowledge also is a particular kind of knowledge produced by the same general conditions as lead to validity only with this difference that some defects or '*doṣas*' such as distance, imperfect nature of organs, etc., are added to it. It is a universally accepted principle that the instrumental causes originating the general are included in those producing the particular, just as the general idea of seed as applied to a tree is included in the particular seed of any special tree. If it be argued that a limiting epithet *mātra* or '*only*' should be added after the common causal conditions of knowledge *(jñāna-sāmānyasāmagrī)* so that the wrong notion might be excluded from the scope of self-validity, the Naiyāyikas pointedly ask whether by being produced by the causal conditions '*only*' in your definition of self-validity, you mean to include or exclude the absence of defects? If absence of defects be included and not excluded in the causal condition, validity does no longer remain self-constituted and self-evident and the definition only explains the Nyāya theory of *parataḥ prāmāṇya.* Again, if it is argued that the absence of defect is not included but excluded in the causal conditions of validity, such an assertion is against experience. For all cases of valid knowledge are accompanied by the absence of defects and invalidity is always characterised by the presence of defects. If there be *doṣābhāva,* there is *pramā* or true knowledge. Absence of *doṣa* is, therefore, not an unimportant factor which can be ignored in a logical definition of self-validity.[63] To this long catalogue of defects urged by the *Naiyāyikas,* the Mīmāṁsists reply as follows : The *Naiyāyika*-objections as to the real definition of self-validity are really beside the point; for evidently, as already shown the *Naiyāyika*-objections are based on their own idea that since *apramā* or invalid knowledge is due to the common causal conditions *plus* defects etc., valid knowledge also must be due to the common causal elements *plus* the absence of defects. But, as has already been discussed, the latter proposition is not a logical corollary of the former. Hence origination of validity may well be defined logically as "due to the common causal conditions of knowledge and as not produced by any condition other than these." The syllogism underlying this may be set out as follows : validity is not produced by any other causal conditions than those of knowledge, because it is something which cannot be the receptacle of invalidity, *e.g.*, the cognition of a jar.[64] It might also be pointed out here that the syllogism while it establishes, the *Mīmāṁsaka's* position also serves to counterbalance the syllogism advanced by Udayana and Gaṅgeśa as already shown and thereby it tends to weaken the *Nyāya* position.

As regards the origination of validity, this is the position of all *Mīmāṁsaka-schools.* But with regard to the cognoscibility of validity *(jñapti)* the schools of *Mīmāṁsakas* differ among themselves since their views as to the real process of apprehension differ from each other. They all agree in taking validity *(prāmāṇya)* to he known through the very elements of knowledge itself. Thus the judgment "I know the pot" while it reveals the knowledge of the pot to me also serves to reveal its validity. As Gaṅgeśa in his *Tattvacintāmaṇi* puts it, while criticising the *Mīmāṁsakas,* the common ground among all *Mīmāṁsā-schools.* in the definition of self-validity is that "self-validity is cognisable by all the common causal conditions of knowledge which at the same time are exclusive of the conditions which produce wrong apprehension."[65] The three well-known *Mimāṁsā* schools differ among themselves when applying this common definition to their respective views of the process of apprehension.

Prabhākara's view

Prabhākara is an advocate of *tripuṭī saṁvit,* according to which the knower, the known, and the knowledge are given simultaneously in every act of cognition. Knowledge reveals itself along with the knower and the known. In the judgment 'I' know this" *(aham idam jānāmi),* we have three presentations of the 'I' or the subject *(ahaṁvitti) 'this'* or the object *(viṣayavitti)* and the conscious awareness *(svasaṁvitti).* Cognition according to Prabhākara is self-valid and self-apprehended. Knowledge is of the nature of light which illumines its own self as well as its objects. It is not apprehended as an object of any other cognition for it then would lead to an infinite regress.[66] All experience comes to us as determinate, *e. g.,* "I know the jar characterised by jarness" *(ghaṭatvena ghaṭamaham jānāmi).* Such an experience reveals the jar, the object and itself as the consciousness of awareness and the subject or *tripuṭī.*[67] *Tripuṭī* explains the judgment as a combination of cognition and after-cognition of *Nyāya.* Hence according to Prabhākara validity is cognised along with the cognition itself and is self-produced because the causal conditions of cognition themselves produce it, knowledge being the locus of validity.[68]

Murāri Miśra's view

The school of *Murāri Miśra* differs from the *Prabhākara* school in holding, unlike the latter, that knowledge itself is not simultaneous combination of cognition and after-cognition. On the contrary, *Murāri Miśra* maintains that the after-cognition *(anuvyavasāya)* comes immediately after the cognition. Thus there is first the cognition 'this is a jar' *(ayaṁ ghaṭaḥ)* and then immediately after arises the introspection that "I know the jar as characterised by jarness *(ghaṭatvena ghaṭamahaṁ jānāmi)*. Now the introspection has its constituent elements—(a) the perception of the jar, (b) the perception of jarness, (c) the perception of the inherent relation between the jar and jarness, *(d)* the perception of consciousness as modified by *a, b* and *c* and *(e)* cognition of the self or 'I' as having an inherent relation with *a, b, c* and *d.*[69] It is thus clear that as soon as the after cognition arises as a result of perception, consciousness of validity at once arises without depending on anything else except the causal condition of perception itself. Hence validity is self-proved.[70] It may be noted that the *Naiyāyikas* who advocate *parataḥ-prāmāṇya* also refer to *anuvyavasāya* or after cognition as revealing knowledge. But a closer study of the two positions will reveal the fundamental difference between the *Naiyāyika* school and that of Murāri Miśra. in the after-cognition or *anu-Vyavasāya* of the *Naiyāyikas,* there is no perception of the inherent relation *(samavāya)* between the jar and jarness.[71] Hence the *Naiyāyika* has to establish validity of cognition by an inference based on correspondence leading to practical success. But such is not the position of Murāri Miśra. His introspection or after-cognition includes within itself the perception of an inherent, relation *(samabāya)* between the presented jar and jarness, thereby unmistakably proving the truth of the perception, since truth or validity implies the apprehension of the real characteristic mark of the thing in the presented object in its proper relation.

Kumārila's view

The *Bhāṭṭa* school diverges from the *Miśra* school in the interpretation of validity revealed by the after-cognition. Murāri Miśra holds that the after-cognition or introspection and its constituent elements are object of direct perception whereas the *Bhāṭṭa* school maintains that knowledge being *atīndriya* or beyond sense perception cannot be perceived and the validity brought forth by the so-called *anuvyavasāya* is not perceived but inferred from *jñātatā* or cognisedness[72] resulting from perception which imparts the revelatory vividness *(prākaṭya)* to the object perceived.[73] Thus according to Kumārila, the judgment 'this is a jar' imparts a sort of cognisedness to the jar whereby it is made vivid; and the revelatory cognition that "I know the jar" is inferred from the cognisedness *(jñātatā)* in regard to the jar. The form of inference is "I know because of the awareness of the cognisedness in me." The validity of knowledge is also to be inferred from the cognisedness *(jñātatā)* to the object.[74] Now this cognisedness which reveals the object is the quality or property of the object cognised; and if the cognisedness modifies the object in the precise form of the jar as it is, the cognition is valid or *pramā* and the syllogism might be put thus : The jar is the object of determinate cognition in which the jar is the object determined and jarness is the determining mark, since the awareness of the cognisedness is qualified by the characteristic mark of the jar.[75] In other words, when we analyse the judgment 'I know the jar' it means that I know the jar as characterised by the essential marks of the jar since the revelatory vividness or *prākaṭya* arises in connection with the object, jar. And this implies that the cognition is characterised or modified by the special form of the object, jar, and this is nothing but the cognition that the perception is valid.

A question may very well be raised here as to how the *Bhāṭṭas* could be called advocates of self-validity *(svataḥ-prāmāṇya)* seeing that they also maintain that validity is revealed through inference—a position held by the *Naiyāyikas* who support the theory of *parataḥ-prāmāṇya.* The enigma however might be explained very well in this way. Self-validity really means that validity is apprehended by the same causal conditions through which knowledge is known or revealed to the knower, and not by something else other than these as held by the *Naiyāyikas.* As we have already seen the three *Mīmāṁsā* schools, though differing from one another in details, accept this as a common principle. Thus according to the *Prabhākara* school, validity is apprehended along with knowledge by the same elements which generate knowledge *(jñānajanaka-sāmagrī), viz.*, the *tripuṭī* of knower, known, and knowledge. According to the *Miśra* school, knowledge itself is known by the after-cognition or *anuvyavasāya* and the same *anuvyavasāya* reveals validity as well. According to the *Bhāṭṭa* school validity is apprehended by the cognisedness or *jñātata* which also makes knowledge known. In the case of the *Naiyāyikas* this does not hold good. For according to them though knowledge is apprehended by *anuvyavasāya* or after-cognition *anuvyavasāya* does not reveal validity. Validity has to be established by an inference based on correspondence leading to pragmatic success. Thus that which reveals knowledge does not reveal validity. In other words, validity is revealed by something other than that which reveals knowledge. But according to the Bhāṭṭas that which reveals knowledge reveals validity. Hence though both the Bhāṭ ṭas and the Naiyāyikas appeal to inference, the former is rightly regarded as an advocate of *svataḥ prāmāṇya* while the latter of *parataḥ prāmāṇya*.

The advaitin's explanation of self-validity

An elaborate discussion of self-validity from the standpoint of the Mīmāṁsists with regard to its origination and cognoscibility has been given above; and a critical study of the Advaita position shows that the Advaitins largely follow the Mīmāṁsakas in these respects. Advaitins, however, differ from the Mīmāṁsakas in their conception of valid cognition. Valid cognition is defined by *Dharmarājādhvarīndra* in his *Vedāntaparibhāṣā* as a cognition which is not previously known and is not also contradicted.[76] The epithet 'not previously known' is designed to exclude memory or *smṛti* from the scope of *pramā* or valid cognition as memory is already known, while the epithet 'not contradicted' is meant to exclude wrong knowledge as it is always contradicted.[77] It might, however, be noted that some Advaita-teachers do not exclude *smṛti* or memory from the scope of valid cognition. Hence from their standpoint the epithet 'not previously known' or *anadhigata* has no utility. If however *smṛti* is to be excluded from the scope of valid cognition by this epithet an obvious difficulty crops up, for the epithet, 'not previously known' would bar out a continuous process of cognition, since these perceptions, as they come after the first, are already previously known. And this would be a manifest absurdity. *Dharmarājādhvarindra* himself realises this difficulty and tries to wriggle out of it by saying that time enters as an element in all perceptions and since the successive moments of a continuous perception remain previously unknown and unperceived the perception may be said to be *anadhigata* or not previously known.[78] But this is not a very happy answer to escape from the difficulty; for time is a common element entering as a category in all judgment constructions and if the particular elements (viśeṣasāmagrī) of the judgment become known in each successive cognition as shown, it is not convincing to argue that they are not previously known, simply because the common factor, the time element, remains unknown.

Real escape from the difficulty may be effected if we take the term *anadhigata* in a technical sense to mean difference or a line of demarcation from a particular kind of knowledge whose essential nature is that it cannot be perceived without being previously known.[79] Defined in this sense, only memory knowledge would be excluded from the scope of validity thus defined and not the successive perception of a continuous cognition; for it is only the nature of memory to be *always* apprehended as previously known. In the case of perception proper the limitation would not apply, for though the second, third and fourth perception of a continuous cognition of the jar might be apprehended as previously known, the first perception is not so apprehended. Thus, the sequence of a perceptual knowledge to another perceptual knowledge of the same kind is only an accident and not the rule as in the case of memory.

Clearly following the Mīmāṁsakas, the Advaitins also explain self-validity as that which is originated by the common conditions of knowledge and not by any additional elements other than those common conditions.[80] Critics however might stand against the exposition of the Advaita teachers and contend that this would exclude eternal, infinite consciousness of God from the scope of self-validity, because it is not originated. The Advaitins have, therefore, to so explain the definition as to include both eternal and non-eternal, infinite or finite cognition in its scope. Hence the true meaning of the definition from the monistic standpoint is that *pramā* or valid cognition is that in which there is an absolute negation of all that is due to the elements other than those common elements. In other words, *pramā* or valid knowledge means the absolute negation of *apramā* or wrong notion; and this absolute negation of wrong notion or *apramā* might apply both to eternal and non-eternal or finite consciousness.[81] The Advaitins further follow the Mīmāṁsakas in drawing this conclusion by similar counter-syllogism refuting the Nyāya-syllogism establishing the theory of *parataḥ prāmāṇya*. It is needless to go into a detailed discussion of the monistic argument as we already discussed the same in connection with the Mīmāṁsaka position. The Advaitins also conclude that because we have to include defects (doṣas) to explain *apramā* or wrong notion, it does not necessarily follow that absence of defects must be included in the causal conditions of valid cognition.

As regards cognoscibility of *pramā,* the monistic teachers closely following the Mīmāṁsakas argue that it is apprehended by the same common elements generating knowledge. At this the critic might include the false cognition of silver in the nacre within the category of *pramā;* for there also the common elements generating the false cognition are there. To this the Advaitins reply that this is not the case; for the consciousness of any defect in the causal conditions and awareness of contradiction which give rise to two kinds of invalid knowledge, doubt and falsity stand as a bar to the notion of validity. The critic might then argue that this means that the absence of the awareness of defect in the causal condition and the negation of the notion of contradiction should then be regarded as causes of *pramā* which is tantamount to the admission of the Naiyāyika-position that valid knowledge is due to absence of defects, etc. The Advaitins point out that this is not so, for the absence of defects (doṣā-bhāva) cannot be regarded as the cause of *pramā;* for what does this absence mean? Does it not mean that as soon as the absence is there, notion of validity shines forth of itself.[82] Besides absence being a negative idea cannot be an operative cause. The truth is that, defects in the causal conditions or the notion of contradiction stand as a bar to valid apprehension and as soon as they are absent validity shines forth of itself. Moreover, if absence of defect (doṣābhāva) be regarded as the cause of *pramā*, it will lead to an infinite regress; the absence of defect, which establishes the first validity, must require another absence of defect as its causal condition and the second absence of defects another and so on *ad infinitum.*[83]

It is now clear that 'absence of defect' cannot be regarded as the cause of the cognoscibility of validity owing to this logical absurdity. Hence Udayana's syllogism "validity has to be cognised by something other (than the common constituents of knowledge) since there may be doubt with regard to the first cognition"[84] is not logically satisfactory. For though doubt may be admitted in the first cognition and though along with doubt it may further be conceded that doubt is due to the extra conditions—organic defects—other than those of normal cognition, it does not follow that cognoscibility of validity should necessarily be explained as due to the absence of defects which generate doubt. Now when the absence of defects, in this way, fails to establish the Nyāya-theory of *parataḥ-prāmāṇya,* the substitution of merit or *guṇa*—a positive idea—as the cause of cognoscibility of validity in addition to the common elements of knowledge, does not fare better. For this introduction of merit or *guṇa* is also not free from difficulties. With regard to perception, the Naiyāyika defines merit or *guṇa* as contact of the sense organs with a considerable number of parts of the object perceived and with regard to inference merit means validity of the middle, etc. Now both these kinds of merit fail to establish validity. In the first place, so far as perception is concerned, we have valid perception of self and forms (rūpa) though they have no parts; and in the case of the false perception of conchshell as yellow, though there is contact of sense-organs with considerable parts of the body, it is invalid. As to inference, it often happens that though the middle or *hetu* is wrong, there is valid inference. Thus, for example, when man infers fire which is accidentally present in the mountain, mistaking the mist for smoke, it cannot be said that the knowledge of the fire is invalid, because the middle term is false. In other words, though the hetu is here false, the cognition of the fire is valid.[85]

Moreover, as already pointed out, the inference of the *Naiyāyika* as to validity being *parataḥ* leads to a twofold *regressus,* The *Naiyāyika* inference—Knowledge is valid because it leads to successful pragmatic results—leads to an infinite regress, because the validity of this inference will have to depend on another inference and that on another and so on. In order to avoid this *regressus,* it might be urged that knowledge or cognition only is the *sine qua* now of practical endeavour and not the consciousness of its validity. But this is not possible as it is against experience. Experience shows that practical endeavour is not possible without a prior consciousness of validity of knowledge leading to it. A closer analysis of experience reveals that practical endeavour is the result of the certainty that the cognition is valid and it cannot be said that practical endeavour may issue when there is a non-cognition of either validity or invalidity. This shows that the *regressus* is unavoidable in the Nyāya theory of *parataḥ-prāmāṇya.* Hence, in order to get over this difficulty such an acute thinker as Vacaspati Miśra in his *Nyāya-Vārtika-tātparyatīkā* had to make the admission that validity of inferential knowledge is self-evident.[86] The *Advaitins,* therefore, contend that if in order to avoid the *regressus,* inference is to be regarded as self-valid, there is no reason why all forms of knowledge including perception should not be regarded as self-evident; since the *regressus* is involved, as already shown, in all forms of knowledge. Moreover, as already pointed out the inclusion of defect or merit in the causal conditions of knowledge is logically unnecessary and fallacious. Hence the conclusion is inevitable that knowledge is not only self-luminous but also self-valid.

REFERENCES

1. Pramāṇatvāpramāṇatve svataḥ Sāṁkhyāḥ samāśritāḥ
Naiyāyikāste parataḥ Saugatāścaramaṁ svataḥ,
Prathamaṁ parataḥ prāhuḥ prāmāṇyaṁ Vedavādinaḥ
Pramāṇatvaṁ svataḥ prāhuḥ parataścāpramāṇatam. —S.D.S., p. 279, Abhyaṅkar Edn,
2. 'Pra'-Valid, 'Ma'-Knowledge.
3. *N. B.*—It is significant and interesting to note that even in the domain of Western Philosophy we have almost parallel theories about the validity of knowledge. The Pragmatic and the Realistic school in modern Philosophy advocates the theory of *Parataḥ-prāmāṇya* and *Arthakriyākāitva* of the Nyāya and Buddhist school. Thus James in his Pragmatism, p. 201, says "Truth *happens* to an idea. It *becomes* true, is *made* true by events. Its verity is in fact an event, a process : the process namely of its verifying itself, its verification. Its validity is the process of its valid action." See also the meaning of truth, pp. 200, 222. Prof. Dewey says, "The true means the verified and means nothing else." Prof. Watts Cunningham in his Problems of Philosophy, p. 120, also explaining the pragmatic test of truth asserts "Utility is the criterion of truth. A judgment is *made* true by being verified and apart from its verification it cannot in any intelligible sense be said to be either true or erroneous. Similarly, Joachim in the Nature of Truth, p. 19, in explaining the correspondence theory writes : "A judgment is true, if the thoughts whose union is the Judgment 'correspond' to the facts whose union is the 'real' situation which is to be expressed. My Judgment is true if my ideas, asserted by me in my Judgment, correspond to the facts. But my ideas are 'real' and 'real' not simply in the sense that they are certain events actually happening in my psychical history. For it is not *qua*-psychical events that my ideas correspond with the facts and in corresponding are true." Similarly an adumbration of the conception of *svataḥ-prāmāṇya* might also be traced here and there. Thus Joachim in his Nature of Truth while criticising the correspondence theory and explaining the neo-Logic and Metaphysics of the Realistic school as represented by Bertrand Russell and G. E. Moore writes: "Truth is what it is independently, whether any mind recognizes it or not." (P. 13.) "We do not create truth, but only find it; we could not find it if it were not there and in a sense independent of our finding." (Pp. 13, 14, p. 20.) "A truth is independently of my thinking it, and again, in independence of the process through which I come to think it." "Truth is discovered, not invented." It must however be recognised that the similarity of the Nyāya and Buddhist position with that of the Pragmatists does not go far enough. A judgment is true or false because of its own causes and conditions and its truth or falsity is made known by verification or contradiction.
4. Nahi svato'satī śaktiḥ kartumanyena śakyate. —S. V. Codanāsūtra verse 47.
5. Pramāṇamavisaṁvādi jñānamartha-kriyāsthitiḥ avisaṁvādanamiti. —Tārkikarakṣā, p. 14.

6. Samyagjñāna-pūrvikā hi sarvapuruṣārthaṣiddhiḥ.—Nyāyavindu, p. 3.
7. *Cf.* James' Pragmatism, p. 201.
   True ideas are those that we can assimilate, validate, corroborate and verify. False ideas are those that we cannot.
8. Indriyārtha-sāmarthyajaṁ jñanaṁ pratyakṣam, na cendriyasyārthasya vā smartuṁ sāmarthyam, savikalpañca smṛtyā kṛṣṭam jātyādi yojanayā upajāyate. —Nyāyaratnākara, p. 161.
9. *Vide* Upaskāra, 8-1-2.
10. Evametāḥ pravartante vāsanāmātra-nirmitāḥ Kalpitālīka-bhedādi-prapañcāḥ pañca kalpanāḥ. —Ny. M. P., 94.
11. sarva evāmī vikalpāḥ paramārthataharthaṁ na spṛśantyeva vikalpāḥ svabhāvata eva vastusaṁsparśakauśalaśūnyātmāna iti. —Ny. M.P., 297.
12. Yathāvagatārtha-prāpakatvamavisaṁvādakatvaṁ prāmāṇyamiti. —Ny. M.P., 24.
13. (a) *Vide* Tārkikarakṣā of Varadarāja, p. 14.
    (b) Nyāyamañjarī. p. 24.
14. Buddhau āropitacaitanyasya viṣayeṇa sambandho jñānam. jñeyena sambandhah cetano'haṁ karomītyupalabdhiḥ, etc. —Haridāsa's Commentary on the Kusutnāñjali, 1-24.
15. In this respect the Sāṁkhyists agree with the Rāmānujists to whom all knowledge is valid *(yathārthaṁ sarvavijñānam)*. We have developed the viewpoint of the Rāmānujists in the chapter," The Epistemology of Illusion." *Vide* the topic "The Satkhyātivāda of Rāmānuja."
16. Marīcikāyāṁ jalalakṣaṇaḥ arthaḥ satyībhūtaḥ pratibhāsamānatvāt ghaṭavat.—Pr. K. M., p. 14.
17. Yadyapyuttarakālaṁ tathā saḥ arthaḥ nāsti tathāpi yadā pratibhāti tadā tāvadastyevānyathā vidyudāderapi sattvasiddhirna syāt.—Pr. K. M., p.13.
18. Yathāvasthitārthagṛhītitvāviśeṣehibhrāntā bhrāntavyavahārābhāvaḥ syāt sarvajñānānām avitathārthaviṣayatvāviśeṣāt.—*Ibid,* p. 13.
19. *Vide* Sāṁkhyapravacanabhāṣya, 1.87. Vācaspati Miśra also in his definition of *pramā* or valid knowledge excludes false knowledge from the conception, of validity.
20. (*a*) Tattvānubhavaḥ pramā,.
    (b) Yathārthānubhavaḥ pramā tatsādhanañca pramāṇam.
21. (a) Yad yatrāsti tatra tajjñānṁ prameti niruktam. Vardhamāna's Kusumāñjali prakāśa, 4.5.
    (b) Kiṁ punastattvam? sataśca sadbhāvaḥ asataścāsabdbhāvaḥ, *sat* saditi gṛhyamāṇaṁ yathā bhūtam avij aritaṁ tattviṁ bhavati asaççā aditi gṛhyamāṁ in tathābhūtaṁ tattvaṁ bhavati. Nyāyabhāṣya, 1.1 1.
    (c) *Vide* Nyāyavārttika and Nyāyavārttikatātparyaṭīkā, 1.1.1.
22. (a) Tatra pramāṇaṁ pramayā vyāptaṁ pramitisādhanaṁ,
    Pramāśrayo vā tadvyāpto yathārthānubhavaḥ pramā.
    (b) Nityānityatayā dvedbā pramā nityāpramāśrayaḥ
    Pramāṇamitarasyāstu karaṇasya pramāṇatā. Tārkikarakṣā, verses 2.3.

23. Sādhanāśrayayoranyataratve sati pramāvyāptaṁ prarnāṇam, tataśca Iśvarasyāpi pramāśrayatayā prāmāṇyasiddher nāvyāptiriti. Tārkikarakṣā, p. 7.

24. (a) Pramātṛtvaṁ pramāsamavāyitvam etacca akāraṇatve'pi pramāyā Īśvarasya siddham, evaṁ pramayā saha ayogavyavacchedena saṁbandhitayā Īśvarasya pramāṇatvam.
Haridāsa's commentary on Kusumāñjali, verse 5, stavaka 4.

(b) Mitiḥ samyak paricchittistadvattā ca pramātṛtā
Tadayogavyavacchedaḥ prāmāṇyaṁ Gautame mate. Udayana's Kusumāñjali 5.5

25. (a) Pramājñānahetvatirikta-hetvadhīnā kāryatve sati tadviśeṣatvāt apramāvat. Udayana's Kusumāñjali. p. 59, Banares edn.

(b) Tattvacintām aṇi, p 211.
Cp Russell, Principles of Mathematics p. 38:
The question is how does a proposition differ by being actually true from what it would be a an entity if it were not true. It is plan that true and false propositions alike re entities of a kind, but that the propositions have a quality not belonging to false ones—a quality which may be called being *asserted*.

26. (a) Utpadyatepi pramā parataḥ na tu svataḥ jñānasāmagrīmātrāt tajjanyatvena apramāpi pramā syāt anyathā jñānamapi sā na yāt.
Tattvacintāmaṇi, pp. 287-88, B.I.S.

(b) Yadi ca tāvanmātrādhīnā bhavet apramāpi pramaiva bhavat
asti ca tatra jnānahetuḥ anyathā jñānamapi sā na syāt.
Udayana's Kusumāñjali, p. 59.

(c) Pramāyā jñānasāmānya-sāmagrī-janyatāmātraśrayatve jñāna-sāmānya-sāmagrī-janyatvena apramrāpi prantā syādiṭarthaḥ. Māthurī on Tattvacintāmaṇi, p. 288.

27. Jñānasāmanyām doṣānupraveśād aprameticet tarhi jñānaviścṣavad apramā pramaviś-ṣah syāt jñānasāmagrī-janyatvāt, tasmāt pramāpramayor vaicitryātguṇādoṣa-janyatvam. Tattvacintāmaṇi, p. 289.

28. Yatkāryam yatkāryavijātīyaṁ tat tatkāraṇavijatīyakaraṇa-janyaṁ, yathā ghaṭ avijātiyaḥ paṭah anyathā kāryava-jātya-yākasmikatvāpatteḥ, ghatjñānajātiyamapi kāryaṁ tadvijātīyakāryakaraṇavijātiya ghaṭendriya-sannikarṣādi-janyam iti na vyabhicāraḥ. Tattvacintāmaṇi, pp. 308-9.

29. *(a)* Evam anityapramātvam anityajñānatvāvacchinna-kāryatva pratiyogika-kāraṇaṭ ābhinna-kāraṇtāpratiyogika-kāryatāvacchedakam anitya jñānatvavyāpya-kāryatāvacchedakadharmatvām apramātvavat ityanitya-pramā-yāmupramāvyāvṛttānugata-hetusiddhiḥ. Tattvacintāmaṇi, pp. 311-12.

(b) *Vide* Vardhamāna-prakāśa, p. 4, stavaka 2.

30. *Cf.* Derke: "all cognitive experiences are knowledge of, not possession of, the existent known (if it is an existent); their validity must be tested by other means than the intuition of the moment." Critical Realism, p. 32.

31. (a) Prāmāṇyaṁ na svatogrāhyaṁ saṅśayānupapattitaḥ. Bh. p., Śl. 76.
(b) Prāmāṇyasya svatograhe anabhyāsadaśotpanna-jñāne tatsaṁśayo na syāt jñānagrahe prāmāṇya-niścayāt, aniścaye vā na svataḥprāmāṇya grahaḥ. Tattvacintāmaṇi, p. 184.

32. (a) Anabhyāsadaśotpannajñānaprāmāṇyaṁ na svāśrayagrāhyaṁ, svāśrayātiriktagrāhyaṁ vā, svāśraye satyapi taduttaratṛtīyakṣaṇavṛtti-saṁśayaviṣayatvāt, aprāmāṇyavat. Tattvacintāmaṇi, pp. 240-41.
(b) *Vide* Vardhamānaprakāśa, p. 9, stavaka 5.
(c) Prāmāṇyaṁ paratojñāyate anabhyāsadaśāyāṁ sāṁśayikatvāt aprāmāṇyavat, yadi ca svato jñāyeta kadācidapi prāmāṇyasaṁśayo na syāt. Udayana's Kusumāñjali, p. 7, stavaka 2.

33. Pūrvotpannaṁ jalajñānaṁ pramā saphalapravṛttijenakatvāt yannaivaṁ tannaivaṁ yathā apramā. Nīlakaṇṭha's Dīpikā, p. 39.

34. Tattvacintāmaṇi, p. 253.

35. Dvitīyādi jalajñānaṁ pramā samarthapravṛttijanakajāitīyatvād adynjñānavat. Tarka-kaumudī, p. 18.

36. Idaṁ jñānamapramā visaṁvādipravṛttijanakatvād yannaivaṁ tannaivaṁ yathā pramā.

Nīlakaṇṭha's commentary on prāmāṇyavāda, p. 187.

37. *Cf.* Joachim: The Nature of Truth, p. 38. For a true proposition, we may say, involves an element which is not contained in a false proposition; and it is this additional element which constitutes its truth. The element in question attaches to the proposition itself. We may adopt Mr. Russell's terminology, and call this element 'assertion.'

38. For an account of extra qualities *(guṇas)* and defects *(doṣas)* see Nīlakaṇṭha's Dīpikā on the Tarkasaṁgraha, pp. 36-37.

39. *Vide* Khaṇḍanakhaṇḍakhādya, p. 239, and Vidyāsāgarī on Khaṇḍana, p. 239.

40. Tattvānubhūtiḥ prametyayuktaṁ tattvaśabdārthasya nirvaktuma-śakyatvāt, tasya bhāvo hi tattvamucyate prakṛtañca tacchabdārthaḥ na cātra prakṛtaṁ kiñcidasti yattacchabdena parāmṛśyate, athānubhūtyā svasaṁbandhiviṣaya ākṣepād buddhisthaḥ kāryate sa tacchabdena parāmṛśyate, tena yasya arthasya yo bhābaḥ tasya tattvāmucyate—iti, na arajatāderapi rajatādyātmanā anubhūtiviṣ ayatāsaṁbhavād asatyānubhūtyavyavacchedāt.

Khaṇḍanakhaṇḍakhādya, pp. 239-40, Benares Edn.

41. Ghaṭādi svarūpaviśeṣasya tattvapadārthatve paṭādipramāyā apramātvāpātaḥ, sakalasvarūpaviśeṣāṇāṁ saṁbhūya tattvapadārthatve ekaika-trāvyāptiriti. Vidyāsāgarī on Khaṇḍana, p. 242.

42. Śuktau hi yo rajatamiti pratyayah so'pi svarūpabuddhirbhavatyeva, na hi

dharmī vā rajatatvaṁ vā na svarūpaṁ, nāpi tayoḥ pratibhāsamānaḥ sambandhaḥ na svarūpamiti yuktam, samavāyo hi tayoḥ saṁbandhaḥ pratibhāti sa ca svarūpameva, satyaṁ samavāyaḥ svarūpam sa eva tu śuktikādau rajatatvasya nāstīti cet maivam, tatra nāstitve'pi svarūpatāyā avyāvrtteḥ na hi gṛhe Devadatto nāstīti svarūpaṁ na syāt.

Khaṇḍanakhaṇḍa-khādya, pp. 243-44.

This criticism of Śrīharṣa proceeds mainly on the linguistic import of the terms used by the Naiyāyikas not having much philosophical significance. Other objections turning on a more profound philosophical import are discussed at a greater length.

43. *Vide* Vidyasāgarī on Khaṇḍana, p. 398.

44. Khaṇḍana, p. 399.

45. *Vide* Khaṇḍanakhaṇḍakhādyam, p. 413.

46. *Vide* Khaṇḍana, pp. 414-20.

47. Kh. Kh., pp. 427-29.

48. Pramā jñānahetvatiriktahetvadhīnākāryatve sati tadviśesatvādapramāvat.

Right knowledge depends on some causes (*e.g.*, absence of defects, etc.) other than the common constituents of knowledge and is an effect just as false or wrong knowledge is an effect originated by causes other than the elements giving rise to cognition.

49. (a) *Vide* T. C., p. 291.

(b) *Vide* T. C. B., p. 292.

(c) *Vide* Varddhamāna's Prakāśa on the Nyāyakusumāñjali, pp. 2-3, stavaka 2.

50. Pramāyā jñānatvena taddhetorjñānahetutayā tadatirikta janyatvasādhane bādhāt. Tarkatāṇḍava, p. 62.

51. (a) *Vide* Tattvacintāmaṇi, p. 291.

(b) *Vide* Tarkatāṇḍava, p. 62.

52. *(a)* T. C., p. 293.

(b) T. C. R., p. 293.

(c) Jñānatvasyeśvarajñānavṛttitvena karaṇāprayojyataya tatprayojakasāmagrya prasiddhyā sādhyāprasiddhiḥ.

Rāghavendra's Tippaṇa on the Tarkatāṇḍava, p. 62.

53. (*a*) Yatkiñcijjñānahetvapekṣayā sarvataddhetvapekṣayā vā atiriktatve indriyādibhiḥ siddhasādhanāt.—T. C., p. 292.

(*b*) T. C. Rahasya, p. 292.

(c) Katipayakāraṇacakravivakṣāyāñcoktarītyā indriyādibhiḥ siddhasādhanat.—Tarkatāṇḍava, p. 63.

54. (a) Vyarthaviśeṣaṇatvañca, vyavartyeśvarajñānasya paraṁpratya-siddheḥ. Varddhamāna's Prakāśa on the Nyāyakusumāñjali, p. 2, stavaka 2.

(b) Tadvyāvartyasya Īśvarajñānasya idānīmasiddherityarthaḥ, pramāyā guṇajanyatvasiddhāveva vaidikapramayāṁ guṇatayā bhagavajjñāna-siddhiriti.—Tattvacintāmaṇirahasya, p. 292.

55. (a) Hetau vijātīyatvaṁ yadi viruddhajātyadhikaraṇatvaṁ tadā pramātvasyā-jātitvenāsiddheḥ.—Tarkatāṇḍava, p. 64.

(b) Idaṁ rajatamityādau dharmyāṁśe sattve'pi, dharmāṁśe abhāvena pramātvasya avyapyavṛttitvāt, jñanatvaparnnniyatatvācceti bhāvaḥ.—Rāghavendra's Tippaṇa on the Tarkatāṇḍava, p. 64.

56. Pākajarūparasādau kāraṇāvaijātye'pi kāryavaijātyadarśanācca.

Tarkatāṇḍava, p. 64.

57. Na caudayanamanumānaṁ paratastvasādhakamiti śaṅkanīyaṁ, prama doṣ-avyatiriktajñāna-hetvatirikta-janyā na bhavati jñānatvāt apramāvaditi pratisādhanagrahagrastatvāt, jñānasāmagrīmātrādeva pramotpattisambhave tadatiriktasya guṇasya doṣābhāvasya vā kāraṇatva-kalpanāyāṁ kalpanāgauravaprasaṅgāt, nanu doṣasya apramā hetutvena tadabbāvasya pramāṁ prati hetutvaṁ durnivāramiti cet na, doṣābhāvasya apramā prati-handhakatvena anyathāsiddhatvāt. Sarvadarśanasaṁgraha, p. 283. Abhyaṅkara's Edn.

58. Pramātve jñāte pravṛttikāraṇatvajñānam, tenaiva ca pramātva-jñānamityanypnyāśrayaḥ.

Tarkatāṇḍava, p. 52.

59. (a) Paratastve prāmāṇyajñānasyāpi prāmāṇyaṁ saṁvādādilṁga-janyānumitirūpeṇa anyena jñānena grāhyam evaṁ tatprāmāṇyamapya-nyeneti phalamukhyekā anavasthā, evaṁ prāmāṇyasyānumeyatve liṅga-vyāptyādijñāna-prāmāṇyasyāniścaye asiddhyādiprasaṅgena tanniścayārthaṅliṅgādyantaraṅ tajjñāna-prāmāṇyaniścayaśca svīkāryaḥ evaṁ tatra tatrāpītikāraṇa-mukhyanyāpītyanavasthādvayāpatteḥ.-Tarkatāṇḍava, p. 41.

(b) *Vide* Tattvacintāmaṇi, p. 182.

(c) Yadi sarvameva jñānaṁ svaviṣayatvāvadhāraṇe svayamasumarthaṁ vijñānāntaramapekṣate tataḥ kāraṇaguṇa-saṁvādārthakriyājñānānyapi svaviṣayabhūtaguṇādyavadhāraṇe paramapekṣeran, aparamapi tatheti na kaścidartho janmasatiasreṇāpi adhyavasīyeteti prāmāṇy ameva utsīdet.

Śāstradīpikā, p. 22.

(d) *Ibid.*, p. 48.

60. Na ca yatra doṣaśaṁkādirūpākāṁkṣā tatraiva saṁvādāpekṣeti nānavastheti vācyam, tathāte pratibandhanirāsārthameva saṁvādāpekṣā na tu prāmāṇyagrahārthamiti manmatapraveśāpatteḥ.

Tarkataṇḍava, p. 41.

61. (a) Guṇasya sato jñānasya prāmāṇyaṁ prati samavāyikāraṇatayā dravyatvāpātāt. Sarvadarśanasaṁgraha, p. 280, Abhayaṁkara's Edn.

62. (a) Prāmāṇyasya upādhitve jātitve vā janmāyogāt, smṛtitvānadhi-karaṇasya jñānasya bādhātyantābhāvaḥ prāmāṇyopādhiḥ, na ca tasya

utpattisaṁbhavaḥ atyantābhāvasya nityatvābhyupagamat ata eva na jāterapi janiryujyate. S.D.S., p. 281.

(*b*) *Vide* Citsukhī, p. 115, Bombay Edn.

63. (a) Kiṁ doṣābhāvasahakṛta-jñānasāmagrī-janyatvameva jñāna-sāmagrīmātrajanyatvaṁ kiṁ vā doṣābhāvasahakṛta-jñānasāmagrī janyatvam, nādyaḥ doṣābhavasahakṛta-jñānasāmagrī-janyatvameva parataḥ-prāmāṇyamiti parataḥ-prāmāṇyavādibhirurarīkaraṇāt; nāpi dvitīyaḥ doṣābhāva sahakṛtatvena sāmagryāṁ sahakṛtatvesiddhe ananyathāsiddhānvaya-vyatirekasiddhatayā doṣābhāvasya kāraṇatāyā vajralepāyamāṇatvāt. S.D.S., pp. 281-82.

(*b*) *Vide* Citsukhī, p. 115, Bombay Edn.

64. Vimatā pramā vijñānasāmagrījanyatve sati tadatiriktajanyā na bhavati apramātvānadhikaraṇatvāt ghaṭādipramāvat.

S.D.S., Jaiminīyadarśanām, p. 283.

65. Tadaprāmāṇyāgrāhaka-yāvaj jñānagrāhaka-sāmagrīgrāhyam.

Tattvacintāmaṇi, p. 122.

66. Saṁvittayaiva hi saṁvit sidhyati na tu saṁvedyatayā.

67. (a) Jñānasya ghaṭādiviṣayasvasvarūpātmarūpādhikaraṇaitat-tritaya-viṣ ayakatvādeva tripuṭī-pratyakṣatā-pravādaḥ Nyāyakoṣa, p. 518.

(*b*) Mitimātṛmeyānāṁ jñānasya eka-sāmagrīkatvāt tripuṭī tat-pratyakṣatā. *Ibid,* p. 518.

68. (*a*) Prāmāṇye svatastvaṁ nāma yāvat svāśraya-viṣayaka-jñāna-grāhyatvam.

(*b*) Svasyaiva svaprāmāṇya-viṣayakatayā svajanakasāmagryeva-svaniṣ thāprāmāṇya-niścāyikā iti guravaḥ.

Māthurī on T.C., p. 126.

69. Ghaṭamahaṁ jānāmītyanuvyavasāyastu ghaṭaṁ ghaṭatvaṁ samavāyañca viṣ ayīkurvanātmani prakārībhūtaghaṭamātmānaṁ tatsambandhī.bhūta-vyavasāyaṁ viṣayīkaroti evaṁ purorvartiprakārasaṁbandhasyaiva pramātva padarthatvena svata eva prāmāṇyaṁ gṛhṇātīti.

Nyāyakoṣa, p. 518.

70. Svottaravartisvavisayakalaukika pratyakṣasya svaniṣṭha-prāmāṇya viṣayakatayā svajanya-svaviṣayaka-pratyakṣa-sāmagrī svaniṣṭha-prāmāṇya-niścāyikā iti Miśrāḥ.

Māthurī on T. C., p. 126.

71. Naiyāyikā api anuvyavasāye viśeṣyatvaprakaratvayorbhānamaṅgīkurvanti; purovartinaṁ ghaṭatvena jānāmi ityākarasyaivānuvyavasāyasyatairaṅgikārāt, parantu purovartini ghaṭādau ghaṭatvādi rūpaprakārasaṁbandhabhānaṁ naṅgīkurvantī. Nyāyokoṣa, p. 518.

72. Jñātatā ca jñāta iti pratītisiddho jñānajanyo viṣaya-samavetaḥ prākaṭyāparanāmātiriktapadārtbaviśeṣeḥ. Tattvacintāmaṇirahasya, p. 126.

73. Vyavasāyotpattyavyavahitottarakṣaṇenotpannānuvyavaṣāya-vyaktereva Bhāṭṭaiḥ jñātatājṅgakānumititvena Miśrādiviśca sākṣāt kāratvenā- bhyupagamāt. Tattvacintāmaṇirahasya, p. 148.

74. (a) Bhāṭṭairapi vyavasāy-apūrvotpannena vyavasāyasamakālotpannena vā smaraṇādyātmaka-parāmarśena vyavasāyotpattīdvitīyakṣaṇe janitayā ahaṁ jñanavān jñātatāvattvādityanumityaiva prāmāṇyagrahā-bhyupagamāt.

Tattvacintāmaṇirahasya, p. 148.

(b) Jñānasyātīndriyatayā pratyakṣāsaṁbhavena svajanyajñātatā liṅgakānumitisāmagrī svaniṣṭha prāmāṇya-niścāyikā iti Bhāṭṭāḥ.

Tattvacintāmaṇirahasya, p. 126.

75. ghaṭo ghaṭatvavadviśeṣyaka-ghaṭatva-prakārakajñanaviṣayah ghaṭa tvaprakārakajñātatvayattvāt.

Nyāyakoṣa, p. 517.

76. anadhigatābādhitārthaviṣayaka jñānatvam pramātvaṁ. Vedāntaparibhāṣā, p. 15. (C. U. Edn.)

See also Bhāmatī: Abādhitānadhigatāsamdigdhabodhajanakatvaṁ hi pramāṇatvaṁ pramāṇānām. See Advaitasiddhi, 1.12.

77. It has already been pointed out that the Nyāya theory of the correspondence of idea and object as the criterion of truth is reflected by the correspondence theory of the Western Realists while the *Arthahkriyā-kāritva* or conductiveness to practical success which is regarded as a test of truth by the Buddhist schools is represented by the modern pragmatic schools of America and Europe. The coherent theory of the Hegelian school represents the view of some Indian Philosophers who regard saṁvāda and saṁvādakatva, *i.e.,* harmony with experience, as the mark of truth. The Advaitins hold a different view according to which the truth and validity of knowledge consists in its non-contradictedness (abādhitatva). This is very much akin to Hegel's own view of truth as resolving and reconciling all contradictions in itself. The Vedāntins proceed to criticise the different theories showing their inadequacies and point out how ultimately all of them might be reduced to their own theory of non-contradictedness. The correspondence theory cannot prove itself; for the question might be urged—how do you know that knowlẹdge and reality correspond? The only way to prove such correspondence is to infer it from the facts of the harmony of experience from consilience of coherence (or saṁvāda as we have seen in the Nyāya explanation of validity of knowledge) which is a foreign method. But even this does not help much for all we can infer from the harmony of knowledge with the rest of experience legitimately is not that knowledge is absolutely free from error but that it is not yet contradicted. What is the guarantee that the future will not contradict it and thus falsify it? To meet this objection the Vedāntins argue that knowledge should be such as to be incapable of being contradicted at all times. The pragmatic test of causal efficiency is also rejected by the Advaitins on the ground that sometimes even a false cognition may lead to the fulfilment of a purpose as when mistaking the *lustre* of a distant jewel for the jewel we approach and get the jewel. Here it is clear that the falsity of the initial cognition which

caused our action is due to its being contradictedness. This criticism of the Advaitins against the sister schools of Indian Philosophy runs on similar lines with Prof. Alexander's criticism against the correspondence theory of the Western Realists; in which he shows how it reduces itself inevitably to the coherence theory.

Vide Alexander's Space Time and Deity, Vol. II, pp. 252-253.

78. Nīrūpasyāpi kālasya indriyavedyatvābhyupagamena dhārāvāhika buddberapi pūrva pūrva jñānaviṣaya tattat kṣaṇaviśeṣaviṣayakatvena na tatrāvyāptiḥ.

Vedāntaparibhāṣā p. 22, C. U. Edn.

79. Yajjātīya-viśiṣṭa-jñānatvāvacchedena samānākāraka-niścayottara-vartitvaṁ niyamaḥ tajjātīyajñānabhinnatvam anadhigatatvam. [M. M. Lakṣmaṇa Śāstrin's interpretation.]

80. Ahurvijñāna-sāmgrī-janyatve satyajanyatā tadanyataḥ pramāyāstat ṣ svatastvamititavidaḥ. Citsukhī, p. 122.

81. (a) Naca ajanyatvādavyāptrirēśvarajñāne tasya ajanyatve'pi jñana-sāmagrījanyatve satyati-riktakāraṇajanyatva-lakṣaṇaviśiṣṭa-dharmavattvā-bhāvāt. Citsukhī, p. 122.

(b) Vijñānasāmagrī-janyatve sati tadatirikta-sāmagrī janyatvaṁ yadapramāsu prasiddhaṁ tadatyantā bhāvavattvaṁ hi lakṣaṇam etacceśvara-jñāne astīti nāvyāptirityarthaḥ.

Nayanaprasādinī, p; 122.

82. *(a)* Na ca jñāna jñapakādeva prāmāṇya grahaṇe mithyārajata buddhiṣu prāmāṇya grahaṇa prasaṅgaḥ, prasaktasyāpi-prāmāṇya grahaṇasya kārana doṣāvagamabādhabodhā-bhyāmapanayāt, na ca tābhyāmapanaye tayorabhāva-jñānasya prāmāṇyagrahaṇahetutvāpattau parataḥ-pramāṇyā pattiriti vācyam, doṣabādha-bodhayoranudaya mātreṇa prāmāṇya sphuraṇarasvīkaraṇāt,

Citsukhī, p. 125.

(b) Navayamaprāmāṇyajñāne kāraṇadoṣa jñāna bādhaka-jñānavat prāmāṇyāvagame tayorabhāvajñānaṁ kāraṇamā-śrayāmahe apitu tajñānānu-dayamātraā tena na parataḥ-prāmāṇyāpattiriti.

Nayanaprasādinī, p. 125.

83. *(a)* Yena hi doṣābhāva jñānena ādyasya prāmāṇyamavagamyate tat prāmāṇyavagamārthamapi doṣā bhāva jñānāntaraṅ gaveṣaṇīya-mevaṅ-kāramuparyapītyanavasthā.

Nayanaprasādinī, p. 125.

(b) *Vide* Citsukhī, p. 125.

84. Pramāparatojñayate anabhyāsadaśāyāṁ sāmśayikatvāt.

85. Napi pratyakṣa pramāyāṁ bhūyo'vayavendriya sannikarṣaḥ, rūpādipratyakṣe, ātma pratyakṣe ca tadabhāvāt, satyapi tasmīṅ pītaḥ śaṅkha iti pratyakṣasya bhramatvācca, ata eva na salliṅgaparā-marśādikamapi anumityādi pramāyāṁ guṅaḥ asalliṅga parāmarśādisthale'pi viṣayābādhena anumityādeḥ pramātvat. Vidānta paribhāṣā, pp. 268-69. (C. U. Edn.)

86. Anumanasya svataḥ pramāṇatayā anvayasyā pi sambhavāt, tathā anumānasyatu parito nirastasamasta-vibhrāmāśaṅkasya svata eva prāmāṇyam anumeyāvyabhicāriliṅgasamutthatvāt.

Nyāya-Vārtika tātparya-ṭīkā, III.

Some of the Naiyāyikas, however, admit the self-evident character of some cognitions. Udayana, for example, maintains that the consciousness of consciousness is self-evident.

APPEARANCE

CHAPTER IV

A CRITICAL EXAMINATION OF THE REALISTIC CATEGORIES

The thesis of *Śaṁkara Vedānta* that there is only one absolute knowledge and that all else is false cannot be established so long as the realistic categories of the *Nyāya-Vaiśeṣika* schools remain unassailed. *Śaṁkara-Vedānta* therefore begins by showing the untenability of the *Nyāya-Vaiśeṣika* conceptions of realistic categories. When subjected to examination they are found to involve self-contradictions. The Neo-Vedāntic teachers critically examined the categories and revealed their untenable nature by pointing out the inherent antinomies in them. The most famous of these teachers are *Śrīharṣa, Citsukha* and *Madhusūdana*. *Madhusūdana* in his monumental work *Advaitasiddhi* mainly refutes the contention of *Vyāsarāja* in *Nyāyāmṛta*. He therefore does not show as much zeal in refuting Nyāya categories as is shown by *Śrīharṣa* and *Citsukha*. Śrīharṣa's criticisms are however all destructive. He directs his energy mainly to the refutation of the categories. He shows that these categories are faulty according to the Naiyāyika's own canons of logic and that all our experiences and the categories which form the bases of our experiences are undefinable and inexplicable. And he concludes that the phenomenal world, being neither true nor false, being in fact indefinable, is unreal. Thus he establishes the Advaita position of the unreality of the world. *Citsukha* is a commentator of *Śrīharṣa*.

He had the critical acumen of his master. But he not only refutes *Nyāya* categories but interpretes the most important concepts of the Advaita-Vedānta and establishes the Advaita standpoint. His criticisms are thus both destructive and constructive. *Śrīharṣ a* spends his zeal more in exposing the contradictions in verbal technicalities and in exposing the fallacy involved in the problems of *Nyāyā* than in establishing the monistic position. His primary concern, as is suggested by the name of his book *Khaṇḍanakhaṇḍakhādya* was to refute the *Nyāya-Vaiśeṣika categories*. The name of Citsukha's book *Tattvapradīpikā* clearly suggests that he wanted to throw light on the Vedānta concept of reality. He however owes much to Śrīharṣa whose method he adopts in assailing Nyāya.

Śrīharṣa's method too cannot be said to be original. He follows in the footsteps of Buddhist philosophers *Nāgārjuna, Candrakīrti* and others. *Nāgārjuna* was the first to lay down this method of refuting *Nyāya categories*. *Śrīharṣa* only continued his method. *Śrīharṣa* however differs in his ultimate conclusion from *Nāgārjuna*[1] In the present chapter we shall follow *Śrīharṣa* and *Citsukha* in their refutation of Nyāya categories such as part and whole *(avayava* and *avayavī)*, substance and attribute *(dravya* and *guṇa)* co-inherence *(samavāya)* universal and particular *(jāti* and *vyakti)*, time and space *(kāla* and *dik)*, cause and effect *(kārya, kāraṇa)*.

Notion of *avayava* and *avayavi*

The table that we see before us is perceived as a thing having an infinite number of parts. To a scientist these parts are nothing but atoms, which are the smallest possible particles of matter beyond the range of ordinary sense-perception.

Now the question arises whether the thing as a whole is, or is not, different from its component imperceptible parts, the atoms. If different, it would occupy a position in space separate from that occupied by its parts, *e.g.*, a jug and a piece of cloth are different things because they occupy different positions in space. But we do not recognise a thing as different from its parts, nor does it occupy a different position in space.[2] Moreover, if the thing were different from its parts, it would possess a separate set of qualities, relation, functions, etc., distinct from those belonging to its parts. But the sense-perception does not corroborate the above view; for in sense-perception we do not meet with a double set of qualities relations, etc., in the perception of a table.

Further, if a thing were different from its parts, both the thing and its parts would be perceived independent of each other just as a table and a chair being different from each other are apprehended independently. But the thing and its parts are never perceived independent of each other. Again, the relation of thinghood to its constituent individual parts is controversial. Does each individual part taken distributively contain the entire thinghood or do all the parts taken collectively contain it? In the first alternative the individual parts would appear as so many things and not as parts of the same thing. Each individual part would appear as a thing by itself so that one individual particle of a thing would occasion the perception of a thing as a whole. Since complete thinghood exists in each part, any change of attribute, such as colour, motion, etc., in any of these parts would appear as change affecting the whole.[3]

Even incompatible changes taking place in different parts of a thing will not warrant the conclusion that the different parts have each a separate entity, as such changes would give rise to a notion of contradictory relation.[4]

The second assumption is open to a worse kind of fallacy. Existence of entire thinghood in all the parts of the thing taken collectively implies thinghood existing in a state of extension. Thinghood in itself is either extended, or unextended. If extended, it has already parts and does not, therefore, require other parts to exist in. Again how is the thinghood related to its primary set of parts? It must exist in those parts taken either distributively or collectively, and the same difficulty would arise again. If thinghood were unextended, and therefore without parts, it could not exist in so many extended-parts all occupying separate locations in space. Again, in that case there would be no valid reason why thinghood of this table would be confined to its own so-called parts and should not be equally related to all objects in the world indiscriminately. The same thing may be said as to the relation of thinghood to its so-called parts, for there would be no reason why entire thinghood should not confine itself to one part only to the exclusion of the rest.[5] Moreover, had thinghood existed in the parts taken collectively, apprehension of thinghood would be possible only when all the parts without any exception would come in direct contact with the operative organ of senses. But this is never the case. For, in every sense-perception only a very small number of the parts of the object comes in direct contact with the sense-organ.[6]

Hence thinghood cannot exist in the parts taken either distributively or collectively.

If thinghood were not different from the parts we are bound to conclude that thinghood as a principle of unity does not exist at all and that it is only the parts that exist.[7] And the so-called thingnood will be nothing more than another name for its parts. Nor will the parts as a group constitute any principle of unity, for the same objections will arise with regard to the relation of the group as unity to its so-called constituents. Hence only the individual atoms, and not the principle of unity exist.

How then can we account for the origin of a conception of an object having a principle of unity, or of a whole having parts as its constituent elements. The subjectivists argue that this conception of whole is nothing but an idea supplied from mind and arises when parts or groups of parts so cluster together as to become an object of apprehension by an organ of sense; *e.g.*, there is no such thing as a forest having objective reality; the notion of forest arises only when trees or groups of trees are so situated together as to produce a simultaneous impression upon our mind and as to make us lose sight, for the time being, of the intervening space that exists between one particular tree and another.[8]

The only conclusion which can, therefore, be legitimately drawn as a result of this analysis and examination is that there is no objective validity of this notion of 'whole'; what appears to be such is nothing but an objectification of the subjective experience itself. The above is the conclusion maintained by the subjectivist school with regard to the ultimate character of 'whole' or a principle of unity, and to this school belong Bauddha, Jaina, Mīmāṁsā, and Vedānta Philosophy.

The subjectivists thus deny the existence of 'whole' which cannot be found to be possessed of any entity when disintegration takes place among the parts composing the whole; what appears as the visible form giving an idea of whole is but a subjectively valid notion arising only when the particles, so grouped together, assume and present a particular shape. In our entire perceptual process, there is nothing to give us any evidence as to the reality of whole; what appeals to our senses is nothing but the taste, colour, etc., of the thing, and not the so-called underlying reality as 'whole.' This is to be particularly noted in this connection that the Buddhists not only deny objective reality of the whole, but hold this idea to be a subjective illusion. In this respect the Buddhist philosophers differ from other subjective schools of philosophy, *viz.*, the Jaina, Mīmāṁsā, Vedānta, etc., which contend that the notion of whole is not an illusion but a subjectively valid notion. We are bound to assume a sort of reality belonging to whole when we note the fact that the whole exerts some influence while serving a particular function in our practical life. But they do not admit the objective reality of whole, inasmuch as any analysis of whole will lead to this conclusion, that the whole is nothing but a transformed condition of the particulars constituting it.[9]

Pārtha Sārathi Miśra, the author of the *Śāstradīpikā,* concludes a sort of subjective reality belonging to whole, but the school does not admit that it has a self-existent reality of its own.[10]

The above position has been subjected to further analysis and elaborated by the author of the *Siddhāntacandrikā,* which is a commentary on the *Śāstradīpikā*. In the analysis of the perception of an object we are aware of the fact that our consciousness of the different parts of the object is accompanied by a simultaneous idea of oneness and the fact of this idea of oneness leads us to conclude that the whole has an entity different from its parts.[11] The question then arises as to the relation between the parts and the whole, and as to whether the whole actually possesses any reality of its own. A closer examination of the thing will reveal to us that the idea of oneness does not transcend our notion of parts but is co-existent with it, and that the comprehension of whole is not possible without comprehending it in relation, to the parts. The relation between the two can, therefore, be best represented as that which subsists between a cause and an effect. But the effect is nothing but a transformed condition of the cause. Therefore, though the whole appears to have its entity of its own, separate from that of the parts, it is not so distinct as the reality of one thing is distinct from that of another thing (*e.g.*, a book and a table). The relation between the two can, therefore, in the opinion of the Mīmāṁsists, be described as *bhinnābhinna*.[12]

In essence the Śaṁkarites also accept this view. In their opinion the whole has got no independent reality apart from the reality of the parts, being nothing more than a specific arrangement of the latter. The relation between the whole and the parts has, therefore, been described by the Śaṁkarites as *tādātmya*. The reality of one has been regarded by them as being identical with that of the other.[13]

Rāmānuja and his school also deny the independent existence of the whole. They look upon parts and whole, *upādāna* and *upādeya*, as being two stages of one substance. Looked at from one standpoint the substance gives us an impression of oneness, *i.e.*, of 'whole' while looked at from a different point of view, we receive from it an objectively valid idea of parts. The relation between the two is thus difference and sameness or *bhinnābhinna* as maintained by the Mīmāṁsists.[14] The Mādhvites also hold the viewpoint of the Mīmāṁsists. They more clearly indicate the relationship that exists between the whole and the parts and among the parts themselves. This school holds that the whole is identical with the parts when the latter are taken collectively. The Mādhvites analyse this thought further and give a definite interpretation of the relationship between the whole and the collection. With any and every collection, the whole does not stand in identical relationship. But only that form of collection that is definite and properly ordered can be said to stand in identical relationship to the whole.

For example, any collection of threads cannot be called a piece of cloth and does not serve any definite purpose, but when this collection has been properly and definitely arranged, we can apply the name to the form and it serves a definite purpose. Thus the relationship between the whole and the collection of the parts is both distinct and identical; it is distinct if the collection is indefinite and vague, but it is identical when the collection is well-ordered and gives rise to the idea of name and form.

But if one of the parts is taken individually and separately from the body of the whole and if we examine the relationship between this part and the whole we find that the relationship between the two is both distinct and identical. It is distinct from one standpoint and identical from another standpoint. It is distinct in the sense that apart from this part the whole can have the name and form and can serve a definite purpose and the idea of the whole remains as it was. Thus from the standpoint of the detached part the relationship is distinct, but from the standpoint of the whole the relationship is identical.

Again, the relationship that exists among the parts themselves is totally distinct. It is true that each part stands in complete isolation from another part, but when any part is related not to another part but to the collection of parts, the relationship becomes an identical one.[15]

To Sum up

It should be noted here that the conception of whole and parts as one of identity in difference is completely borrowed from Kumārila's system of Mīmāṁsā metaphysics. Śaṁkara here subscribes to Kumārila's position from empirical standpoint, as in the case of other empirical categories. Being an absolute monist the absolute reality of these categories cannot be admitted by Śaṁkara as has been done by Rāmānuja, Mādhva, consistently with their realistic philosophy. This fact has been plainly stated by Citsukha. In course of discoursing on the unreality of the phenomenal order, Citsukha singles out this case of whole and part, as illustrative of his thesis *(e. g.,* unreality of phenomenal world). The whole, he argues, is non-existent in the parts, because it is an effect being made up of parts on the Naiyāyika's own hypothesis. Now the relation of cause and effect has been proved to be an illusory super-imposition like that of silver on the shell. The effect cannot be regarded as absolutely identical with the cause as in that case the causal relation would be inconceivable, nor can it be held to be absolutely distinct since in that case anything could be regarded as the effect on the ground of its difference. If the pot is regarded as the effect of the clay on the ground of the difference from clay the cloth also could be thought of as the effect of clay by: the same logic. Śaṁkara also hints as the essential unreality of these categories, *e. g.,* whole and parts when he says they are related in the relation of identity and difference which is a contradiction in terms. The whole thing can be easily disposed of by the following dilemma.

Is the whole something different or non-different from the parts? If the latter alternative be accepted then the position of the realist that the whole is a distinct entity produced from the parts falls to the ground. If it is different we cannot understand how the two can be related. The relation of co-inherence-*(samavāya)* is an illogical assumption as we shall see later on and as such cannot be pressed as an explanation of these categories. In short all these realistic categories are found to be fraught with self-contradiction when logically examined.[16]

Substance and attributes

In our sense-perception, the object appears to us, as a substance having certain attributes. The attributes can never be perceived independent of the substance nor can the latter be cognised divested of the former. They are so related that the knowledge of the one invariably presupposes that of the other. A careful examination reveals that what we apprehend as the substance does not exist at all as a reality without its attributes.

Now the point at issue is whether the substance is different from its attributes or inseparably related to the latter.

If we admit the first alternative, the substance will be perceived in itself apart from and independent of the attributes. If we assume that the substance and the attributes are quite distinct in their nature but we have the cognisance of them together, the question would be, how do we come to the knowledge of the substance independent of the attributes? We do not derive the idea of such a substance through any of the five senses because the five sense-organs can give us only the knowledge of the attributes and not of the substance underlying the attributes. Therefore, we must be endowed with a new sixth sense-organ to have the perception of such a substance. But such an organ is not known to exist; hence no such idea of substance is valid.

Again we may accept the other alternative, *i.e.,* the idea of substance is is separably connected with that of the attributes. Then it is evident that the substance is nothing more than an aggregate of attributes. Now this conclusion breaks up the idea of unity that is necessarily involved. The attributes can never be understood if there exists no principle of unity in them. The substance tends to unify these attributes. The substance is not merely the sum-total of attributes, it is something more. It is not wholly immanent in the attributes, *i.e.,* the idea of the substance is not completely exhausted in the attributes. It is transcendent as well, and in this aspect the substance supplies the principle of unity that we are clearly conscious of in our sense-perception. Again, the attributes are ever-changing and have their meaning only in and through permanence. There is a permanent underlying substance and the changes have their seat in the former and this supplies the connecting link that runs through the series of changes. This one that supplies the connecting link is substance or *dravya.*

The consideration of these difficulties, that are rightly urged against the Buddhists, led the later thinkers of Indian Philosophy to conclude that the substance or the principle of unity cannot be denied. The Jaina school holds that the attributes are not self-sufficient and cannot exist in themselves. Further the same fact becoming the object of perception and touch-sensation proves that there is an underlying basis that gives rise to these different sensations.[17] Kumārila Bhaṭṭa in his *Ślokavārtika* and Pārtha sārathi Miśra in his *Śāstradīpikā* draw the same conclusion.[18] The Vedāntins also hold the same view.

The *Nyāya-Vaiśeṣika* systems admit the notion of the substance or the principle of unity and that of the attributes. But the *Naiyāyikas* and *Vaiśeṣikas* differ from the system of *Mīmāṁsā, Sāṁkhya* and *Vedānta* with regard to the determination of the character of the substance and that of the attributes and the relation that exists between the two. *Nyāya-Vaiśeṣika* systems of thought hold that the substance and the attributes are independent and self-sufficient categories and there arises a third entity namely, *samavāya* that connects these two separate categories in our experience.

A careful examination reveals that the Nyāya-Vaiśeṣika systems are at war, as it were, with the Advaita-Vedānta as they accept the independent existence of three categories, namely, (1) *substance,* (2) *attributes,* and (3) *samavāya.* The definitions, they set forth to determine the true nature of these three concepts are strongly criticised by the Śaṁkarites.

Śaṁkarites dialectical criticism of the definition of substance advanced by the Nyāya and Vaiśeṣika schools

First, let us examine the definition of substance as is given by the Nyāya-Vaiśeṣika schools. They define substance *(dravya)* as the seat of properties *(guṇaśraya).* Gitsukhacarya and Śrīharṣa, the and two well-known critics and staunch exponents of the Śaṁkara- Vedānta, strongly criticise this definition. It is vitiated in two ways : it is wider in one sense and narrower in another sense. Therefore, it is erroneous in two respects.[19]

The definition is wider because *guṇāśraya* or the seat of properties is the definition of the substance and this definition can rightly be applied to the attributes themselves for they are also the seat of properties as they are characterised by number *(saṁkhyā)* and separateness *(pṛthaktva)*. Thus colour is an attribute but it may have other attributes. A particular colour may be light or deep and it may be of many kinds. It may be one or many.[20] The teachers of the Nyāya-Vaiśeṣika systems were clearly conscious of these defects and tried to meet these shortcomings by saying that the attributes are attributeless and motionless in their nature.[21] The properties, number and *pṛthaktva* really inhere in the substance but are only falsely applied to the attributes. This conclusion does not appeal to the Advaita-critics as there is no ground of such false application; and it can be interpreted conversely as well, *i.e.,* we can say that the attributes, number and *pṛthaktva,* etc., really belong to the attributes themselves and are erroneously applied to the substance.[22]

Again, the definition is too narrow. If the substance is *guṇāśraya* or the locus of properties, it implies that the relation is one of cause and effect. The substance stands for the cause and the attributes represent the effect. The cause must precede the effect in point of time, and there must be a moment when the cause exists in itself devoid of any effect. Therefore, the substance must have a condition in which it is divested of all attributes; and this definition in its ordinary sense cannot be applied to the substance in that state. So this definition errs in being narrower as it excludes that substance which is free from attributes.

In order to meet this objection the Naiyāyikas explain *guṇāśrayatva* to mean *guṇavattvātyantābhāvānadhikaraṇatva* or the state of not being the substratum of the absence of having properties. They say that though at the time of origination there are, according to their own admission, no qualities in the substance, still the substance is not the substratum of the absolute negation of qualities, for in the second moment qualities inhere in it. But this roundabout explanation of the concept *guṇāśrayatva* does not help the Naiyāyikas, for then the definition of substance becomes too wide. Absolute negation of having qualities *(guṇa-vattvātyantābhāvaḥ)* may be characterised as not being the substratum of absolute negation of having qualities which is the characteristic of substance,[23] for nothing can be its own receptacle.

Again this characteristic mark of substance will be found even in *guṇas* themselves. For *guṇas* or qualities also are, as we have shown above, endowed with some other *guṇas, e.g.*, number, separateness, etc., and so they cannot be the substratum of the absolute negation of having qualities.[24]

Further does the definition of substance imply the absolute negation of one quality or of all?

The definition would be too narrow in either case. The *guṇas* or qualities are twenty-four in number, and what is the receptacle of one quality, *e.g.*, colour, may be characterised as the substratum of the absolute negation of another quality, *e.g.*, *rasa* or taste, and thus an entity—endowed with colour may not be determined by the definition of substance. Again, since there is no substance endowed with all qualities, therefore, nothing can be characterised as not being the substratum of the absolute negation of all qualities.[25]

As this definition is beset with difficulties, the Nyāya-Vaiśeṣika thinkers advance another definition of substance. The definition runs thus : substance is what is organically related to thinghood *(dravyatvajāti yogitvaṁ dravyalakṣaṇam)*. Chitsukhācārya is not satisfied with this definition and strongly criticises it. Wherefrom do we derive the idea of thinghood that attempts to define the substance? To have the idea of thinghood, we must have a pre-supposition of something that supplies this idea and that something must be of the same nature and character as those of the substance itself. Therefore, to possess the idea of thinghood we must previously be conscious of the thing itself.[26]

Śaṁkarites' criticism of the definition of attributes

The definition of the attributes as given by the Vaiśeṣika school does not also appear to be convincing. The Vaiśeṣikas define the attributes thus : The attributes are inherent in the substance and are totally divested of any quality and motion. They are not the causes of conjunction and separation.[27] The author of the *Nyāyakandalī* defines attributes as attributeless *(aguṇa)* and organically related to the universal characteristics of *guṇa (sāmānyavān)*. If we analyse this definition and make a careful scrutiny we find that it involves the fallacy of begging the question. In order to have a clear conception of *aguṇa* we must have the pre-conception of *guṇa* itself.

It has already been proved in the examination of the definition of substance that the attributes are not totally divested of qualities. They are characterised by number and separateness, etc.

The author of the *Kiraṇāvalī* defines attributes in a different form when he says that the attributes possess the characteristic of universality, *i.e., guṇatva* and lie beyond the range of touch-sensation though inhering in the substance and they form a separate category from motion or karma.[28] This definition involves four factors. We have already discussed the first epithet and there remain three more factors to be carefully analysed and critically examined.

We have no objection against *Kiraṇāvalī* when it declares that the attributes inhere in the substance and lie beyond touch-perception, but we cannot accept the last characteristic without doing violence to reason. When we fully analyse the term *karmātiriktaḥ* we see that it involves the following stages:— (1) distinct knowledge of *karma,* (2) the conception of *guṇa* and (3) clear understanding of the difference or distinction that lies between the two, To understand the nature of *karma* we must have a pre-conception of *guṇa* and that of the relation between the two. Again, to know *guṇa,* we must be familiar with the nature of *karma* and its distinctive characteristics. Thus each, in its turn, leads to the other. There is neither beginning nor any end. The process is never-ending and it commits the fallacy that is technically known as arguing in a circle.[29]

Śaṁkarites' criticism of the definition of 'samavāya'

We have seen that in the *Nyāya-Vaiśeṣika* systems substance and attributes are two distinct categories. They can never be cognised in such a way, so far as our experience is concerned, we know the substance in and through the attributes and the attributes in and through the former. Now, these systems are logically forced to admit the independent existence of a third category, *viz., samavāya* to account for the cognition of the substance through the help of the attributes and of the attributes in and through the substance. Praśastapāda defines *samavāya* as a category that brings into connection two concepts that cannot exist independently though standing in the relation of the container and the contained.[30]

Śrīdhara, in his *Nyāya-Kandalī,* attempts to render a thorough interpretation of this definition.[31] All instances of the relation of the container and the contained do not represent *samavāya* relation. For example, a particular book is placed on a table and they stand in the relation of the container and the contained; but this relation is not one of *samavāya* but of *saṁyoga*. *Samavāya* relationship is distinguished from *saṁyoga* relationship by the fact that in the former both the entities that are related together cannot stand independent of each other, while in the latter, they can so stand. In the previous illustration, the book and the table can both exist independent of each other, but a piece of cloth cannot exist independent of the threads that constitute its materials, though the latter can stand independent of the former. Thus both can never stand independent of each other and this relation illustrates the distinctive nature of *samavāya* relation.

Citsukhācārya strongly criticises this definition as being too wide. When we cognise the negation of a certain object, *viz.*, a particular pot on a particular place, we see that these two ideas cannot stand independently and express the relation of the container and the contained. Though all the requirements of *samavāya* relation are satisfied here, the Naiyāyikas themselves hold that this example is not one of *samavāya* relation. The relation is one of *viśeṣaṇa-viśeṣya-lakṣaṇa, i.e.*, the thing and its adjuncts.[32] Now the Nyāya-Vaiśeṣika systems modify this definition by adding that *samavāya* relation has its validity only in the case of two entities that are positive in their nature and it does not hold good in the instances in which even one is negative. This modification also is not satisfactory and to the Advaitins, it is equally fallacious. For example the sound has its existence in ether *(Iha ākāśe śabdaḥ)*. Here both the entities are positive and thereby all conditions are satisfied, still, the Naiyāyikas themselves do not hold this to be a case of *samavāya* relation. Therefore, the definition is too wide. Again, the definition unwarrantably assumes the epithet *ādhāryā-dhārabhūta* that necessarily follows from *ayutasiddha.*[33]

Samavāya is an independent category and relates two concepts, *viz.*, the substance and the attributes, etc. Now when it establishes the relation between the two, it itself stands in a certain relation to the substance. Therefore, in order to have the cognisance of the substance in and through the attributes and the latter in and through the former, we accept *samavāya* relation, and in connecting the two, *samavāya* itself is related to the substance. Now the question arises, how do we become aware of this relation that exists between the substance and *samavāya?* To account for this if we accept another *samavāya* and so on, we are led to an infinite regress *(anavasthā)*.

This fallacy of infinite regress led the Vedāntins to reject this *samavāya* relation as an entity standing independent of the substance and the attributes.[34]

Śaṁkara has pointed out in his *Bhāṣya* that the *Nyaya-Vaiśeṣika* systems cannot fully explain the real nature of the substance and that of the attributes, and their relation though they admit *samavāya* to be a third category. In refuting these systems Śaṁkara points out that they are self-contradictory as they admit the existence of six independent categories, substance, attributes, etc., and hold, at the same time, that five categories *guṇa,* motion, etc., entirely depend on the first, *viz.*, substance. Thus they affirm and deny the same truth in the same breath. Categories are at once independent and dependent, an absurd conclusion.[35]

It may however be contended that subordination does not do away with independence. As for example, smoke having originated from fire depends on it, though smoke and fire have both got independent existences. Similarly, attribute, etc., though dependent on substance, do not, on that account, lose their independence.

Attributes and other entities are dependent in the sense that they cannot be cognised unless they are related to the substance.

Upon this contention, Śaṁkarites argue that this example of smoke and fire does not hold good and it fails to explain the nature of subordination. It is a case of false analogy. Smoke and fire can be cognised independently and we consider them as distinct and separate. But the attributes cannot be cognised apart from their relation to the substance. Hence, the idea of distinctiveness and uniqueness is not clear in the case of the attributes.

Advaitin's decision

Thus, if experience be the last court of appeal, we find that the idea of the substance cannot be had apart from that of the attributes and the idea of the attributes equally depends on that of the former for its cognisance. So, there is no clear-cut distinction between the two. They are the two aspects of the same entity. Substance expresses itself in attributes and the latter have their perfection and consummation in the substance. The two are identical in essence. Attributes exist when the substance is there; they lack existence when the substance is wanting. So the substance expresses itself in different forms in different stages and assumes different names. But through these different names and forms runs a principle of unity that is known as substance.

Vācaspati Miśra in his *Bhāmati* explaining the nature of the substance and that of the attributes says that the attributes cannot be defined and conceived of as independent of the substance to which they belong. Whenever we have the cognisance of any attribute we conceive in reality the substance in one of its forms. Therefore, the attributes are not separate from and independent of the substance, but the universal character of the substance is illustrated in and through some particular attributes.[36]

Universal and particulars

When we perceive an object it appears to us a particular individual possessing characteristics, some of which are common to the class while others are specially its own. For example, a cow which we perceive before us, has two sets of qualities : (1) those that are common and essential to all cows in the world and (2) others that are particular to this cow only. The first set implies the pure essence which are common to all cows. The realistic philosophers are of opinion, that such essence found in different classes of things is not merely accidental points of resemblance. They indicate self-existent, eternal, unchangeable realities, *e.g.*, universals belonging, as it were, to a separate world of their own.[37] It is by virtue of their participating in the same universal that the particular individuals of a class happen to possess the so-called common and essential attributes.

As regards the existence of the universals and their relation to the particulars, there are other thinkers who hold a different view. They admit the class concepts or universals but do not think them as existing apart from particulars.

Realistic explanation of universal and particulars

The realistic philosophers maintain that these universals are objective entities and are revealed in perceptual cognition as much as individual objects, as the idea of universals is given in sense-perceptions. The existence of these universals can be demonstrated by a regular syllogistic inference also. Our perceptual experience is not only of the particular cow, but contains a reference to another distinct principle, which is not confined to the individual concerned but inheres in other individuals in the same manner and the same degree. Had we been cognisant of the particular individual alone the cognitions would have been distinct and separate and there would be no class-concept, put this is not the case; there is the sameness of cognition in our cognitions different cows, cows, this identity of reference linguistic and psychological alike, can be accounted for only on the assumption of a universal element super-added to particulars.[38] The existence and non-existence of an objective reality and determined by the arbitration of experience alone and the dictum[39] that excess in knowledge presupposes a correspond excess in the objective order should be accepted by all believers in extra mental reality. So the particular and universal should be accepted as equally true and equally real and there is no contradiction or logical incompatibility in these two factors coalescing in one substratum.

According to the subjectivists, *jāti* is merely a creation of our own mind without any objective counterpart at all. The Buddhists urge that the existence of the universal can be proved neither by sense-perception nor by inference. It is impossible that sense-perception should give us the knowledge of the universal. Sense-perception is confined to particulars only and has no valid application beyond them. Nor can inference or testimony, being ultimately based on perception, supply us with the knowledge of the universal.[40]

There are two forms of perception, *Nirvikalpa* and *Savikalpa* and none of these is sufficient to prove conclusively the universal that underlies the particulars. Indeterminate or *Nirvikalpa* perception is occasioned as soon as the so-called object comes in contact with a particular sense-organ just before the subjective contributions from within have any opportunity to modify the pure sensuous processes. Determinate or *Savikalpa* perception, according to this theory, is due to subjective contributions added to the stage of pure perception. These subjective contributions not being in kind of touch with the object itself, cannot affect the true nature of the object. Hence, even when we seem to apprehend them sensuously this knowledge must be taken to be an illusion without any validity. And the sensuous perception of the universal depends upon a comprehensive apprehension of the particulars participating in the same universal. But as sense-perception is by its nature confined only to the presentative elements, other elements will have to be represented in consciousness in order to occasion a comprehensive apprehension of the object. If the universals were sensuously perceived, it would be either by means of presentive elements or by representative elements or by means of both in co-operation. The knowledge of the universal involves a comparative consciousness of the particulars and this consciousness requires the presence of both the presentative and representative elements. But sense-perception supplies us only with presentative elements. Now as the latter elements are wanting in sense-perception, it is not the only source of knowledge of the universal. Representative elements, again, not being in direct touch with any present object, cannot occasion any sensuous apprehension even if they seem to establish a true relation with the presentative elements. Representative elements are the creations of the mind and hence illusory. They cannot therefore in any way prove the objective validity of the universal.

If it were argued that the presentative and representative elements, by their co-operation occasion the sensuous perception of the universal, the same reply would be given. So far as the representative elements are concerned, the apprehension of the universal, resulting from them, cannot be sensuous; because the representative elements unlike the presentative ones, are occasioned by a process of memory revival *(smṛtyanantarabhāvī)* and not by any inter-action between the object and the sense organ. Though ordinary experience apparently shows that we perceive the universals sensuously, a deeper analysis discloses the fact that representative factors constitute the major portion of sensuous perception and that there is not a bit of sensuousness in representative factors. Hence no sense-perception of the universal is possible. Inference, again, being based on perception, equally fails to stand as a source from which we might derive the knowledge of the universal. The degree of subjective complexity is much greater in inference than in sense perception. So we conclude that neither perception nor inference can warrant any knowledge of the universal.

If we admit the existence of the universal, the question arises, what is the relation between the universal and the particular? Is it one of difference or of identity ! If the universal is different from the particulars, it would be perceived independently of the latter. If identical, it would cease to exist as a principle of unity. If different and identical at the same time, it is inconceivable.[41]

Further, if the universal were different from the particular, it would exist either everywhere in the world or only in the particulars belonging to the class. If it existed everywhere, it would be perceived not only in the objects other than its so-called particulars but also in a space not occupied by any object; the universal 'cowhood' would be perceived in a horse also. It may be argued that though the universal is ubiquitous, it is manifested only in that particular class because only these individuals have (while other individuals have not) the capacity to manifest it. The reply would be that since the universal is ubiquitous, there is no reason why it should not be perceived in all the objects in the world indiscriminately. Moreover, since the universal is ubiquitous and stands in the same relation to all objects in space, there is no reason why some objects should and others should not have the so-called capacity to manifest the universals.

If it were assumed that the universal is not ubiquitous but exists as confined to the particulars only, then in the case of a new-born individual, first coming into relation with the universal, either the universal is born along with the particulars or comes to it from another particular already existing. In the first alternative, the universal would not be external; in the second, it would not be unchangeable. Moreover, the particular which the universal abandons in order to be associated with the newly-born one would be without any universal. Similarly, if a particular were annihilated the universal already present in it would either be annihilated with it or remain unsupported in the same locality or go to a second particular to reside in. In the first alternative, the universal would not be eternal; the second one is inconceivable and in the third alternative, the second particular would have two universals simultaneously present in it which is an absurdity.[42]

The manner of existence of the universal in the particulars is equally inconceivable. For, the entire universal is present either in a single particular only (in which case other particulars will be without any universal) or in all particulars taken distributively (in which case the universal would not be a partless unity) or in all particulars taken collectively (in which case it would be perceived only when all the particulars are simultaneously perceived).

Hence the universal is merely a subjective fiction without any objective counterpart.[43]

Now the question arises that if it be a subjective fiction, how do we become conscious of oneness, *anugata-pratyaya* that runs through different individuals of a class? We find, for example, two cows and believe that they belong to the same species. This cognition of the principle of unity cannot be satisfactorily explained if we do not admit that, behind these particular cows, there is a universal cowhood in which all the particular cows participate. Therefore, the universal has its objective validity on the ground of the consciousness of the principle of unity, that runs through the individuals and makes a class concept possible. The Buddhists contend, however, that this feeling of the general essence is also a subjective fiction and it is not essential that the universal should have an existence to give rise to this form of consciousness. The notions of the genus and the species, substance and attributes, etc., are all fictitious without corresponding realities; and this kind of notions has its origin in the mind when it finds that two or more particular individuals serve the same purpose in our practical life. The capacity of the individuals to serve the same purpose gives rise to this notion of the principle of unity,[44] and the realists erroneously hold that corresponding to this notion of the principle of unity there lies a universal or *jāti* in the real facts of nature.

Citsukha's criticism against Nyāya

Following the mode of arguments advanced by the subjectivists' school discussed above Citsukha says that neither by perception nor by inference *jāti* as a separate class-concept can be established. What is exactly meant by class concept? Does it mean the apprehension of a cow in one animal just as we have it in another animal? Or does it mean the apprehension of the nature of a cow inhering in all cows? Or does it mean the apprehension of a characteristic common to them all? In none of these senses the class-concept be established. In the first case even without the class-concept we can apprehend each of the animals as a cow by seeing some peculiarities common to them just as we can apprehend the moon in its several reflexions in many vessels of water.[45] In the second case the nature of the cows is not determined, or if determined the class-concept becomes useless. In the third case, it can be said that just as we have the perception of a man as holding the stick *(daṇḍī, daṇḍavān)* so we have not the perception of a cow as having the characteristic of cows *(gotrī, gotvavān)*. It is only from the perception of cows that we can gather the characteristic of cows, *viz.*, the possession of dewlap, etc. In this case we can have the apprehension by means of the differentia and there is no need of a class concept. Again what indicates the *jāti* and where does it reside? If it be said that the indicator resides where *jāti* resides then there arises fallacy of mutual dependence; for without the knowledge of the indicator we cannot have the idea of *jāti* and again without the knowledge of *jāti* we cannot have any idea of the indicator which co-exists with *jāti*.[46]

Admitting *jāti* the question arises : how is *jāti* related to individuals? The relation between *jāti* and individuals can neither be one of contact *(saṁjoga)* nor of coherence *(samavāya)* nor of identity *(tādātmya)*. The relation cannot be one of *saṁyoga;* for in that case the *jātis* being eternal and all-pervading it will be possible for them to be in contact with all substances, so we might perceive cowhood in things other than cows as well as in them. The *samavāya* category has been already refuted. If the relation is said to be one of identity then cowhood being identical with existing cows, it cannot apply to a newly-born cow as it is distinct from existing cows with which *jāti* is identified and as it has no motion and no parts it cannot adhere to the new cow.[47]

Advaitins' Conclusion

For all these difficulties the Advaitins reject *jāti* and hold that there is one principle of unity which is a purely subjective contribution without any objective reality necessitated by the demands of understanding.

Time and Space

The ideas of Time and Space are inherent in the very cognition of finite beings. To have a clear understanding of any object, we study it as standing in three relations; it must be in Time, it will occupy Space, and be bound to other objects by the tie of Causality. The very fact of sequence involves the notions of Time, Space and Causality. These three factors constitute the common cause of the being and comprehension of any finite object. All schools of Indian thought, in one sense or other, have accepted the truth of these notions.

The Nyāya system on Time and Space

The past, present and future have no meaning if we do not accept the concept of 'Time.' Time is the cause that give rise to the distinction of the two as older and younger. Days, months, years, etc., are nothing but the limitations of Time.[48] All these considerations led the Naiyāyikas to admit Time as an eternal entity that conditions itself in finite times. Let us see however whether these considerations can be explained in another way, and then there would be no necessity of assuming the existence of an eternal Time.

It is also objected that the idea of Time is not essential to explain the notion of day, month, year, young and old, etc. These ideas of young and old do not originate from the belief in eternal Time; they are simply the modes of the finite experience.[49] The notion of day, month, year, etc., depends on the various movements and evolutions of the planets and does not require a pre-supposition of Time as a separate category. This notion, therefore, being a mode of motion, belongs to '*karma*' category.[50]

In reply to the first objection, it is argued that time is a fact of independent perception in any cognition and cannot therefore be denied. In any cognition the idea of delay or swiftness or the idea of sequence, etc., appear like the adjuncts or qualities that specialise that form of cognition. These special qualities must have a basis to stand upon; and this fundamental basis is Time which is thus perceived in cognition. Similarly, space also is perceived when we see a thing as located in a particular space. It may be contended, however, that perception is possible only when the object comes in direct contact with the sense-organ. Spaces and time though standing as qualitative adjuncts, being devoid of smell, colour, etc., do not come in contact with the sense-organs and lie beyond perception. This contention, however, is not satisfactory. It is not necessary that the object of perception must appeal to sense-organs through their respective objects such as smell, touch, taste, colour, etc. Whatever is clearly manifested in cognition is taken to be a fact of perception. Time and space qualifying the objects of cognition are clearly manifested to us, though smell, taste, etc., are wanting. For example, the notion of specific gravity is an instance of perception, though it fails to appeal to the different sense-organs but still it is perceived. Time and Space are also perceived in the same way. Again, if we concede validity to these objections and hold that time and space are inferential, it does not invalidate their being.

In reply to the second objection it may be argued that the succession of day and night, year, etc., cannot be finally explained by the revolution of the earth round its axis or by the movements of the planets. The movements of the planets also depend for their explanation on the idea of time. The sun rises and sets. The understanding of this proposition presupposes time. Therefore, time is the fundamental idea that expresses itself in the movements of the planets and in the succession of day and night. Movements of planets have their being in planets only and have no relation to finite events. Therefore, the succession of day and night, month and year, etc., cannot be explained by these movements as there is no point of similarity between them. Thus we are forced to believe time as an entity that underlies sequence. This time is eternal, all-pervading and partless just as ether is.[51]

Similarly, Space is another aspect of sequence and is eternal, all-pervading and partless like Time. So Time and Space are in their nature eternal and all-pervading; but from the phenomenal standpoint, they are perceived no longer as eternal and all-pervading but limited when they stand in relation to finite objects. Just as one eternal ether breaks down, as it were, and manifests itself in particular pots; so eternal Time and Space lose as it were their eternity and manifest themselves in particular events and finite objects as limited. Thus, in themselves, Time and Space are eternal, but they are looked upon as limited in relation to finite events and objects.

To sum up

In our previous discussion we have examined the Naiyāyika-position and have found that one, eternal Space and Time cannot explain the facts of perception. The Naiyāyikas hold that the idea of day, month, year, etc., is due to the relations of the movements of the sun to the finite objects. According to the variation of this movement, variation or change in Time order is produced. It may be asked here, the movements exist in the sun and how can they be related to the objects of physical nature? According to the Naiyāyikas, the factor that establishes this relation is to be known as time. Time is thus the source or cause of giving rise to this idea in us.[52]

Citsukha's criticism against the Nyāya position

Citsukha here observes that the idea of Time has its origin in the movements of the sun; but we are conscious of time when the movements of the sun are related to finite objects. The Naiyāyikas lay exclusive stress on the principle that establishes this relation and take this principle to be time. Citsukha points out that the relation is not a potent factor in the consciousness of time. That the true knowledge of time lies in the movements of the sun and the relation between these movements and the finite objects can be explained by any other eternal factor and does not necessitate time. There is one, eternal and all-pervading self, which, as substrate, establishes unity in diversity and harmonises all the objects that seem to be detached from one another, can explain the relation between the movements of the sun and the finite objects.[53] Further, the idea of day, month, year, etc., depends purely on the movements of the sun. Therefore, the motion of the sun is the final solution of the secret of Time. Every experience involves Time and Space as inherent in it. But this does not go to prove the separate and independent entity of Time and Space.

Finite objects are explained by the idea of finite time; but the current of time is infinite, because origination and destruction cannot be explained if we do not hold belief in infinite time. If we affirm that there was a period when time was not, and there will be a period when time will cease to exist, it will presuppose time as we have already explained. Thus Time is proved to be infinite. Citsukha observes that infinite time is inconceivable. We are conscious of time when the movements of the sun are related to the finite objects, *i.e.,* we know the meaning of 'before' and 'after' through relation. But when there is no relation between the movements of the sun and the finite objects, time exists in the motion itself as a form of energy. Thus there is no necessity of assuming one infinite time.[54]

Similarly, Citsukha proves that space is not infinite. The idea of space dawns on us when the sun touches the various parts of its orbit in its different movements. The first point of contact is known as the eastern gate and in reference to this point we come to know the ten quarters. When the sun's path or line of movement is related to finite objects we are conscious of space, and this does not necessitate the concept of an infinite space. Here also the relationship is established by the absolute Self.[55]

Cause and effect

Citsukha refutes also the Nyāya category of cause and effect. *Pūrvakālabhāvitva* or antecedence in time cannot be the criterion of a cause. For, in that case the washermans ass, which stands just before the fire is lighted, will be the cause of fire. If, however, the expression *niyata* or invariable is prefixed to *pūrvakālabhāvitva* or antecedence, then also the ass becomes the cause as only when the ass is present the fire is kindled. If again the expression *ananyathā-siddha* be added, that is the cause be regarded as the invariable antecedent *sine qua non,* then also the ass being that without which the washerman who is the cause of fire, cannot do, will be the cause. Space without which fire cannot be kindled will also be the cause of fire. The objection that space being common and all pervasive cannot be the cause of fire cannot be raised by the Naiyāyikas, for the same objection will hold true of the soul which they regard as the cause of the production of pleasure and pain. The cause cannot be defined as that which being present the effect follows, for the seed cannot produce sprouts without accessories and therefore according to this definition the seed will not be the cause. If the accessories are introduced as the cause then there arises the fallacy of *ātmāśrayatva,* for if the cause be explained by a reference to the secondary causes, then cause is sought to be explained by causes. Again the dictum that cause is that which being present the effect follows and which being absent the effect does not follow invalidates plurality of causes; for since fire can be produced by many different agencies, some will be present in one and others in another case. Fire will be kindled even in the absence of some factors and the definition of cause will thus be invalidated for these absent factors may also produce fire, on other occasions. It is absurd to define cause as collocation of causal factors, for then cause will to be determined by causes.[56]

The Nyāya interpretation of cause thus being proved to be untenable the conception of effect which depends on the conception of cause cannot be logically determined.

Now we turn to prove the untenability of Nyāya explanation of effect and to discuss in this connection the doctrine of causation as held by different schools of Indian thought.

The doctrine of causation

Causality is the central category of experience. In every experience we find that each phenomenon is connected with another phenomenon by the law of causation. No event in the universe is totally detatched from the rest. Experience becomes possible only when we presuppose causation.

Three lines of thought run through the history of Indian Philosophy in explaining the law of Causation. *Ārambhavāda* or *Asatkāryavāda, Pariṇāmavāda* or *Satkāryavāda* and *Sad-vivartavāda* or *Sat-kāraṇavāda.*

Naiyāyika conception of causation Asatkāryavāda or Ārambhavāda

Ārambhavāda admits of two forms, *Asatkāraṇavāda* of the Buddhists and *Sat-kāraṇavāda* of the Naiyāyikas. The two schools of thought agree so far as the nature of the effect is concerned, *i.e.,* it is asat, non- existent. *Asat-Kāryavāda* or *Ārambhavāda* of the Naiyāyikas is a commonsense theory and we generally assume the truth of this theory in our every day experience. It adopts the empirical standpoint and holds that the effect is non-existent before its creation. The activity of the agent creates a kind of new effect from the cause, which did not exist before the operation of the agent. For instance, a jar, although made of clay, is non-existent *qua* jar before the potter moulds the clay into this form. The potter creates a new effect from the clay. Hence prior to its production, the effect as such is non-existent. Though the effects have no permanent reality, they have a temporary existence. They suddenly come into being and soon vanish away. The Naiyāyikas try to explain everything by means of the atoms. By the conglomeration of atoms, everything comes into existence that had no prior existence. This theory runs counter to the Sāṁkhya theory which holds that the effect is implicitly and potentially present in the cause. The cause and the effect are identical. But the Naiyāyikas hold that the cause and effect stand in the relation of sequence and can never be identical. Cause and effect appear in our consciousness as separate. We never identify a piece of cloth with the thread of which it is made. The cloth was '*asat*' but the threads were existent, *sat*. When so made, we do not look upon it as threads arranged in a certain order but as cloth. So too, a jar is not identical with its cause clay.

Criticism

This theory suffers from many difficulties. At the very outset, it appears to us to be inconsistent when we think that bodily substances can have their origin in a bodiless substance. Non-existence can never be transformed into existence. If the effect were absolutely non-existent before its production, it could by no means be brought into being. We can, for example, extract oil from mustard-seeds, but never from sand. Every effect exists potentially in its material cause, and is only manifested as such through the activity of the agent. The jar in question exists in clay even prior to its being moulded as such. The potter's activity is only a suitable occasion for its manifestation as a jar.

Further, if we accept the hypothesis of *Ārambhavāda,* we are forced to admit the principle of the plurality of causes. If the effect suddenly comes into being spontaneously and does not exist potentially in the cause prior to its being manifested, we are forced to believe that anything can come out of anything else; and there is no certainty that the same cause will produce the same effect. We know that the causal connection is a necessary relation and we get oil from mustard-seed only because oil is inherent in the seed; but we cannot derive oil from sand and the reason is to be found in the fact that there is no necessary relation between oil and sand, or in other words, oil does not implicitly inhere in the sand.

Thus if we hold that the same cause will give rise to the same effect, we are called upon to admit at the same time that the effect remains implicit in the cause before its manifestation.

Thus we see that the effect is not *'asat'* or non-existent prior to its production. It is to be found inhering in the cause, and by the activity of the agent what was implicitly contained in the cause is explicitly expressed in the effect. The effect is hidden from our view before its production and it is presented to us under favourable conditions. Limits to knowledge are not the same thing as limits to existence. We cannot, therefore, argue that because we do not see the effect before its production it does not exist. But it does exist though only implicitly. No foreknowledge is possible if the effect is non-existent. The effect-form is, therefore, potentially existent in the cause. It is not purely *'asat'* before it is produced.

Naiyāyika theory, though it gives a better interpretation of the Law of Causation and removes the shortcomings of Buddhism, is not fully satisfactory; because in refuting the Buddhists, it adopts some view that are logically false. The Naiyāyika-difficulties did strike the Sāṁkhyists who render a better explanation of Causation. These three schools represent the different stages of development of the same thought in so far as Causation is concerned.

Sāṁkhya theory of Causation

This school holds that the effect is real or *sat*. Whatever comes into being cannot be non-existent. The effect, before its production, is implicitly present in the cause and under suitable conditions the cause manifests itself in the effect. The cause and the effect are not two different realities. The cause appears in the effect; the two are different aspects of the same phenomenon. Before transformation it is known as cause and after transformation it is known as effect. The author of *Siddhāntaleśa* defines causation as a process of becoming in which the cause gradually changes and reappears in the effect. The effect can be described as the immanent finality, the formative principle realising itself through successive transformations till it reaches the final growth and development. It is the generally accepted theory of causation in metaphysics.

Advaitin's explanation of Cause and Effect

The monistic doctrine of causation is known as *Vivartavāda*. The effect is not the transformation of the cause, as the Sāṁkhyists hold, but it is the manifestation of the cause; in this manifestation the cause is not affected in any way. According to Sāṁkhya, the cause and the effect are identical, because it is the potentiality that comes into actuality. But Advaitism denies this truth and hold that the relation is inexplicable, *anirvacanīya*. So far as our experience is concerned, we can say this much that the effect cannot be understood independent of its material cause, *i.e.,* a pot cannot exist independent of clay. Thus it stands in opposition to the Nyāya-Vaiśeṣika systems that hold that the effect is a separate and independent entity. The relation is not identical; because the activity of the agent fails in this affirmation and the expression 'the agent makes a thing' is emptied of all meaning. Neither can it be considered as *bhedābheda* as these are two contradictory terms which cannot inhere in the same object at the same time. Hence the nature of the effect is unspeakable or *anirvacanīya*. This is the view of the Sāṁkarites.

Advaita Vedānta explains the relation between the cause and the effect as *ananya*. The term does not mean *abheda* or non-difference as used in Sāṁkhya. It means, on the other hand, that the effect has no being or reality apart from that of the cause.[57]

Vācaspati Miśra in explaining the term *ananya* says that it is neither *bheda* or different nor *abheda* or identical. In introducing this term Advaitism differs from the *Nyāya-Vaiśeṣika* systems on the one hand, and *Sāṁkhya* and *Pātañjala* on the other. If the cause and the effect are different, we fail to trace out any causal link between two separate, independent and different entities.

The activity of the agent becomes useless if the cause and the effect are identical. This objection can be met by the Sāṁkhyists by saying that the activity of the agent is necessary to bring potentiality into actuality as we have seen in the examples of the Sāṁkhyists. This contention being-granted, the theory cannot be considered as beyond dispute. What do we mean by the transformation of the cause into the effect? If transformation implies a complete change of cause, knowledge Would be impossible, for it makes every state of existence different from the previous state. If it means, on the other hand, that transformation is not of the whole but of the parts only, the question arises whether these parts are different from or identical with the entire cause. If we affirm the first alternative, we have to admit the synthesis between the two and this is logically absurd. The other alternative is meaningless, because if the parts are identical with the entire cause and get themselves transformed, what is the ground of objection to the whole being changed?

Again, the application of the law of transformation on universal sequence leads to further difficulties. What is the nature of the entire cause that is transformed into diversified forms? Is it partless or is it endowed with parts? If it be partless, it goes to prove that complete change is produced in the primordial cause in every form of transformation and the effect must be eternal. If we accept the second alternative, the primordial cause becomes no longer eternal but perishable.[58]

All these defects and shortcomings of the Sāṁkhyists lead the Advaitins to accept the theory of *vivarta,* evolution, or self-alienation, *i.e.,* the process of reflection in which the effect does not possess the same amount of being as the cause.[59] This is also transformation, but a new form of transformation, *i. e.,* manifestation. The effect is a mere appearance and is valid only empirically from the phenomenal standpoint. Causality holds good as long as we are confined to the empirical world, but when we transcend the phenomenal world and judge the effect from the metaphysical standpoint, it is non-existent or false. Experience must presuppose the chain of causation, but beyond experience it has no validity.

Bauddha view of causation and its comparison with that of the Advaitins

The Buddhist logicians, who advocate *asatkāryavāda* or production of a previously non-existent effect as held by the Naiyāyikas, also ultimately come to the monistic conclusion that the effect is non-existent and false. The Sautrāntika, on being questioned why the same seed should produce oil and not any other substance, though it is all equally non-existent in the causal entity, only says in reply that there can be no questioning with regard to the ultimate laws of nature, which are unthinkable and beyond the scope of Philosophy. They are to be accepted as facts without question.[60] There is no means of divining the inner powers of things by intuition; they can be known only when particular effects are seen to be produced. There is an unknown law which regulates the powers of things and the determinate effects that are seen to issue from particular causes are determined by this unknown law. But it has been urged that determination connotes the idea of delimitation, and when the other limit, *viz.*, the effect, is absent, how can you speak of determination? It is understandable if the effects are existent in some form or other, otherwise, it is only a word without meaning.[61] The Buddhist allows the justice of the objection that the word 'determination' is inapplicable in the absence of the other limit, *viz.*, the effect. But the position he seeks to establish simply amounts to this : that the causal entity, the unique fact which is seen to be invariably attended by another entity styled the effect, is undeniable as a real, substantive fact, though the particular expressions usually employed to characterise it may fail to convey a correct idea of its real nature. Words are but convenient symbols, employed according to the taste and purpose of the speaker and are by no manner of means to be regarded as integral parts of things-in-themselves. So the objection with regard to an expression does not touch the essential nature of things. However objectionable and defective the language one may use to interpret the causal relation may be the existence of the two entities, one following closely on the heels of another, is unquestionable. All existents being momentary can have neither a past nor a future history and their momentary existence is interpreted as origination by a necessary fiction of the understanding.[62]

The question of their previous existence or non-existence cannot, therefore, arise, as a momentary entity is *ex hypothesi* destitute of all continuity. It is, however, by a fiction of the understanding, supposed to be non-existent in the past, as it is only seen to emerge closely on the heels of another entity. But in reality neither existence nor non-existence can be predicated of it, as a non-existent can never be existent or *vice versa.* The idea of one thing being the cause and another being effect is also an intellectual fiction—a mere form of understanding called into being by the necessity of interpreting the relation of two events, which, however, has nothing to do with the objective order of reals. What happens in reality is that one entity follows closely another.[63] And this is endorsed by an *ipse dixit* of the

Lord Buddha, "O thou Mahāmate (take it) that all these phenomena have no origination, as neither existent nor non-existent can be produced."[64]

This account of the *Sautrāntika* throws overboard the theory of causation *in toto.* It reduces causation to a mere mechanical sequence and confesses its inability to explain the character of necessity, which distinguishes causal relation from cases of accidental sequence. The *Sautrāntika* plays into the hands of the *Śūnyavādin,* who declares that causation is an appearance and not reality. The *Śūnya-vāda* and the theory of *Māyā* have, however, the virtue of logical consistency to their credit, as they make no scruple to declare that the phenomenal order of things is unintelligible and inexplicable, that the entire cosmos is a mysterious appearance.

Nāgārjuna and Śaṁkara, with their keen logical acumen, have shown in unmistakable language that causation is the hidden rock, on which the ship of realism must suffer shipwreck.

REFERENCES

1. For a detailed account of the above a reference may be made to Dr. S. N. Das Gupta's History of Indian Philosophy, Vol. II, Chap. XI.
2. Yo hi yasmād vyatiriktaḥ sa tadadhiṣṭhita-deśavyatiriktadeśādhiṣṭhāna upalabhyate ghaṭādiva paṭah. Ny. M., p. 549, Benares Edition.
3. S. B. p. 468 (Bombay Edition). Pr. P., p. 18.
4. p. 468.
5. P. P., p. 18.
6. (a) Ny. M., p. 549.
   (b) Bha. (Bombay Edition), p. 468.
   (c) S. B., p. 568.
7. P. P., p. 18.
8. (a) P. P., pp. 18-19.
   (b) Ny. M., p. 549.
9. Pr. K. M., p. 162.
10. S. D., p. 106 (Bombay Edition).
11. S. C., p. 106 (Bombay Edition).
12. S. D., p. 108 (Bombay Edition); Ny. M., p. 649.
13. S. B., p. 464 (Bombay Edition).
14. *(a)* Upādānātiriktaṁ kāryadravyaṁ nāstīti sādhyate avasthābheda-mātram

avikṛtamekasyaiva dravyasya avasthābhedādupādānopādeya-bhāva iti. T. M. K., p. 41.

(b) Tantava eva vyatiṣaṅga-viśeṣabhājaḥ paṭa iti nāmarūpa-kāryāntarādikaṁ bhajate. R. Bh., 2. 11. 16.

15. *(a)* Aṁśinoṁśairabhedoyamaṁśenatu bhidābhidā
Parasparaṁ tathāṁ śānāṁ bheda eva prakīrtitaḥ.
S. T. R., p. 12 (Mādhvavilāsa Book Depot).

(b) Aśeṣāṁśairvinā abhāvāt aṁśino, bhedaḥ bhedābhedāvanubhavasiddhāviti. *Ibid,* p. 12.

(c) Aṁśinaḥ sarvāṁśairabhedaḥ ekaikāṁśena tu bhedābhedau tadvināśe'pi aṁśinaḥ. sthiteḥ. *Ibid,* p. 12.

16. Aṁśinaḥ svāmśagātyantabhāvasyapratiyoginaḥ aṁśitvāditarāṁśīva digeṣaiva guṇādiṣu. Vimataḥ paṭaḥ etattantuniṣṭhātyantābhāvapratiyogī avayavitvāt, paṭ āntaṛavat, evametad guṇa-karma-jātyādayopi tattattantuniṣṭhātyantābhāva pratiyoginaḥ tattadrūpatvāditara-tattadrūpavadityevamādi-prayogaḥ sarvatraivohanīyaḥ. cit., pp. 40-41.

17. Pr. K. M., p. 162.

18. S.V., pp. 181-183; S.D., pp. 42-43.

19. Avyāpterapyativyāpterdravyaṁ naivaguṇāśrayaḥ
Ādye kṣaṇe guṇābhāvād guṇādāvapivīkṣaṇāt. Cit., p. 175.

20. Guṇādiṣvapi caturviṁśatirguṇā ityādi saṁkhyā guṇānvayavīkṣaṇā-dativyāpteḥ. Cit., p. 176.

21. Guṇādir nirguṇakriyaḥ.

22. Citsukhī, p. 176.

23. Yo'pi guṇavattvātyantābhāvaḥ so'pi svasyānadhikaraṇameva svasmin svasyāvṛtteḥ.

Na yanaprasādinī, p. 176.

24. Asminnapi vakralakṣaṇe guṇādiṣvapi saṅkhyāpṛthaktva-guṇayoḥ pratīteḥ kathaṁ nātivyāptiḥ.

Cit., p. 177.

25. ūpādīnāṁ guṇānāmanekatvāttadekaguṇādhikaraṇasyāpi taditaraguṇāty antābhāvādhikaraṇatvādeva tadatyantābhāvānadhikaraṇatvābhāvāt, sarvaguṇavattvātyantābhāvānadhikaraṇatvasya sarvasminnasambhavāt. satiḥ sarvaguṇādhikaraṇatve sarvaguṇātyantābhāvānadhikaraṇatā syāt, na ca sarvaguṇādhikaraṇatvamekaikasyāstīti kathaṁ nāvyāptiḥ. Citsukhī, p. 176.

26. Pravyatvajātiyogitvamapi no dravyalakṣaṇam
Tajjātivyañjakābhāvāttanmāuasyānirūpaṇāt. Cit., p. 178.

27. Dravyāśrayī na guṇavān saṁyoga-vibhāgeṣvakāraṇaṁ nirapekṣaḥ (guṇaḥ). V. S., p.94.

28. Sāmānyavān sparśarahito dravyāśrayaḥ karmātirikto guṇaḥ.

29. (a) *Cit.,* pp. 181-84 (Bombay Edition).

(b) Kh. Kh., p. 580 (Benares Edition).

(c) Yadi guṇād bhedena karmajñānaṁ syāt karmātiriktatā guṇasya jñāyeta naitadasti guṇānirṇaye tadvyatirekasyāpi karmaṇo jñātumaśakyatvāt, etallakṣaṇena guṇaṅ niścitya tato'tiriktaṁ karmajñātvā tadatiriktatva Viśeṣaṇajñanaṁ vāñchataścakrakāpattiriti. N. Pr. P. 181.

30. Ayuṭa-siddhānāmādhārjādhārabhūtānāṁ yaḥ saṁbandha iha pratyayahetuḥ sa samavāyaḥ. P. Bh., p. 14.
31. *Vide* Nyāya-Kandalī, p. 14.
32. Nasyādayutasiddhādi samavāyasyalakṣaṇaṁ viśeṣaṇaviśeṣyatva-sambandhe vyabhicārataḥ, iha bhūtale ghaṭābhāva iti viśeṣaṇa viśeṣyabhāva-lakṣaṇe' pi saṁbandhe lakṣaṇasyātivyāptiḥ asticādhāryādbāra bhāva iha pratyayaśca. Cit., p. 199.
33. *Cit.*, p. 199.
34. (a) S. B., p. 511.
    (b) B. Bh. 2.2.13.
35. S. B., 2.2.17.
36. Guṇādayo na dravyādyanadhīna nirūpaṇāḥ api tu yadā yadā nirūpyante tadā tadā tadākāratayaiva prathante, na tu prathāyāmeṣāmasti svātantryah, tasmannatiricyante dravyat api tu dravyameva sāmānyarūpaṁ tathā tathā prathate.

    Bhā., p. 517.
37. According to the Nyāya-teachers *jāti* is not a class concept, for a class concept is subjective but *jāti* has an objective reality and it exists even though there is no individual in which to inhere. *Jāti* thus corresponds to Plato's 'Ideas' which are informed in individuals. *Jāti,* though independently existent, has its manifestation in and through individuals. *Jāti* corresponds to 'quiddity' of Schoolmen.
38. Tasmādekasya bhinneṣu yā vṛttistannibandhanaḥ sāmānya śabdaḥ sattādāvekadhīkaraṇena vā.

    V. (Ākṛtivāda, Sl. 12.
39. Viṣayātiśayamantareṇapratyayātiśayānupapātteḥ.

    Ny. M., p. 314.
40. Na tāvat sāmanyagrahaṇa nipuṇamakṣajaṁ jñānaṁ bhavitu-marhati.. nacānumānaṁ śabdo va sāmānya syarūpa vāstavatva vyavas-thtapana-sāmarthyamaśnute.

    Ny. M., p. 297.
41. Pṛthaktve vyaktito jātirdṛśyeta pṛthageva sā
    Abhede vyakti mātraṁ syād dvedhācennavirodhataḥ.

    S. D., p. 98 (Bombay Edition).
42. Nāyāti na ca tatrāsīdasti paścānna cāṁśavat
    jahāti pūrvvaṁ nādhāramahovvyasanasaṁtatih.

    S.D., p. 98.
43. S.D., p. 98; Ny. M., p. 307.
44. Yadeva vāhadohādi karyamokena janyate
    gopiṇḍena tadevānyairiti teṣvanuvṛttidhiḥ. Ny. M., p. 301.

45. Tatkimekavyaktivadvyaktyantare gaurityavabhāsaḥ, uta vyaktīnāmekagosvabhāvāvabhāsah, ekadharmavattayāvabhāso vā, nādyaḥ, ekavyaktergosvabhāvavadvyaktyantareṣvapi gosvabhāvatvād antareṇāpi sāmānyamanekodakabhājaneṣvayarii candro'yam candra itivadavabhāsopapatteḥ. Cit., p. 303.
46. Jātiṁ svīkurvatātadvyañjakaṁ kiñcid vācyam, tadapi, kutra vartate iti paryanuyoge yatra jātistatra vartata ityuktāvanyonyāśrayatā. Cit., p. 304.
47. Nāpi piṇḍasarvagatā jātiḥ, pratyagrajāyamāna-khaṇḍamuṇḍādipiṇḍeṣu piṇḍāntarasthitāyā jāteḥ sambandhābhāvaprasaṅgāt. Cit., p. 306.
48. Bh. P. and S, M. on Sl. 44. Dinakarī, p. 193 (Benares Edition).
49. Na tāvad gṛhyate kālaḥ pratyakṣeṇa ghaṭādivat
cirakṣiprādibodho hi kāryamātrāvalambanaḥ. Ny. M. P., 136.
50. Na caiṣa grahanakṣatraparispandasvabhāvakaḥ
Kālaḥ kalpayituṁ yuktaḥ kriyāto nāparo hyasau.
Ny. M. P., 136.
51. Sa cāyamākāśavat sarvatraikaḥ kālaḥ...sarvatratadvyavaḥārād vibhuḥ avayavāśrayānupalaṁbhānniravayavaḥ, anāśritaścānāśritatvādeva dravyam avayavavibhāgādināśakāraṇānupapatternitya iti. Ny. M., p. 139.
52. Idānīṁ ghaṭa ityyādipratītiḥ sūryaparispandādikaṁ yadi viṣayīkaroti tadā sūryaparispandādinā ghaṭādeḥ saṁbandho vācyaḥ kāla eva tatsaṁbandhaghaṭakaḥ kalpyate. S. M., p. 195.
53. Divākara-parispanda-piṇḍasaṅgati-saṁbhavāt
vyāpinaścetanādeva kathaṁ kālaḥ prasidhyati. Cit., p. 320.
54. (a) Ubhayavādisaṁpratipannātmanaiva vastūnāmupādhisaṁbandhasiddheratirikta-dravya-kalpanāyāṁ kalpanā-gauravaprasaṅgāt. Cit., p. 322.
    (b) *Ibid,* p. 323.
    (c) N. Pr., p. 323.
    (d) Kh. Kh.., pp. 567-572.
55. (a) Suraśikhari-śikhara-paribhramanmārtaṇḍa-maṇḍala-prathamasaṁyogādyupādhyupadhāne tenaiva pūrvādi-pratyayānāmanyathāsiddhatvāt. Cit., p. 324.
    (b) *Ibid,* 324-327.
    (c) Kh. Kh., pp. 563-567.
56. Citsukhī, pp. 314-317.
57. (a) Kāraṇāt pṛthak sattāśūnyatvaṁ kāryasya sādhyate naikyamityarthaḥ. R. P., 2. 1. 16.
    (b) Na khalvananyatvamityabhedaṁ brūmaḥ kintu bhedaṁ vyāsedhāmaḥ tataśca nābhedāśrayadoṣaprasaṅgaḥ. Bh., 2. 1. 14.
58. *(i)* Bhāmatī, 1. 1. 4.
    (ii) Kalpataru, p. 117, 1.1.4.
59. S. L., p. 108.
60. Niyatacintya-śaktīni vastunī'ha pratīkṣaṇam,
bhavanti nānuyojyāni dahane dāhaśaktivat. T. S., Sl. 438.

61. Avadhīnām aniṣpatterniyatāstena śaktayaḥ
sattve tu niyamās tāsāṁ yuktāḥ sāvadhiko nanu.

T. S., Sl. 29.

62. Vastūnāṁ pūrvāparakoṭiśūnyānāṁ kṣaṇamātrāvasthāyī svabhāva evotpāda ityucyate. T. S., p. 33.

63. (a) Utpādo vastubhāvastu so'satā na satā tathā,
sambadhyate kalpikayā kevalaṁ tvasatā dhiyā.

(b) Yadidaṁ vastuno rūpam ekānantaramīkṣyate,
Prāgāsīnneti tadvījaṁ prāgbhūte tvidamasti na. T. S., Sls. 32-33.

64. Anutpannā mahāmate sarvadharmāḥ sadasatoranutparunatvāt. T. S., p.32.

CHAPTER 5

NATURE OF PHENOMENAL APPEARANCE

The theory of phenomenality of this order of existence has a long history behind it; it was later on developed by the *Neo-Vedāntic* teachers of the *Advaita-Vedānta* school. Gauḍapāda, the first systematic exponent of the *Advaita-Vedānta* wrote a chapter on the phenomenal character of this worldly existence. His philosophy was perhaps greatly influenced by the *Vijñānavāda* and the *Mādhyamika* schools of Buddhism. To him the worldly existence is a pure subjective illusion and the sense-perception of our waking consciousness is just akin to the dream impressions.[1] Gauḍapāda has applied the very same arguments as advanced by the Buddhistic teachers.

Next comes Śaṁkara who has repudiated the doctrine of unreality of external objects as propounded by the *Vijñānavāda* school. But he maintains the phenomenality of the creative order and explains this appearance to be a seeming expression of A-logical reality. According to the *Vijñānavāda* the creative order is a mere subjective illusion. The waking consciousness is similar to the dream consciousness. But according to Śaṁkara, the world of existence is not a subjective creation or a mere illusion. The waking consciousness is different from dream consciousness, inasmuch as the former has got a pragmatic validity while the latter has got none.

The world neither is, nor is not, and so its nature is indescribable. While it is different from being and non-being it shares in the character of both. All finite things, as Plato says, are made up of being and non-being. Phenomenal appearance is, in the words of Bosanquet, "the great ultimate contradiction of the finite infinite nature." Heaven and Earth shall pass away, our body decays, our senses change and our empirical egoes are built up before our eyes. None of these is ultimately real. The whole chain of phenomenal existence is a manifestation or an expression of reality and is itself false as an independent existence.

Now the problem which faces us here, is what is the true nature of falsity attributed to the phenomenal appearance by the teachers of the *Advaita-Vedānta.* The *Mādhvites,* who hold the worldly appearance as real, seriously question the standpoint of the *Śaṁkarites,* Vyāsarāja, the author of the *Nyāyāmṛta,* puts forward and critically examines all plausible interpretations of falsity and comes to the conclusion that none of them is logically cogent to give a rational explanation of falsity of the phenomenal world. Thus contending against the position of the *Neo-Vedāntic* teachers, Vyāsarāja asks the Advaitins what is the real nature of falsity predicated of the phenomenal appearances? The Advaita-teachers advance fivefold logical explanations of the concept.[2] Madhusūdana Sarasvatī in his *Advaita-Siddhi,* the monumental work of the *Neo-Vedāntic* school, has given a brilliant exposition of the concept against a good number of objections of Vyāsarāja and his school; and he has thus pointed out the real essence of the five-fold explanations of falsity put forward by the masters of the Advaita school. In replying to the question of Vyāsarāja, Madhusūdana, on the basis of the exposition of the *Pañcapādikā* of Padmapāda, defines falsehood or *mithyātva* as something inexplicable and inconceivable in the sense that it is neither the receptacle *(adhikaraṇa)* of existence and nor of non-existence.[3]

Vyāsaraja's objections against the defintion of Padmapāda

Against this explanation of Padmapāda, Vyāsarāja contends that *sadasadanadhikaraṇatva,* which according to the view-point of Padmapāda, is the criterion of falsehood, is a concept which stands against all logic and reason and connotes nothing logically valid. Padmapāda's expression admits of three possible interpretations but none of them is free from fallacy of one kind or another. The three probable interpretations brought forward by Vyāsarāja are :—

(a) The absolute negation of non-existence characterised by existence,

(*b*) The dual character of the absolute negation of existence and that of non-existence,

(*c*) The absolute negation of non-existence as determined by that of existence.[4]

Inadequacies of the interpretations pointed out by Vyāsarāja

In pointing out inadequacies in the given interpretations Vyāsarāja contends that the first exposition is untenable because phenomenal appearances by non-existence determined by existence *(sattva-viśiṣṭāsattva)*. The Mādhvites admit absolute existence of the phenomenal appearance and totally deny non-existence advocated by the monistic teachers. And non-existence or *asattva* being negated therein, the worldly appearance cannot be characterised by any particular form of non-existence *(sattva-viśiṣṭā-sattva)* for a substantive aspect *(viśeṣyāṁśa)* of a concept being denied all special features which determine the nature of the substantive *(viśeṣya)* must also be necessarily negated.

Fallacy of *Sādhyāprasiddhi*

Further such an exposition commits the fallacy of *śādhyā-prasiddhi* or attempting to prove something which is nowhere known to exist, *sādhya* or the major or what is to be predicated of the minor must be a known fact. Non-existence characterised by existence, which is the suggested criterion of falsity, is a concept which is totally devoid of any factuality according to the Mādhvites. Hence there arises the fallacy of *sādhyā-prasiddhi* or reasoning from something which is nowhere known to exist.[5]

Inadequacies pointed out by Vyāsarāja in the second interpretation of Falsity

The second interpretation is unsatisfactory because it involves contradiction or *vyāghāta*. Of the two characteristics which are quite contradictory in their nature, if one is negated in a phenomenon, the other is posited by the negation of the first one, but the two cannot reside simultaneously. Now if the absolute negation of existence is denied in the phenomenal appearance, its contradictory, the negation of non-existence, is posited therein; and again if the absolute negation of non-existence is negated, the negation of existence is posited in the worldly existence.

The charge of *Vyāghāta*

For the test of the two concepts '*sattva* and *asattva*,' existence and non-existence, is contradiction and non-contradiction. Worldly existences are *sat* because they are not contradicted; and the oyster-silver, rope-serpent, etc., are *asat* because they are contradicted. If *sattva* or *abādhyatva* be negated in a phenomenon it logically follows that the phenomenon is *asat* or *bādhya*. The exposition under consideration positing two contradictory characteristics, *viz.*, the absolute negation of existence and of non-existence in the worldly appearance commits an unavoidable contradiction or *vyāghāta*.[6]

The charge of *Arthāntaram*

Secondly, the interpretation is faulty as it might be turned against the Advaitin's position in twofold manner. In the first place, it may be argued that *Brahman* being devoid of all determinate qualities can be said to be marked by the negation of existence and that of non-existence. Hence if this dual characterisation, *viz.*, negation of existence and non-existence be the creterion of falsity, *Brahman* itself becomes false. Then again if *Brahman* thus characterised be taken as absolutely real, the worldly appearance should also be regarded as real as it is, on the Advaitin's own admission, marked by these two dual negative characters. This is what is called one of the 'occasions of rebuke' *(nigrahasthānam)* known as *Arthāntaram, i.e.*, the argument leads to a position which is not intended.[7]

The charge of *Sadhyavaikalya*

The position is again untenable, because the major or *sādhya* cannot be proved from the given explanatory example as the explanatory instance is inadequate. In the syllogism under discussion 'negation of existence and of non-existence' is the major or *sādhya* and the oyster-silver rope-serpent, etc., are the given explanatory instances. Now the Mādhvites contend that the absotute negation of existence may exist in the nonest oyster-silver, etc., but the negation of non-existence can in no way be admitted in them because they are unreal or *asat* in their character. Thus only a part of the major is proved by the explanatory instance. Hence the instance is *śādhya-vikala.*[8]

It may be argued in reply that if the major of the syllogism under discussion being partly negated in the oyster-silver and such other explanatory examples, makes the inference a faulty one, the well-known syllogism 'the earth differs from other categories for its smell'[9] also becomes fallacious. For in this syllogism, water, ether, etc., form the explanatory examples, and 'the difference of all other categories' forms the major *(sādhya)*. Now in a particular example, say in water, difference of all other categories except its own self can be held, but the difference of water in water can in no way be acknowledged; and in this way all explanatory instances fail to prove the mutual negation of all categories of the major of the given syllogism. And the examples being partially invalid in their nature invalidate the syllogism.[10]

The charge of *sādhya vailkalya* cannot be urged in the purely negative inference – the negative inference commits the fallacy of *sadhya-prasiddhi*

But the argument is not convincing, for, the given syllogism being purely negative *(kevala-vyatireki)* in its character does not require a positive instance to prove its major and the question of *sādhya-vaikalya* being one of the defects of the example homogeneous with the proven, cannot be urged in the case of purely negative form of inference. Such an inference is based on the negative form of *vyāpti* or concomitance between the negation of the major and that of the middle. Even then, a question may naturally be asked that such a major cannot be established because the instance of such a concomitance cannot be found anywhere else. It is found only in the earth where it is doubted and has to be proved by the syllogistic argument. Hence the charge of *sādhyaprasiddhi* or the improbability of the major invalidates the whole chain of reasoning.

The charge of *sādhyāprasiddhi* can not stand in the Nyāya syllogism under discussion

To refute the charge it may be argued that the major — the difference of all categories—is not to be understood individually or separately but collectively by a particular determinate cognition *(viśiṣṭa-buddhi)* in which the aggregate itself is presented as its object *(samūhālambanajñāna)* . Thus in a particular instance, *e.g.*, in water, the difference of water itself may appear as an absurdity, but the negation of totality or *samūha* in any particular case is logically established. And in this way, the given major may be proved in all heterogeneous instances and the charge of *sādhyāprasiddhi* is a futile one.[11]

Advaitin's refutation of the charge of *sādhyāprasidhi*

By the application of the same logic which establishes the difference of all categories in earth on account of its smell, the Advaitins avoid the opponent's charge of *sādhyāprasiddhi* or of improbable predication.Of the two noted characteristics of the major the negation of existence may be found in the oyster-silver and that of non-existence in the phenomenal appearance; but the two can nowhere be found in a single substratum. For this reason the charge of improbability major has been urged in the Advaita-interpretation of falsity.[12] In repudiating the Mādhvites' charge of *sādhyāprasiddhi,* the Advaitins contend that the two characteristics, *viz.*, negation of existence and of non-existence, are jointly and collectively apprehended as the counterpart *(pratiyogi)* of one absolute negation; and the oyster silver, rope-serpent, etc., which, though incapable of being characterised by the negation of non-existence, can be logically determined by the negation of both the characteristics taken jointly. For the negation of both in the substrate of one is a well-admitted fact in the science of reasoning.

Sādhyāprasiddhi being thus refuted advaita syllogism commits the fallacy of aṁśataḥ-_siddha-sādhanatā_

Now the Mādhvites contend that such a position may refute the charge of *sādhyāprasiddhi* but one of parts of the major being already admitted the explanatory example, *e. g.*, oyster-silver, the Advaita position can in no way avoid the charge of *aṁśataḥ-siddha-sādhanatā* or proving what is partly proved.[13]

Vyāsarāja's criticism of the third interpretation

The third interpretation of falsity in which the two independent negations of existence and non-existence, as they are understood in the second interpretation, are combined in a single notion of two component parts, one being the qualifying epithet, and the other a noun qualified. The absolute negation of existence and of non-existence related as noun and adjective would not give the Advaitins any relief for all the shortcomings, mainly based on the two negative marks, *viz.*, (1) *vyāghāta* or contradiction, (2) *arthāntaram* or shifting of topic and (3) *sādhya-vaikalya* or inadequacy of instance pointed out in the second interpretation, may be shown to have crept in the third one as well. Of the two other fallacies, *viz.*, (1) *sādhyāprasiddhi* or improbability of the major and (2) *aṁśataḥ-siddha-sādhanatā* or proving what has been partly proved, the charge of *siddha-sādhanatā* does not lie in this interpretation; for a major thus characterised has nowhere been partially known. The question of *aṁśatah-siddha-sādhanatā* occurs in cases in which the distinctive marks of the major *(sādhyatāvacchedaka-dharma)* are not one but many; and of the many marks of the major, some already exist where they are to be proved. In the second explanation of falsity, the major was characterised by its two constituent parts and one of them, *viz.*, the negation of existence was already preadmitted in the oyster-silver, thus the charge of *aṁśataḥ-siddha sādhanatā* has been urged in the second exposition. In the third one, the combined notion *(viśiṣṭa-buddhi)* has been taken as the major and the distinctive feature of the major *(sādhyatāvacchedakadharma)* is a unique one comprising the two constituents in a single determinate notion.

It is a third notion distinct from the two and relating the two as a limiting adjunct and the noun qualified, in other words, the distinctive mark of the major is not identical with the characteristics of the determinate factor and that of the noun *(viśeṣaṇatāvacchedaka* and *viśeṣyatāvacchedaka). Viśiṣṭa-buddhi* or determinate notion is one distinctive judgment which unites the two or more independent notions in one single whole and originates as a third apprehension springing out of individual notions which are united in one whole. And this wholeness being the distinctive feature of the major the major in its entirety is nowhere established and thus the charge of *aṁśataḥ-siddha-sādhanatā* cannot be urged in the third exposition.[14]

The charge of superfluity of the substantive portion of the major

When this wholeness forms the characteristic of the major, a new defect creeps into the exposition. The combined concept, which is the distinctive feature of the major has, as we have already noticed, the two component parts related as noun and its determining adjuncts. Now to establish falsity of the phenomenal appearances, if the Advaita-teachers prove the absolute negation of existence *(sattvātyantābhāva)* in the worldly existences against the Madhvites who advocate their reality, the Advaita proposition can be affirmed and the portion which forms the limiting adjunct *(viśeṣaṇāṁśa)* of the entire judgment forming the major is quite enough to establish the Advaita tenet of falsity and the portion representing the main component *(viśeṣyāṁśa)* appears to be redundant, for, the absolute negation of non-existence in the phenomenal existences is an admitted fact in the thesis of the Mādhvites. Thus the charge of *vyartha-viśeṣyatā* or superfluity of the subjective aspect of the major renders the interpretation faulty.

Against this the Advaitins might argue that the charge of *vyartha-viśeṣyatā* or redundancy of the substantive aspect of the major cannot be brought against the monistic thesis. For to establish the falsity of the phenomenal world which has been characterised by the Advaitins as neither being nor non-being, such a superfluity of the major is rather helpful and intentional. The Advaita teachers, establishing such a redundant major in the minor, *viz.*, in the phenomenal appearance, characterise it as false in the sense of being indescribable in its nature. The worldly appearance is neither existence nor non-existence. It partakes of the character of both being and non-being. It is neither ultimately real as it has got no permanent substratum of its own nor does it share in the nature of sky-flower, hare's horn, etc., as they are absolute nought. The world appearance takes a middle course between the two extremes. We do not and cannot know its nature. It is inconceivable and inexplicable. To attribute falsity in this peculiar sense, the Advaitins deem such a superfluity as an absolutely necessary part of the major and the charge of redundancy in the monistic proposition is beside the point.

The charge *of sādhyāprasiddhi*

Even granting for the sake of argument that the charge of superfluity of the substantive portion of the major *(vyartha-viśeṣyatā)* can be met in the above way, the Mādhvites return to the charge and contend that the charge of *sādhyāprasiddhi* cannot be got over and seems to be a formidable objection to the Advaita syllogism. It might be contended that though such a determinate major can no where be established, the different parts of it might be proved separately. Thus the existent proves the negation of non-existent and the non-existent proves the negation of existent. But such proof by parts cannot establish the totality *(samudāyasiddhi)* which is the essence of the given major. Moreover any such attempt to prove the total major by part would banish the fallacy of *sādhyāprasiddhi* from the science of reasoning. In the universally accepted instance *of sādhyāprasiddhi, viz.*, the 'earth is scratched by the hare's horn because it is earth,"[15] the hare's horn being an impossibility, the syllogism suffers from the fallacy of 'unknown predication.' The real absurdity of the proposition lies in the fact that there is no inherent relation between the hare and the horn. And it is no answer to the fallacy to say that the two terms 'hare' and 'horn' can be taken separately as real entities. Since such separation of elements of the complex major is against the real essence of the argument, the two parts are to be taken as a collective notion and the charge of *sādhyāprasiddhi* will apply whenever there is any such disjunction of parts.

The charge of *vyāghāta* cannot stand

To refute the charge put forward by Vyāsarāja against the expression of Padmapāda, Madhusūdana Sarasvatī contends that the objections are not to the point. The charge of contradiction or *vyāghāta* as pointed out by Vyāsarāja in the second interpretation, Madhusūdana observes, cannot stand. The real essence of Vyāsarāja's charge of contradiction lies in the fact that of two absolute negations of diverse character, *viz.*, the absolute negation of existence and of non-existence when one is negated, the other is invariably posited and *vice versa;* but the two cannot reside in a single substrate. Against this, Madhusūdana argues that Vyāsarāja's charge is mainly based on what the two terms *sattva* and *asattva,* existence and non-existence, connote here. Are they to be taken in the sense that (1) one is the absolute negation of the other *(paraspara-viraharūpatayā),* or that (2) one invariably and universally pervades the absolute negation of the other *(paraspara-virahavyāpakatayā),* or that (3) the absolute negation of one is to be pervaded by the other *(paraspara-viraha-vyāpyatayā).* These are the three possible interpretations which might bring about the charge of contradiction in the Advaita-position. To explain the position further : if existence be taken in the sense of the absolute negation of non-existence and non-existence as that of existence, they cannot reside in the same substrate; if again they are located in the same substratum, they are not of the said nature. If the negation of existence *(asattva)* be characterised to be located in the substrate of the absolute negation of existence, *asattva* cannot be defined as the absolute negation of existence. In other words, if the negation of non-existence exists in the substrate of that of existence, the two concepts *sattva* and *asattva* cannot be characterised as mutual absolute negation. For example, the negation of existence *(sattvā-bhāva)* exists in the substrate of the negation of existence, thus existence cannot be characterised as the negation of existence. Similarly, if the negation of existence exists in the substrate of that of non-existence, non-existence and existence cannot be defined as mutual absolute negation.[16]

Explanation of the second alteration

Again, if *asattva,* negation of existence, is to be located in substrate of that of existence, *asattva* second alternative. cannot invariably and universally pervade the negation of existence. As for example, *sattva* or existence, which can be negated in the substrate of the negation of existence, cannot pervade the negation of existence, so is non-existence. On the other hand, if *sattva* or existence is to be located in the same location with the negation of non-existence, *sattva* cannot pervade the negation of non-existence.[17]

Explanation of the third alternative

If *asattva* resides in the substrate of the negation of existence, the negation of existence is not to be pervaded by *asattva* and *vice versa.*[18] All these contra-reasonings definitely prove that *sattva* and *asattva* cannot reside in the same substrate and this invalidates the Advaita-proposition which characterises the worldly existence with the dual negation of both existence and non-existence. Here lies the real logic of contradiction *(vyāghāta)* pointed out by Vyāsarāja.

Monistic explanation of *sat* and *asat*

In repudiating Vyāsarāja's charge of contradiction Madhusūdana contends that none of three interpretations of the concepts *sattva* and *asattva* is free from defects. That *sattva* and *asattva* are to be taken as mutual absolute negation *(paraspara-viraha-rūpa)* is a position advocated by the Mādhvites but thoroughly discarded by the Śaṁkarites. The Advaitins explain the criterion of *sattva* as free from contradiction of all times *(trikālā-bādhyatvam)* and *asattva* as what does never form the object of cognition as reality in any substrate.[19] The sky-flower, hare's horn, etc., which have no objectivity at all, are never cognised as real in any substratum; they are therefore styled as '*asat*' or unreal. Phenonmenal appearances, which satisfy the demand of our pragmatic life, have objectivity of their own and are apprehended as real. They, therefore, cannot be classed with the nonest sky-flower, hare's horn, etc. The pot, carrying water, occupying a particular space-position, is cognised as real and cannot be charged with unreality as explained by the monistic teachers. All phenomenal objects which serve the pragmatic affairs of life, cannot be defined as absolute nought; nor can they be explained as real in the absolute sense of the term. They, therefore, do not come under the category of either "is" or "is not" and their nature is different from both. The world-appearance has got an empirical existence of its own. As it is not existence in the pure and absolute sense of the term, it is also not false in the sense of non-existence which is the characteristic of sky-flower, hare's horn, etc. The world appearance is thus styled *sadasadanadhi-karaṇa* by Padmapāda, and the Mādhva charge of contradiction *(vyāghāta)* is beside the point.

Contradiction cannot stand in the sense that one pervades the absolute negation of the other

It is now seen from the previous discussion that the Mādhvites' charge of contradiction cannot stand in the sense that *sattva* and *asattva* are the two contradictory terms and one is the absolute negation of the other *(parasparaviraharūpa)*. Now if the two concepts, existence and non-existence, be explained in the sense that one invariably pervades the absolute negation of the other *(paraspara-virahavyāpaka),* the opponents' charge seems to be an absurdity." Of the two phenomena so connected, one is called the *vyāpya or gamaka* (the sign, mark or indicator) and the other *vyāpaka or gamya* (the thing signified, marked or indicated). In the relation of fire and smoke, for example, smoke is the *vyāpya* or *gamaka* (sign or mark); and fire, the *vyāpaka* or *gamya* (the thing signified or marked). Now the relation of *vyāpti* between A and B may be either unequal or equipollent *(viṣamavyāpti* or *samavyāpti)*. When A is the sign of B, but B is not the sign of A, the *vyāpti* is one-sided or unequal and here a *vyāpti* is said to exist between A and B and not between B and A. For example, smoke is the sign of fire but fire is not universally a sign of smoke. When, therefore, the relation of *vyāpti* is an unequal one, as between smoke and fire, it is expressed in the proposition whenever the *vyāpya* (sign or mark, *e.g* , smoke) exists, the *vyāpaka* (the thing signified or marked, *e.g.*, fire) also exists. From this it follows by necessary implication (a sort of *arthāpatti)* that whenever the *vyāpaka (e.g.,* fire) is absent, the *vyāpya (e. g..,* smoke) is also absent *(vyāpakābhāve vyāpyābhāvaḥ)*,[20] This being the essence of *vyāpya-vyāpaka-bhāva* or the relation of the sign and the thing signified, the two concepts *asattva* and *sattva* which are thus related through their negation would be explained as wherever the *vyāpya, i.e.*, the negation of existence—*sattvābhāva,* the mark, the sign—exists, the *vyāpaka, i. e. asattva* also exists. In other words, wherever the *vyāpaka, e.g., asattva* is absent, the *vyāpya* or the negation of existence is also absent. And again wherever the *vyāpya, i.e.*, the negation of non-existence *(asattvābhāva)* exists, *sattva,* the *vyāpaka* also exists; and wherever the *vyāpaka, i.e., sattva* does not exist, the negation of non-existence, the *vyāpya* also does not exist. This is the position which has been advocated by the Mādhvites, but thoroughly, discarded by the Advaitins. If the *vyāpya, i.e.*, the negation of existence or that of non-existence as the case may be exists in the absence of the *vyāpaka, viz. (asattva* or *sattva)* the unbroken uniformity *(avyabhicāritva)* which is the criterion of the *vyāpya* falls through and the ascertainment of a mutual relation between the two phenomena of the invariable, unconditional concomitance *(vyāpti-nirūpakatva)* which is the true characteristic of the *vyāpaka* or the ubiquitous also falls to the ground. The judgment where there is a fire, there is smoke *(dhūmavān vahneḥ)* is fallacious because the said relation of the *vyāpya* and *vyāpaka* or the mark or sign and the thing signified, does not exist between fire and smoke, for as is evident in the overheated iron-ball, fire, the *vyāpya* or the so-called sign does exist without smoke or the *vyāpaka*. Thus the unbroken uniformity which is the criterion of the sign or *vyāpya,* falls and the capability of ascertainment of *vyāpti* or unconditional, invariable relation *(vyāpti-nirūpakatva)* or the real essence of the *vyāpaka* also falls through.

The same logic might be applied by Madhusūdana in the case of *sattva* and *asattva* characterised as *paraspara-virahavyāpaka* by the Mādhvites. The Mādhva explanation of *sattva* and *asattva* implies that wherever *sattvābhāva* is, *asattva* is; and again where *asattvābhāva* exists, *sattva* exists. Madhusūdana, standing against the so-called relation of invariable concomitance between *sattvābhāva* and *asattva,* contends that such a relation is faulty. Because in the case of oyster-silver super-imposition, *sattvābhāva* exists in its absolute sense or in the sense in which *sattva* has been defined by the Advaitins, *asattva* also does not exist in its extreme sense or in the sense in which it is read in the sky-flower and such other absolutely non-existents. For *asattva* has been defined by the Advaitins as what does never form the object of cognition as reality in any substrate. And in this sense it cannot be urged in the oyster-silver superimposition which by its false appearance, occupies the middle position between reality and non-reality in their extreme sense. Again *asattvābhāva* exists in the oyster-silver, but *sattva* does not exist. Madhusūdana's definition of *sattva* and *asattva,* as we have studied before, clearly implies that *sattvābhāva* can exist even in the absence of *asattva* and *asattvābhāva* in the absence of *sattva.* Now the said relation of *niyata-sāhacarya* or unbroken uniformity which depends on the ascertainment of an invariable, and unconditional concomitance between *sattvābhāva* and *asattva* and again *asattvābhāva* and *sattva* totally falls to the ground. And the charge of contradiction on the basis of a relation of the sign *(vyāpya)* and the thing signified *(vyāpaka),* stands only on the Mādhvites' utter ignorance of the Advaita-position.

Contradiction cannot stand in the third alternative

The charge of contradiction cannot at all arise in the third alternative in which *sattva* and *asattva* have been explained as the *vyāpya* or the sign or mark of their mutual absolute negation. In this case, *sattvābhāva* and *asattvābhāva* are taken as *vyāpaka* or *gamya* and *sattva* and *asattva* as *vyāpya* or *gamaka*. And the proposition means wherever *sattva* and *asattva* or *vyāpya* or *gamaka* exist, *asattvābhāva* and *sattvābhava* also exist, and again wherever the *vyāpaka-sattvābhāva* and *asattvābhāva* do not exist, the *vyāpya-asattva* and *sattva* also do not exist. From this syllogistic argument, it does not logically follow that the *vyāpaka-sattvābhāva* and *asattvābhāva* cannot exist without the *vyāpya-asattva* and *sattva*. Such a syllogism only proves that wherever *asattva* is, *sattvābhāva* is. *Sattvābhāva* and *asattvā-bhāva* being *vyāpaka* or more extensive than their *vyāpya-asattva* and *sattva* respectively, can exist in a third entity where the *vyāpya-asattva* and *sattva* do not exist. An example will make it clear : in the proposition 'wherever cowhood exists, the negation of horsehood exists *(asattvābhāvavān gotvāt);* and again horsehood implies the negation of cowhood *(gotvābhāvavān aśvatvāt)*. In other words, wherever the negation of horsehood is absent, cowhood is also absent; and again when the negation of cowhood is absent, horsehood is also absent. Thus, cowhood and horsehood are styled *(parasparavirahavyāpya)*. But negation of cowhood and horsehood *(gotvābhāva* and *aṣvatvābhāva)* which are *vyāpaka,* ubiquitous or more extensive than their *vyāpya* or *gamaka, i.e.,* horsehood and cowhood respectively, may be found in a camel.[21] And such an apprehension of the negation of cowhood and horsehood in a camel does not stand against the unbroken uniformity *(niyatasāha-carya)* or the relation of the sign and the thing signified *(vyāpyavyāpakabhāva)* between the cowhood *(i.e., vyāpya)* and the negation of horsehood *(vyāpaka)* and horsehood and negation of cowhood. Now, though *sattva* and *asattva* are characterised as *paraspara-virahavyāpya* or in other words, wherever *sattva* and *asattva* exist, *asattvābhāva* and *sattvābhāva* exist, the dual negation of *sattva* and *asattva* can be apprehended in a third phenomenon, e.g., oyster-silver. The oyster-silver is neither *sat* nor *asat* and thus the absolute negation of both *sattva* and *asattva* in the extreme sense of the terms as explained by the monistic teachers, can be found in the silver of the oyster-silver super-imposition.

In the interpretation under consideration, the charge of contradiction advanced by the Mādhvites appears to be a logical absurdity because the dual negations of the two entities which are styled as *parasparavirahavyāpya* can be logically established in a third entity and thus there arises no room for contradiction. The real implication of the Mādhvites' charge of contradiction lies in the fact that if the negation of the two phenomena can be found in a third phenomenon, the two phenomena cannot be characterised as *parasparavirahavyāpya.* It is not substantially proved that the *vyāpaka* phenomenon being more extensive in its character does exist even in the absence of the *vyāpya.* phenomenon and the presence of the *vyāpaka* in the absence of the *vyāpya* does not stand against the principle of logic and reason. What is needed in the invariable co-existence of the *vyāpya* and the *vyāpaka* is that in the presence of the *vyāpya,* the existence of the *vyāpaka* is an absolute necessity but not *vice versa.* The said invariable co-existence or concomitance of *asattva* (the *vyāpya)* and the absolute negation of *sattva* (the *vyāpaka)* can be found in sky-flower, hare's horn, etc., and again in the highest reality, the co-presence of *sattva* (the *vyāpya)* and the negation of *asattva* (the *vyāpaka)* can be apprehended; and thus the demanded relation of *vyāpya* and *vyāpaka* or the sign and the thing signified might be proved. And again the dual negation of *sattva* and *asattva* which were the *vyāpaka* phenomena in the said *vyāpti* can be, the Advaitins argue, observed in the phenomenal appearance.[22] Now the proposition or general maxim, which urges that the two phenomena, the absolute negation of which exists in the same location, *e.g.* a third phenomenon, cannot be characterised as *parasparavirahavyāpya* or indicative mark of their mutual negation[23] becomes absolutely fallacious. More clearly the Mādhva doctrine that if the negation of non-existence *(asattvābhāva)* co-exists with the negation of existence in a particular location *(e.g.,* oyster-silver, etc.), non-existence *(asattva)* would not be *vyāpya* or the invariable, unconditional mark or the sign of the negation of *sattva (sattvābhāva),* altogether fails being contrary to all logic and reason.

The charge of *sādhya-vaikalya* cannot stand

The charge of *sādhya-vaikalya* or inadequacy of the given explanatory example, which has been urged by the Mādhvites on the ground that of the dual character of the absolute negation of existence and that of non-existence, the negation of non-existence cannot be admitted in the oyster-silver and other explanatory instances as in these cases non-existence is always present, and thus the part of the major being negated in the explanatory example, the example itself suffers from the fallacy of *sādhya-vaikalya.* Against this Madhusūdana contends that the charge stands on the Mādhvites' misapprehension of the Advaita position as regards the connotation of *sattva* and *asattva.* The Advaitins explain the two concepts *sattva* and *asattva,* as we have already seen, not in the sense of contradiction and non-contradiction as defined by the Mādhvites; they explain *sattva* as absolute truth not to be contradicted in all times and *asattva* as 'what does never form the object of cognition as reality in any substrate. The oyster-silver, the given explanatory example appears as something existent and at the same time is negated at the dawn of knowledge of oyster itself. Hence the oyster-silver can be characterised neither as real nor as non-real in the absolute sense of the terms, but occupying a middle position, it can be marked out by the dual negation, *viz.,* the negation of existence and that of non-existence. And the charge of *sādhya – vaikalya* cannot be levelled against the monistic position.

Madhusūdana's refutation of the charge of arthāntaram or shifting of topic

As regards the opponent's charge of *arthāntaram* or shifting of topic which had been turned against the Advaita position in a two-fold manner, namely Brahman which is devoid of all attributes can be marked out by the absence of existence and non-existence—the criterion of falsity—and thus Brahman itself —becomes false. Then again if Brahman thus characterised be taken as absolutely real, the creative order which, on the Advaitin's own admission, is determined by the absence of both of position and negation of existence should also be taken as real in the absolute sense of the term. In other words, the definition by denying to the world order both position and negation so much widens its bound as to obliterate the line of demarcation between Brahman and the phenomenal appearances and in defining the world order, the Advaitins have defined the absolute. To meet the charge the Advaitins argue that Brahman which is pure Being-Bliss-Consciousness in the Advaita-Vedānta is *pūrṇa* in itself.

Brahman cannot be regarded as false

It is as the Śruti says, an a-logical Being neither cause nor effect, neither substance nor attribute, neither subject nor object. It lies at the back of this cosmic regarded as false. existence. It is the substrate of all substrates wider and larger than the totality of defined and determined systems that express themselves in this universe. Had there been no underlying substratum of this cosmic order, the whole order of phenomena would have appeared as so many puzzling sensations bewildering our sense organs without satisfying the logical demand of intellect or falling in harmony with our pragmatic life. This permanent substratum is according to the Advaita-Vedānta, unmarked, featureless pure being. Though featureless, it seems to manifest itself through an infinity of changes which is the creation of *Avidyā,* the *causā-materia* of all operations in this universe. To attribute falsity to this A-logical Being is an absurdity in the domain of the Advaita-Vedānta. And the questions now turn to the other point namely, world-appearance may be regarded as absolutely real just like the Brahman itself.

The phenomenal appearance cannot be taken as absolutely real

Against this Madhusūdana argues that the creative order has got an existence which is only empirically valid. Brahman which is absolute existence expresses itself in and through the concrete manifolds, which, therefore, partially share in the quality of existence. The 'isness' reflected in the world order is to be referred to Brahman which forms its ultimate substratum. It is due to the apparent identituy with the permanent substratum Brahman that the worldly appearances are cognised as true. It is rather unnecessary and superfluous to introduce a plurality of existences as the whole order of universe may be explained by being referred to one transcendental reality which runs through all diversity.[24] This is the real position of the Avaita-Vadānta. The realistic schools of Vedānta which advocate the world order as true, standing against the standpoint of the Advaitins, may argue that the judgment constructions 'the pot is real,' etc., on the basis of perceptual proof, demand reality of the phenomenal appearances. The Advaitins, who hold the worldly existences as only empirically valid, contend that the so-called reality implied in the given judgment may be explained as due to its apparent identity with the Absolute Being as a result of superimposition. The perception of reality in the pragmatic appearances is not a valid perception. It is a mal-observation to be negated by the inference under discussion which establishes the falsity of the world order. Again the reality of existences which may be established on the basis of perception cannot be absolute as the perception itself is only empirically valid. Brahman is the only absolute reality as demanded by the *śruti* texts and it is that Absolute Being which runs through the diversified would and has been identified with this world order as its substrate and appears as a limiting adjunct *(viśeṣaṇa)*. To admit plurality of existences, in rendering a rational explanation of the so-called reality reflected in the particular experiences is unphilosophical or unscientific because such an admission, the Advaitins argue, cannot give any consistent *(anugata)* exposition of reality. For on such a supposition the nature of reality and its cognition must vary according to the varied nature of existences and one has to admit a plurality of existences and their different forms of apprehension which would render the process of apprehending truth rather cumbrous.[25] The bone of contention lies in the fact that the Mādhvites and other theistic Vedāntists following the path of the Naiyāyikas advocate the absolute reality of the cosmic order which has been denied by the Advaita teachers. But no philosopher can deny the experience of the 'pot' which satisfies the demand of practical life, as real. The reality of the pot carrying water is experienced in every-day life. Now the question is how to explain the reality of the worldly appearances? Is it empiric or absolute? The Advaitins hold the former view while the realistic schools advocate the absolute reality of the world order. Madhusūdana in repudiating the opponents' charge of *arthāntaram* or shifting of topic fully explains his own position and observes that the position held by the Mādhvites is not free from defect.

The Mādhva explanation of the wordly existence is also untenable

The Mādhva contention that the worldly appearances are as real as *Brahman* itself,[26] is unsatisfactory. The inert world which is subject to the antecedent and consequent non-existence or every-day change and decay cannot be characterised as real as *Brahman* which is Pure Being-Bliss-Consciousness and ever was, ever is and ever shall be. Existence of *Brahman* can be explained by its own nature, self-luminous, one, unique consciousness which is directly contradictory to inertness, the essential nature of the ever-changing world. Thus the Mādhva-proposition which makes the world order as real as Brahman seems to be an absurdity. And to admit such an absolute reality which is diametrically opposed to inertness *(jaḍatva)* is only to attribute falsity to the world order as is evident in the cognition of silver in the oyster. In the oyster-silver cognition, silver is false because being or reality of oyster is totally contradictory to that of silver and the notion of silver is false as it has been characterised by the existence not of its own but of its locus-oyster.[27] Oyster and silver are endowed with different grades of realities and it is due to the obliteration of distinction between the empiric and imaginary existences that silver is wrongly apprehended. Now the Mādhvites advocating the absolute reality of the world order in the sense of Brahman ignore the obvious distinction of the absolute and pragmatic realities and such an attribution of absolute reality to the empirical appearance rather leads to its falsity. Reality or existence is thus to be construed in the sense that 'What does never form the counterpart of negation of all times and space.' In this sense reality is ascribable to Brahman and not to the concrete manifold.

The phenomenal appearances should not be regarded as endowed with independent reality like *Brahman;* they appear as real because they are kindled with the Highest Reality. They are the seeming expression of reality and not real existence. *Sureśvarācārya* thus rightly observes that "the world has come out of *Sat,* loses itself in *Sat,* so the entire world is real, but viewed apart from *sat* is false." To advocate absolute reality of the worldly existences is to admit plurality of existences which would render the process of apprehending truth a cumbrous one. Thus the Mādhva charge of shifting of topic or *arthāntaram* does not stand.

The opponents in charge of *Aṁśataḥ siddhasādhanatā* cannot ṣtand

The Advaita-syllogism which predicates the dual character of absolute negation of existence and non-existence of the world order cannot escape the charge of *aṁśatoḥsiddhasādhanatā;* for the Mādhvites, advocating the absolute reality of the phenomenal appearance admit the negation of non-existence—a part of the major—in the world order. Against this the Advaitins argue that the charge of *siddhasādhanatā* can only be brought against the syllogism in which the major with all its characteristics *(sādhyatāvacchedakadharma)* is proved of the minor with all the special characteristics or distinctive features of its own *(pakṣatāvacchedakadharma)* and not in the given minor alone. The real essence of the argument lies in the fact that in order to establish the major in the minor which is the result of an inferential reasoning the major with all its distinguishing marks should be proved of the minor, determined by all its own particular inherent characteristics and not merely by the special sign or mark which serves the function of the middle in the syllogism. For otherwise all valid syllogisms would suffer from the fallacy of *Siddhasādhanatā* or establishing what has already been established. When we infer fire in a hill from the proposition 'the hill is fiery' because it is smoky, *vyāpti* or invariable, unconditional concomitance, between fire and smoke, helps us to the conclusion that the hill is on fire, because the agreement in absence *(vyatireka)* between fire and smoke with the non-observation of the contrary *(vyabhicārādarśana)* is the foundation of our knowledge of *vyāpti* between fire and smoke. Now from such an observation, fire is inferred in the hill because the hill was found to be smoky. The presence of the middle (smoke) in the minor (hill) is also a necessary factor of the inference. The moment we perceive smoke in it we infer that it has fire also. But the question arises, is the fire inferred in the hill as hill with all its hill aspects or as the repository of smoke the middle or *hetu* or means of proof? If we accept the latter view this syllogism also suffers from the fallacy of *siddhasādhanatā* because, as is evident from the universal concomitance between fire and smoke, fire the major is an universally admitted fact in the smoky things and in this respect it is already proved in the smoky hill. The real significance of the syllogism is to prove fire in the hill as hill and not as something smoky. *Pakṣa* or the minor has been defined as the subject in which the major is doubted. The hill which is perceived to be smoky, with its hill aspects serves the function of the minor or *Pakṣa* where fire, the major is doubted. And the syllogistic reasoning proves fire in all smoky hills with their hill aspects in which the ascertainment of fire cannot be made with the help of perception or observation. Any hill is not minor, hills endowed with smoke are styled minor or *pakṣa* of the syllogism. Smoke is the sign or the ground of inference and it is with this ground that fire is proved in the yonder hill as well as in all other hills characterised by their distinctive features, hillness *(parvaṭatva)*. The universal conclusion of the syllogistic reasoning which might be drawn from the proof of fire in the hill as hill could not be deduced from the inference of fire in the yonder hill as something smoky (with all its distinctive marks being hidden). Such an inference could no doubt prove the major in the minor marked out only by the presence of the middle and not by its own distinctive features. Again the proof of the major also means presence of the major with all its distinctive marks. Thus the charge of *siddhasādhanatā* occurs only in cases in which the major with all its distinctive features is pre-established in the minor endowed with all its characteristic marks. In such cases inference or syllogistic reasoning proves only what is already proved. This fact has been implied by Madhusūdana by saying that the fallacy of *aṁśataḥ-siddha-sādhanatā* occurs in the syllogisms in which the characteristics of the major and those of the minor are many in number and some of them are previously established in some particular parts of the minor.

In order to repudiate the charge of the Mādhvites Madhusūdana argues that to establish what has already been established is, no doubt, a serious type of error in the domain of logic and reason and it stands against all syllogistic arguments and invalidates the inferences. The previous proof, as a logical error, stands only in these cases in which the syllogisms do not give any new idea and prove the major in the same light in which it has been proved. But when inferences add novel features in the major in which it has not been proved, the charge of *siddhasādhanatā* totally falls to the ground. In the Advaita syllogism under discussion, the major, the dual negation of existence and non-existence forms one unique determinate cognition *(viśiṣṭabuddhi)* combining two in one single notion. Duality itself constitutes the determining mark of the major and not the two singularities forming the duality. And the Advaita inference proves this duality of negation which constitutes one unity in the given minor. Such is the essence or intention of the monistic proposition which cannot be served by the previous proof of a particular part *(e.g.,* the negation of the non-existence) or parts constituting the duality and such a partial proof cannot stand against the intended inference of the Advaita Vedānta. The two parts of the dual major form one indivisible determinate term giving rise to a unique conception, distinct from the component notions and the presence of one of the parts of this unique major in the minor cannot be said to involve the fallacy of *siddhasādhanatā*. It is sheer folly to bring forth the charge of *siddhasādhanatā* when the syllogism unfolds new truth or establishes the major in the sense in which it has not been previously seen. In order to strengthen his own position, Madhusūdana points out the well-known Mīmāṁsā syllogism in which to explain away the charge of *siddhasādhanatā,* the same truth has been advocated by the Mīmāṁsists against the Naiyāyikas, the masters of logic.

Explanation of the Mīmāṁsā syllogism

The Mīmāṁsā syllogism[28] implies that *bhedābheda* or difference and sameness is the relation between the property *(guṇa),* action or motion *(kriyā)* and generality, etc., and their respective seats. To establish the theory of *bhedābheda* Mīmāṁsists advance *samānādhikṛtatva* as the middle or *hetu* of their syllogism. But as the expression *samānādhikṛtatva* admits of different interpretations the question arises, what is its proper connotation here? It cannot mean the notion deduced from the words or terms bearing the same case endings *(ekavibhaktyanta-pada-vācyatvam).* For in that case the middle becomes too wide because the two terms pot and pitcher *(ghaṭaḥ* and *kalasaḥ)* with the first case-ending may be characterised by the middle but the said major, *e.g.,* difference and sameness is wanting.

It also does not mean the capability of usage as noun and its qualifying epithet *(viśeṣya-viśeṣanabhāvena vyavahriyamāṇatvam);* for here again the middle becomes too wide as is evident from the judgment 'the pot is on the earth' in which the earth and the pot are related as noun and its limiting adjunct but the major is inapplicable. The real essence of the middle, according to the view-point of the Mīmāṁsakas, is the capacity of being apprehended as noun of a determinate cognition in which the subject and the predicate are related in an identical or appositional relation *(abhedasahsargaka-dhīviśeṣyalva-yogya-tvam), 'Dhī'* or the determinate cognition introduced in the conception of the middle must be a valid one, for otherwise the middle becomes too wide in the case of oyster-silver super-imposition in which the oyster, the subject of the false notion, satisfies all the marks of the ground or means of proof. The middle thus explained, the Mīmāṁsakas argue, does not suffer from the fallacy of one kind or other. As regards *vyāpti* or the invariable unconditional concomitance between the said middle *(samānādhikṛtattva)* and the major *bhedābheda,* or difference and sameness it might be argued that if the said middle does not invariably and unconditionally exist in the said major it, may exist either in the case of extreme identity *(atyantā bhinna)*, *e.g.*, the pot and the pitcher *(ghaṭaḥ* and *kalasaḥ)* or in the case of absolute difference, *e.g.*, the pot and cloth *(ghaṭaḥ* and *paṭaḥ)*. But an examination shows that the said middle exists in neither but only in the case in which both *bhedābheda* difference and sameness, is found in apposition. Thus the appositeness of the middle is wanting in either case of extreme identity or of difference, and is to be found only in the case in which both difference and sameness can be simultaneously apprehended. The given argument leads the Mīmāṁsists to infer the duality of difference and sameness *(bhedābhedobhayatva)* in the minor, *e.g.*, the property, etc., with their respective seats. Similarly the Advaita-syllogism also proves the dual negation of existence and non-existence as one determinate cognition. If the phenomenal be real or *sat,* it cannot be called perceptible *(dṛśya)* for perceptibility or *dṛśyatva* does not invariably co-exist with reality, *e.g.*, in the case of Brahman. Again if the phenomenal appearance be styled unreal or 'asat,' it cannot be characterised by the middle 'perceptibility' as the nonest hare's horn, etc., are not perceptible. In other words, if perceptibility exists even in the absence of the mutual or absolute negation of existence it might exist in Brahman where it is not; and if it be found in the absence of the negation of non-existence it might be found in the hare's horn, etc. Now if the phenomenal appearance is to be determined by perceptibility, the phenomenal appearance must be characterised by the dual negation of existence and non-existence. And duality itself forms the characteristic mark of the major *(sādhyatāvacchedaka dharma)* as one determinate cognition.

The real purpose of the whole syllogistic argument is not to prove or establish the major as two distinct and separate parts forming an aggregate of independent judgments linked together by copulative conjunctions but as an aggregate in which the two component judgments form one unique duality as the characteristic mark which was not known before. So the opponents' charge of *siddhasādhanatā* falls to the ground. The world order is proved as neither being nor non-being; it is inexplicable or false.[29]

REFERENCES

1. Svapnajāgarite sthāne hyekamāhurmanīṣiṇaḥ
Bhedānām hi samatvena prasiddhenaiva hetunā
Ādāvante ca yannāsti vartamāno'pi tattathā
Vitatthaiḥ sadrśāḥ santaḥ avitathā iva lakṣitāh
Saprayojanatā teṣāṁ svapne vipratipadyate
Tasmādādyantavattvena mithyaiva khalu te smṛtāḥ. M.K.G., 5, 6, 7, Ch. II.

2. (a) Sadasattānadhikaraṇatvam,
(b) Pratipannopādhau traikālika-niṣedha-pratiyogitvam,
(c) Jñānanivartyatvam,
(d) Svāśrajaniṣṭhātyantābhāvapratiyogitvam,
(e) Sadviviktatvaṁ mithyātvam.

The first definition has been suggested by Padmapāda in his *Pañca-pādikā,* second and third by Prakāśātman in his *Vivaraṇa,* fourth by Citsukha in his *Tattvapradīpikā* and fifth by Ānandabodḥa in his *Nyāya-dīpāvalī.*

3. Sadasadanadhikaraṇatvamanirvācyatvaṁ mithyātvamiti. P. P., p. 8.

4. Tat kiṁ sattva-viśiṣṭāsattvābhāvaḥ, sattvātyantābhāvāsattvātyantā-bhāvarūpaṁ dharmadvayam, sattvātyantābhāvatve sati asattvātyantābhāva-rūpaṁ viśiṣṭam. N. Mr., p. 22.

In explaining Padmapāda's expression Vyāsarāja takes his stand only on the grammatical and syntactical formation of the expression. *Vide Siddhivyākhyā, p.* 48.

5. *Sadhyaprasiddhi* is a fallacy of reasoning based on the improbability of *sādhya* or major. When in a syllogism, the major which is affirmed or denied of the subject or the minor; becomes an unknown factor, the syllogistic argument commits the fallacy of unknown predication. For example, in the syllogism "a mountain has golden fire, because it has smoke,' the golden fire or the major of the syllogism is not known to us and hence such a factor cannot be predicated of the mountain and the syllogism becomes fallacious.

6. (a) *Vide* Nyāyāmṛta, p. 22.
(b) Niṣedhasya anyataravidhinantarīyakatvāt sattvātyantābhāve sādhye vyāhatiḥ, evamasattvātyantābhāve sādhye sattvasyaiva prāptyā punaḥ tadatyantābhāvasādhane vyāhatirityarthaḥ. N. Mr., p. 22.
(c) Sattvābhāvasādhane asattvasya prāptyā punarasattvābhāva-sādhane vyāhatirityarthaḥ. N, Mr. T., p. 10.

7. (a) Nirdharmaka-Brahmavat sattvarāhitye'pi sadrūpatvenāmithyātvopapattyā arthāntarañca. N. Mr., p. 24.
(*b*) Rajataṁ vināpi śuktyādau rajata-pratīti-vyavaḥārādidarśanāt satpadārthaṅ vināpi satpratltyāderupapattāvatilāghavamiti Brahmāpi sadrūpam na sidhyet, pramitatvat Brahma sadrūpamiti jagatyapi tulyam. N. Mr. T., p. 11.

8. *Sādhya-vikala* is one of the four fallacies of the positive explanatory instance, for example, if in the syllogism, sound is eternal because it is without a cause, and what is without a cause is eternal the antecedent non-existence or *prāgabhāva* be brought forward as an explanatory instance, the instance

being negated at the origination of its counterpart or *pratiyogī* cannot be characterised as eternal and the major of the syllogism thus does not exist in the explanatory example and the example is styled *sādhya-vikala.*

9. Pṛthivī itarebhyo bhidyate gandhavattvāt.
10. (a) N. Mr., p. 24.
 (b) Pṛthivītarabhinnetyatrāpi trayodaśabhedānāṁ sādhyatvāt jalādau tejaḥprabhṛtidvādaśabhedānāṁ sattvepi jalabhedasya abbāvāt sādhya-vaikalyam. N. Mr. P., p. 24.
 (c) N. Mr. T., p. 12.
11. (a) N. Mr., p. 24.
 (b) Jalāditrayodaśānyonyābhāvānāṁ tejaḥprabhṛtiṣu pratyekaṁ pratyekaṁ jñānānantaraṁ trayodaśānyonyābhāva iti sam ūhālambanarūpaika-jñānārūḍhānāṁ prasiddhi-sambhavena vyatirekanirūpaṇaṁ saṁbhavati. N. Mr. P., p. 24.
 (c) Ekaikānyonyābhāvasya na sādhyatāvacchedakāvacchinnatvam, sādhyatāvacchedakasya samūhālabanaika-jñānopārūḍhatvasya vyāsajya-vṛtterdharmasya pratyekābhāveṣvaparyāpteḥ. N. Mr. P., p. 12.
12. Ekādhikaraṇyāvacchedena sādhyasiddheruddeśyatvena atra ekādhi-karaṇyāvacchedena sādhyaprasiddherabhāvāt aprasiddhaviśeṣaṇatā syādeva. N. Mr. P., p. 24
13. Pṛthivītarabhinnā pṛthivītvādityatra trayodaśānyonyābhāvānāmiva atrāpi sattvāsattvātyantābhāvayoḥ pratyekaṁ prasiddhatvena kathañcida-prasiddhaviśeṣaṇatvābhāve'pi asattvātyantābbāvāṁśe siddhasādhanācca. N. Mr., p. 24.
14. (a) Sādhyatāvacchedakaikyannāṁśe siddhasādhanatvam. N. Mr., p. 25.
 (b) Prakṛte viśiṣṭasya ekasya sādhyatvena sādhyatāvaccheda-kaikyena tadavacchinnasādhyasya asiddhatvānnāṁśe siddhasādhanāvakāśaḥ. N. Mr., p. 25.
15. Bhūḥ śaśa-viṣāṇollikhitā bhūtvāt.
16. Asattvaṁ yadi sattvābhāva-samānādhikaraṇa-svabhāvakaṁ syāt, tadā sattvābhāvarūpaṁ na syāt; yat yadabhāvasamānādhikaraṇa-svabhāvakaṁ tat na tadabhāvarūpamiti evaṁ sattvaṁ yadi asattvābhāvasamānādhikaraṇa-svabhāvakaṁ syāt, tadā asattvābhāvarūpaṁ na syāt.
 Viṭṭha, the gloss on the G. B., pp. 50-51.
17. *Ibid,* p. 51.
18. *Ibid,* p. 51.
19. Kvacidapyupādhau sattvena pratīyamānatvānadhikaraṇatvam. Ad, S., p.51.
20. The Positive Sciences of the Ancient Hindus, pp. 2747-75.
21. Gotvāṣvatvayoḥ parasparavirahavyāpyatve'pi tadabbāvayoruṣṭrādā vekatra sahopalambhāt. Ad. S., p. 65.
22. Asattvādau sattvādyabhāvasamānādhikaraṇa-svabhāvakatva-rūpāpā-dakopagame'pi vyāpakasya adhikadeśavṛttitayā vyāpya-tvābhañjakatayā tucchādyantarbhāvena sattvādyabhāvavyāpya-tvopa-pattisambhavena mūla-śaithilyāditi. Viṭṭha, p. 53.
23. Yo yadabhāva-samānādhikaraṇa-svabhavakaḥ sa na tadabhāvavyāpya iti. *Ibid,* p. 53.

24. Ekenaiva-sarvānugatena sarvatra satpratītyupapattau Brahmavat prapañcasya pratyekaṁ satsvabhāvatā-kalpane mānābhāvāt. A. S., p. 55.

25. (a) *Vide* Siddhivyākhyā, pp. 55-56.

    (b) *Vide* Gauḍa-Brahmānandī, p. 56.

26. Yādṛśam Brahmaṇaḥ sattvaṁ tādṛśam syāt jagatyapi.

27. Svaprakāśādvitīyacaitanya-rūpameva Brahmaṇaḥ sattvaṁ tadeva cej-jaḍasyāpi jagataḥ tadā rajatatva-virodhiśuktisattayā rajatasyeva jaḍatva-virodhisvaprakāśa-sattayā jagataḥ svarūpato mithyātvopapatteḥ. Ad. S, p. 334.

    N.B.—To strengthen his own position Madhusūdana quotes the Mīmāṁsā syllogism because the position which has been advocated by the Mīmāṁsists on the basis of the syllogism, has been accepted by the Mādhvites, the staunch opponents of the Advaitins. *Jayatīrtha,* one of the great founders of the Mādhva school of Vedānta in his *Pramāṇa-paddhati,* in refuting the relation of inhesion *(samavāya)* between the property, etc.; and their seats, explains the relation in the light of the Mīmāṁsists. And the charges launched against the Advaitins by the Mādhvites might be brought forward even against the Mīmāṁsā syllogism as it is very akin to that of the Advaitins and the Mādhvites in criticising the Advaita postion criticise their own position.

28. Guṇādikaṁ guṇyādinā bhinnābhinnaṁ samānādhikṛtatvāt.

29. At the outset, we saw that Madhusūdana began by taking three possible interpretations of falsity on the basis of exposition of the *Pañca-pādiiā:* Firstly, whether it is the negation of non-existence characterised by existence; secondly, whether it is the dual negation of existence and non-existence; and thirdly, whether it is negation of non-existence characterised by the negation of existence. So far we have been discussing the problem from the point of view of the first and second alternative interpretations and we have seen how Madhusūdana successfully meets the charges levelled against him by the opponents, the Mādhvites and the Naiyāyikas. With regard to the third alternative it may be pointed out that it is not necessary to discuss it in detail as Madhusūdana has dealt with the second alternative as a special complex notion almost identical with the third and all the arguments brought forward to establish the second alternative would apply *mutatis mutandis* to the third. The commentators have however tried to distinguish between the second and the third alternatives on certain grammatical reasons, but such distinction does not affect the real philosophical position underlying them. Thus the third alternative requires no separate interpretation.

CHAPTER 6

IS FALSITY OF THE PHENOMENAL APPEARANCE FALSE?

In the previous chapter falsity of the phenomenal appearance has been logically defined and proved by the Advaitins. Now Vyāsarāja contends that if, for argument's sake, the falsity of the world order as advocated by the Advaitins be admitted, the Advaita position cannot escape logical errors. In order to point out the fallacious character of the Advaitins' standpoint, Vyāsarāja asks, is the falsity itself, which has been attributed to the phenomenal world, true or false? If the Advaitins accept the former view, in other words, if falsity itself be taken as true, the monistic proposition totally fails, for there comes the question of duality or of two absolute realities, *viz.*, *Brahman* itself and the falsity of the phenomenal appearances. So the position that Brahman alone is real and everything else is false, becomes untenable. To explain away the charge of duality it might be argued that the falsity of the phenomenal world as true or uncontradictable *(abādhya)* does not mean that it is an independent absolute reality apart from its substratum. It is *Brahman* the permanent substratum which negatively appears in the phenomenal appearances and speaks for the truth or absoluteness of falsity. To explain further, that is false which is negated universally in all times in its substratum. While mistaking an oyster for silver we get a false perception of silver superimposed on the oyster. Here the substratum is oyster and really the silver is negated in the oyster by all men in all times and under all circumstances. So in the case of the world its substratum is *Brahman* as it sustains and supports all concrete manifold and the worldly existence is negated in *Brahman* in all times in all circumstances and hence false.

The Mādhvites question the position of the Śaṁkarites by arguing that if the universal negation of this worldly existence in *Brahman* be true the non-duality of the Advaita-Vedānta is denied; for the universal negation comes in as existing negatively while *Brahman* remains a pure existence. Along with the existence of the latter there lies the existence of the former and the monistic premise that *Brahman* alone is real and all else is false, falls to the ground.

In repudiating the charge of the Mādhvites the Śaṁkarites argue that negation has no independent existence apart from its locus, for example the earth itself is the negation of the pot. Hence the universal negation of the world order is *Brahman,* the locus consciousness itself. So the question of *duality, i.e.,* the existence of *Brahman* along with the existence of the universal negation cannot arise at all.

The Mādhvites again contend that the given exposition of the Advaita-position which identifies falsity with *Brahman* itself is unsatisfactory because the two, falsity and *Brahman,* widely differ in their character. Question of identity occurs in cases where there is no difference at all. *Mithyātva* or falsity, as its definition implies, has been datermined by time, space and other causal categories and thus cannot be identified with A-logical *Brahman* which lies beyond all conditions and limitations. Falsity of the silver in the oyster-silver cognition is not cognised so long as the man is under delusion. He runs after yonder substrate only because he is unconscious of his own mistake. But the fact is to be noted here that the substrate of a false notion, though its special features are hidden for the time being, is real and not to be doubted even at the time of mistake and cannot remain unknown and unnoticed as locus, for in that case no false notion would arise. Thus the locus of a false cognition and the object superimposed do not belong to the same category and are not of the same nature. *Brahman* in the Advaita-Vedānta is the substrate of all substrates. It is due to super-imposition on the permanent substratum, *Brahman,* that the worldly appearances are apprehended as true. This permanent substratum being an ever certain factor, can in no way be identified with falsity having uncertainty for its criterion.

Secondly, in the case of identification, perceptibility, the middle term of the Advaita-syllogism,[1] suffers from a fallacy in regard to the falsity itself. The question under discussion is whether the falsity of the phenomenal appearance is false or true? If falsity be taken as identical with *Brahman,* the Mādhvites contend, that 'perceptibility,' the middle term of the Advaitins, cannot exist in the major. In other words, the middle failing to prove the major becomes inconclusive or *anaikāntika.*[2]

Falsity cannot be styled as false

The defects enumerated above will not allow falsity to be styled as true or uncontradictable *(abādhya).* It also cannot be taken as contradictable or false *(bādhya)* for the following defects. If 'the Advaitins' inference, the Mādhvites argue, proves, as monistic principle demands, the falsity of the phenomenal world as false or contradictable. the syllogism suffers from the fallacy of *siddha-sādhanatā.* That falsity of the phenomenal world is false is a position which is advocated by the Mādhvites. The Mādhva-teachers hold that the phenomenal appearances are absolutely true. It is only due to ignorance that falsity has been attributed to them. And the falsely attributed falsity of the world order, is subject to contradiction and thus cannot negate realities of the phenomenal appearances; they are thus styled as real. The Advaitins, holding the falsity of the world order as false, establish what has already been established in the Mādhva doctrine.

Again such a position would infer realities of the phenomenal appearances against absolute monism. "The world is real as it is endowed with falsity which itself is false, as for example the self."[3] The self is a self-revealed and self-valid reality and falsity of the self is an erroneous notion. And when this erroneous notion is apprehended the real nature of self is revealed. The real essence of the argument lies in the fact that when falsity is perceived in a particular substance, such perception veils the inherent truth of the substance and when the falsity itself is cognised as erroneous the veil of nescience which hides the underlying truth is lifted up and the substance is apprehended as real. Thus in all cases in which the falsely attributed falsity itself is cognised as erroneous the notion of truth invariably becomes manifested. And the Advaitins, advocating the falsity of the world order as false, are bound to accept the reality of the phenomenal existences,

But the validity of the Mādhva-inference might be challenged by the Advaitins as the relation between the said major *(satyam)* and the middle *(mithyābhūta-mithyātmakatvāt)* is not an unconditional one. The concomitance or *vyāpti* of the given syllogism has been rendered faulty by the *upādhi* or condition. Take for example the *upādhi* or limitation of *ātmatva* or selfhood. The determining condition, selfhood or *ātmatva* invariably accompanies the major as seen in regard to self but being absent in the minor—the phenomenal appearance, does not always accompany the middle or *hetu* which must be present in the minor. *Upādhi* or determining condition is "that which always accompanies the major *(sādhya)* but does not always accompany the middle or *hetu*"[4] "The *upādhi* is the 'condition' which must be supplied to restrict a general middle term. If the middle term as thus restricted is still found in the minor term, the argument is valid, if not it fails. It does in the examples 'The mountain is smoky because it has fire' (for it rests on the false premise that all fire is accompanied by smoke). Now if we add 'wet fuel' as the condition of 'fire,' the proposition is valid; for if the mountain has wet fuel as well as fire, of course it will have smoke."

"It would be correct to say that a *vyāpti* exists between greenwood fire and smoke as well as between smoke and green-wood fire. The question, therefore, is : what is the relation between fire and smoke? The relation between fire and smoke is a conditional relation, *i.e.,* on condition that fire is green-wood fire, it would be a sign of smoke. But a *vyāpti* implies an unconditional invariable concomitance, and the relation between fire and smoke is not therefore a *vyāpti* (natural unconditional concomitance), for fire requires a 'condition,' *upādhi, viz.,* green wood, to be followed by smoke. Smoke on the other hand, requires no 'condition' to indicate fire. For the purposes of inference, therefore, relation between phenomena may be considered as of two kinds : (1) contingent or conditional relation holding good on the fulfilment of a certain condition or *upādhi* and (2) *vyāpti* or unconditional invariable relation between a mark and that which it marks, a relation without any *upādhi* or determining condition *(upādhividhuraḥ sambandhaḥ)*. It is the latter kind of relation that serves as the ground of inference." As unconditionality of the concomitance is essential to a *vyāpti*. "We have therefore to examine the case carefully to see if there is any determining condition *(upādhi, i.e.,* some hidden or undetected but really operative or indispensable accompaniment) which conditions the relation between the supposed sign or mark *(gamaka)* and the supposed signate (thing signified *gamya).*" *Upādhi* or condition, as we have already seen, is a circumstance which always accompanies and is always accompanied by the supposed signate (the thing signified, *gamya),* but does not invariably accompany the "supposed sign or mark' *(gamaka)*. If, therefore, in the set of positive instances where both the sign and the signate are present, nothing else is constantly present, there can be no '*upādhi.*' Or again, if in the set of negative instances where both the sign and the signate are absent, no other material circumstances is constantly absent there is no '*upādhi.*' This follows from the very definition of an *upādhi*. It is impracticable to fulfil those requirements rigorously, till every one of the accompanying circumstances (of course, of likely ones) may be taken successively and it may be shown that the concomitance continue even when the suspected *upādhi (śaṁkitopādhi)* is absent, and therefore it cannot be the *upādhi*. And this is to be fortified by the observation of uniform uninterrupted agreement in absence *(vyatireka)* between the two concomitant phenomena. In this way, when we have disproved all suspected *upādhis* we conclude by establishing the *vyāpti*. "This is the real essence of *upādhi* in the science of Indian Logic. *Upādhi* or condition points out the fallacy of the middle term and thus undermines the very ground of inference." It is in order to prove the fault of generality in a middle term that the 'condition has to be employed.' "All true conditions reside in the same subjects with their major terms and their subjects being thus common, the (erring) middle term will be equally too general in regard to the condition and the major term. "The meaning of this is that it is in consequence of the middle term being found too general in regard to the condition, that we infer that it is too general in regard to the major term; and hence the use of having a condition at all. Thus, where the condition invariably accompanies an unlimited major term, we infer that the middle term is too general *(Vyabhicāri)* in regard to the major term, from the very fact that it is too general in regard to the condition, as for example, in the instance "The mountain has smoke because it has fire," where we infer that the 'fire' is too general in regard to 'smoke,' since it is too general in regard to 'wet fuel;' for there is a rule that what is too general for that which invariably accompanies must also be too general for that which is invariably accompanied. But where we take some fact or mark to determine definitely the major term which the condition is invariably to accompany— there it is from the middle term's being found too general in regard to the condition in cases possessing this fact or mark that we infer that the middle term is equally too general in regard to the major term. Thus in the argument "B is dark because he is Mitrā's son" the middle term, "the fact of being Mitrā's son," is too general in regard to the *sādhya* "dark colour" because it is too general in regard to the *upādhi,* "Feeding on vegetables "as seen in the case of Mitrā's second son.[5]

Advaitin's *vyabhicārānumāna* against the Mādhvites

Having followed this logic the Advaitins on the basis of the condition or *upādhi* shown in the Mādhva-syllogism,[6] infer the variability or too general character of the middle term and thus destroy the very ground of the syllogistic reasoning. The Advaita inference runs as follows: Falsehood which itself is false is too general in regard to truth because it is too general in regard to selfhood or *ātmatva,* the shown condition, which is equipollent with truth, as for example, the oyster-silver.[7]

The Mādhvite's reply

Against this the Mādhvites contend that the erroneous or too general character of the middle of Mādhva-syllogism, as urged by the given inference is not to the point. In the Mādhva inference falsity which itself is false *(mithyābhūta-mithyātmakatva)* forms the middle and truth or *satyatva* as the major. The said middle and the major are related as invariable concomitance and hence it cannot be said that the middle exists even in the absence of the major. Now to prove the middle as too general on the strength of condition or *upādhi* the disputant is to establish the fact that the middle term or *hetu* does not always accompany the condition and hence must not also necessarily accompany the major or *sādhya* as the major and the condition are equipollent and thus related as the mutual sign and the signate *(vyāpya* aud *vyāpaka)*. For what is absent in the *vyāpaka* must as a rule be absent in the *vyāpya* (the major). But if it is proved that the middle invariably co-exists with the condition or *upādhi* it must co-exist with the major or *sādhya* which is the sign or mark of the said condition. And the charge of too generality of the middle totally falls to the ground. In the syllogism under discussion,[8] the Mādhvites argue, truth or *satyatva* is the major and selfhood or *ātmatva* which pervades the major is the given condition. Examination shows that *mithyābhūta-mithyātmakatva* the middle of the syllogism invariably exists in the selfhood or *ātmatva* or the shown condition. The selfhood or *ātmatva* is endowed with the middle and it is for this reason that *ātmā* or self forms the explanatory example of the Mādhva syllogism. From the given arguments, it is definitely proved that *mithyābhūta-mithyātmakatva,* the said minor of the Advaitin's counter-inference cannot be marked off or characterised by the given middle *ātmavyabhicāritva.* Or, in other words, the presence of the middle in the minor *(hetoḥ pakṣadharmatā),* one of the most important conditions of the valid middle failing, the middle suffers from the fallacy of *svarūpāsiddha* or the unreal in itself.[9] And on the strength of this fallacious reasoning or of the given condition, the Advaitins attempt to prove the too general character of the middle *mithyābhūta-mithyātmakatva* in regard to truth, the major of the Mādhva inference, is an absurdity.

The Advaitin's *Satpratipakṣānumāna*

Now the reason, not existent in the subject, might lead the Advaitins to bring forward a counterbalanced inference *satpratipakṣānumāna*[10] and thus by advancing an argument of an equal weight render the middle of the Mādhva-inference inconclusive. "The world is characterised by the negation of truth because it is determined by the negation of self, *e.g.*, the oyster-silver or the self, which is not endowed with the negation of truth, is not endowed with the negation of selfhood."

Anukūla tarka or argument in favour in the Mādhva syllogism

Such a counter-balanced inference which takes its stand on the shown condition or *upādhi* gives rise to doubt in the main inference and weakens the very foundation of the syllogistic reasoning. In the case of counter-balanced arguments involving two inferences of equal weight fresh arguments in favour should be sought for to establish the main proposition. If there are arguments in favour which are wanting in the reason proving the contrary, *satpratipakṣa* or the counter-balanced reason does not stand. In the Mādhva proposition, there are arguments in favour *(anukūla tarka)* helping the formation of *vyāpti* or invariable concomitance but no reason can be advanced to lead to or the counter-reason of the Advaitins. In the Mādhva-inference the truth or uncontradictability of the phenomenal appearance forms the major and *mithyābhūta-mithyātmakatva* as the middle. *Mithyā-bhūta-mithyātmūkatva* connotes truth. Now the charge which challenges the appositeness of the middle that the middle exists and the major does not exist, commits a flat contradiction. And such a contradiction *(vyāghāta)* helps the formation of *vyāpti* between the said middle and the major in the Mādhva-syllogism.

The counterbalanced inference of the Advaitins does not stand

But there are no such arguments which might prevent the too general character or inappositeness of the Advaitin's middle and help the formation of *vyāpti*. In the counter-balanced inference, the negation of the truth of the world has been inferred on the ground of the negation of selfhood *(ātmatvaohāva)*. As there might be things other than the self which might be true, the negation of selfhood does not always accompany the major, the negation of truth; in other words, the given middle cannot be the *vyāpya* or *gamaka* the sign, mark or indication of the said major, the *vyāpaka gamya* or the thing signified. Thus selfhood or *ātmātva* cannot be the condition in the Mādhva-inference which urges the truth or absolute reality of the phenomenal world. For it is evident from the given counter-inference that the negative concomitance between truth or the major of the Mādhva-syllogism and the shown condition or *ātmatva,* does not stand to reason and the truth or selfhood thus cannot be called equipollent *(samavyāpta), i.e.,* what constitutes the true criterion of *upādhi* or condition. *Upādhi* is, as we have already noticed, a circumstance which always accompanies and is accompanied by the supposed signate or the thing signified. From this it follows that *(a)* where the major is, the condition is; *(b)* where the condition exists the major exists; *(c)* when there is no condition, there is no major; *(d)* where there is no major, there is no condition. Now if truth or *satyatva* exists in the absence of selfhood or the negation of the said condition the relation of mutual sign and the signate *(vyāpya* and *vyāpaka)* as expressed in the given proposition fails and *ātmatva* cannot be the true condition of the Mādhva-syllogism.

No such discovery of contradiction disproves the inappositeness of middle of the Mādhva inference and helps the formation of a valid concomitance in favour of the Advaitin's counter-balanced reason. For *mithyābhūta-mithyātmakatva* (the middle of the Mādhva proposition) and *asatyatva,* negation of truth or the major are two contradictory terms, when one is affirmed the other is denied and *vice versa* and the two cannot reside in a substrate. But such a charge of contradiction cannot be brought forward between *anātmatva,* the negation of selfhood (the middle terms of the counter-balanced reason of the Advaitins) and truth or *satyatva* (the negation of the major) as there may be realities other than the self. Negation of selfhood does not therefore mean negation of truth. And the two are not quite contradictory in their nature and there arises no possibility of contradiction.

The Advaitins now point out the fallacy in the Mādhva Inference

From the above discussion it has been proved that the charge of condition or *upādhi* pointed out by the Advaitins falls to the ground. Now the Advaitins launch a new attack against the Mādhva proposition by arguing that the middle term of the Mādhva inference is too general, because the false oyster-silver, where even the notion of falsity is erroneous, might be characterised by the said middle but not by the said major and thus the middle becomes too general or *sādhāraṇa* in its character.[11]

The Mādhvites refute the charge of the too general character of the middle

To repudiate the Advaita charge of the extreme generality of the middle, the Mādhvites argue that of the two contradictory concepts, if one is affirmed in a particular substrate, the other is denied and *vice versa*. But it should be noted here that the question of co-presence of the two contradictory notions in a particular substrate, namely *mithyābhūta-mithyātmakatva* or truth and the negation of truth in the oyster-silver, creates a doubt as to the real nature of the substrate oyster-silver and leads us to the following deduction. The oyster-silver cannot be the substrate of falsehood, which is itself false, because it cannot be the receptacle of truth which contradicts falsity. What does not form the receptacle of notion directly contradictory to its truthful existence cannot also form the receptacle of the falsity of the same notion contradicting its negation. As for example, the cow cannot form the receptable of cowhood directly contradictory to the valid notion of cowhood; it also thus cannot form the receptacle of falsity of the notion of cowhood directly contradictory to the absolute negation of cowhood.[12] This syllogic definitely proves the fact that what does not form the receptation *(adhikaraṇa)* of truth which is directly contrary to falsehood *(satyabhūta, mithyātvaviruddha-satyatva)* cannot be the substratum *(adhikaraṇa)* of the falsity of falsehood *(mithyābhūta-mithyātva)*; for truth and falsity are of the nature of mutual contradiction. The notion of truth of the oyster-silver is not correct but erroneous and hence the oyster-silver cannot be called true which is contradictory to falsehood, it therefore cannot be marked by *mithyābhūta-mithyātmakatva*—the given major of the said deduction. For wherever the *vyāpya,* the sign or the mark is absent the *vyāpaka* or the signate must necessarily be absent. *Mithyābhūta-mithyātmakatva* being thus wanting in the oyster-silver, the oyster-silver cannot be characterised by truth or what is quite contradictory to its own falsehood. And the charge of the too generality of the middle urged in the main syllogism of the Mādhvites falls to the ground.[13]

It might be contended against the Mādhvites that as the oyster-silver cannot be characterised by *satyabhūta-satyatva* or *mithyātvaviruddhasatyatva,* it cannot also be endowed with *satyabhūtamithyātva,* falsehood which is held as true, as the oyster-silver—the *dharmin,* receptacle of all the marks is itself false. And the falsity of what itself is false must necessarily be false and not true *(satyabhūtā).*[14] To prove this the Advaitins advance the following syllogistic reasoning in their favour. Both *satyatva* and *mithyātva,* truth and falsehood, which might be attributed to the oyster-silver are false because they are the characteristics *(dharmas)* of a substance which itself is false like the being and non-being *(astitva* and *nāstitva)* of an elephant seen in a dream.[15] This inference establishes the falsity *(mithyātva)* of the falsehood residing in the nonest silver. The too general character of the middle in regard to the oyster-silver as urged by the Advaitins against the Mādhvites remains still a formidable objection.[16]

The Mādhva charge of counter-balanced reasons against the Advaitins

Against this the Mādhvites contend that the given Advaita-syllogism (which establishes falsity of the falsehood of the nonest silver) is counter-balanced *(satpratipakṣita)* by the given Mādhva-syllogism which negates *mithyābhūtamithyātva* of the oyster-silver.[17] The Mādhva-syllogism is based on an all-admitted universal law, namely of the two contradictory notions when one is affirmed in a substrate, the other is denied and *vice versa.* The inference being based on sound logic would invalidate the Advaita-proposition and the Advaitins, charge of the extreme generality of the middle in regard to the oyster-silver totally falls through.

The Advaitins reply

Against the charge of the counter-balanced reason the Advaitins argue that the disputant's objection is not to the point. The underlying principle upon which the opponents' argument has been based should be applied in cases where both the characteristic and the instance thus characterised are marked by the same grade or reality *(samānasattāka).* Here the silver itself is nonest or false and how can, its falsity or *mithyātva* be styled valid? So the opponents' inference proving the falsity of the nonest silver as true stands against all logic and reason. For in that case the *dharma* or characteristic becomes more real than the substance characterised which is an absurdity.

Again the given counterbalanced inference suffers from condition or *upādhi, amithyātva* (negation of falsity) which exists in the cow, the explanatory instance of the counter-balanced reason, invariably accompanies the major and as it does not exist in the minor, *e.g.,* the false oyster-silver, it does not always accompany the middle or the *vyāpya* or the sign or the mark which must be present in the minor. The said condition would deduce the too general character of the given middle in the sense that as the middle does not invariably accompany the given condition, it must not accompany the major, for the major and the condition are equipollent in their character. The middle thus not existing in the subject or the major, suffers from the falacy of the unreal in itself and, therefore, cannot afford the basis of any valid reasoning. The counter-balanced reason advanced by the Mādhvites is thus invalidated by the said condition and cannot stand against the Advaita-syllogism which establishes falsity of the wrong notion or *mithyābhūta-mithyātmakatva* of silver superimposed on the oyster and the Advaitins' charge of the extreme generality of the middle in the Mādhva proposition in regard to the oyster-silver stands good.[18]

Again the *vyāpti* or the invariable concomitance on which the counter-balanced reason of the Mādhvites has been, based, *viz.*, of the two contradictory notions when one is affirmed in a particular substrate, the other is denied and *vice versa,* is not valid. And to prove the invalidity of the said *vyāpti* the Advaitins contend that the barren women's son cannot called fair because the black colour has been negated in him. In other words, when blackness or *śyāmatva* is negated in a barren woman's son, whiteness or *gauratva* is not affirmed by that negation on the ground that the said two marks blackhood and whiteness are styled contradictory because they never co-exist *(sahānava-sthānalakṣaṇa-virodhaḥ)*. In a barren woman's son both *śyāmatva* and *gauratva* or blackness and whiteness are called false because the barren woman's son itself is false.[19]

It might here be argued in support of the said *vyāpti* or universal concomitance that the mutual contradiction or *paras-paravirodha* introduced in the *vyāpti* does not mean the *mere* absence of co-presence *(sahānavasthāna)* but it means, as evident from the explanatory instance, cowhood and the negation of cowhood *(gotva* and *gotvābhāva),* that the two concepts are so related that the one involves the absolute negation of the other or *parasparaviraha-vyāpaka*. *Virodha* or contradiction explained in this sense cannot be applied to blackness and whiteness *(śyāmatva* and *gauratva)* as these two marks are not contradictory and thus has to be taken as *parasparaviraha-vyāpya* and not as *paraspara-viraha-vyāpaka* [20] or one is absolute negation of the other. Thus the charge of variability against the said *vyāpti* is not to the point. Such an answer also cannot establish the validity of the said *vyāpti*. Both being and non-being, reality and unreality of the elephant seen in a dream, though they can be styled as *paraspara-viraha-vyāpaka* or directly contradictory to each other, are false and hence the *vyāpti* fails in the case of the nonest dream-elephant. Similarly it might not also be applied in the false oyster-silver and the so-called truth and falsity of the silver, though apparently contradictory is characterised as false.[21]

The Mādhva vyāpti thus failing in the nonest things should be restricted to cases in which the substance or the seat of the contradictory characteristic is not false but pragmatically valid. This view questions, in regard to the oyster-silver and the dream-elephant, etc., the universal co-presence of *mithyābhūta-mithyātmakatva*—the middle and the major of the Mādhva thesis as demanded by the said *vyāpti* and the Mādhva logic, establishing the reality of the phenomenal world on the ground of its falsity being false, totally falls through.

The Mādhavites reply against the Advaita charge of invalidity of the *vyāpti*

To explain away the charge (the too general character of the middle *mithyābhūta-mithyātmakatva* in regard to truth) the Mādhvites contend that the Advaita inference [22] which has been based on the argument that characteristics of the nonest things must necesarily be nonest, is not convincing, for the nature of the characteristics does not always depend upon the nature of the things characterised. We can independently understand the *dharmas* without understanding the *dharmins*. For example, we may refer to the Advaitins' concept of falsity. Falsity or *mithyātva,* according to the Advaitins' own admission, has been defined as what forms the counterpart of the absolute negation of all times in any accepted substratum;[23] and it is mainly based on the *dharmas* independent of the *dharmins*. Falsity, when it arises, removes the so-called notion of truth or being residing so long in the false thing, it stands as directly contradictory to the preconceived notion of being or reality abiding in the so-called real things. For, otherwise the Advaita-proposition which proves the falsity of the phenomenal world suffers from the fallacy of *siddhasādhanatā* or establishing what has already been established.[24] From this it can be said that being or existence of the sign or mark *(dharmasattā)* does not always depend upon being of the thing signified *(dharmisattā)*. And such independent *dharmas* can be independently understood as true or real when their respective seats are apprehended as false. The fact might be proved from the false notion of the barren woman's son. The barren woman's son, though nonest, is characterised as the counterpart of an absolute negation and such a characteristic mark in the nonest barren woman's son is not nonest but a logically valid concept. Hence the proposition that the characteristic marks of nonest things are nonest, falls to the ground and the Advaita syllogism, urging the falsity of the silver as erroneous on the ground of unreality or non-existence of silver itself[25] becomes invalid. In other words, the appositeness *(prayojakatva)* of the middle *(avidyamānadharmikatvāt)* in the said proposition has been challenged in regard to the Advaitins' concept of falsity as we have noticed before.

Against this it might be argued that the shown inappositeness of the middle goes against the universally admitted maxim that the *dharmas* cannot exist in the non-existence of their *dharmins*. How can the *dharmas* stand without their respective seats *(dharmyasattve dharmāsattvam)?* The disputant however may contend that the maxim is not universal. It is confined only to those cases in which the *dharmas* or the characteristics are dependent on and not independent of the *dharmins, e.g.,* the colour, taste, etc. The sign falsity which has been defined as the counterpart of the absolute negation *(atyantābhāva pratiyogī)* does not depend upon the being or existence of its counterpart. For the nonest things, *e.g.,* the barren woman's son, sky-flower, etc., may form the counterpart of the valid absolute negation. But the validity of concepts of colour, taste, smell, etc., of the *alīka* or nonest things is an absurdity. Thus the *dharmas* are classified into two groups:—dependent upon their *dharmins* and independent of their *dharmins*. The notion of taste, colour, etc., belongs to the former class while the notion of falsity to the latter. And the maxim *(dharmyasattve dharmāsattvam)* is applicable to the former case and not to the latter. Because falsity or *mithyātva* is, as its definition implies, nothing but the negation or denial of truth or *satyatva* of the *dharmin,* which forms the counterpart of the negation. It thus in no way depends upon the being or existence *(sattā)* of its counterpart, rather it destroys the so-called validity of the counterpart. It is the inherent nature of the absolute negation that it arises as a contradiction of the so-called being or existence of its counterpart.[26] Hence the appositeness *(prayojakatā)* of the middle *(avidyamānadharmikatvāt)* is questioned. And the falsity of the notion of silver as false is not proved. On the contrary, falsity of the silver is proved as valid. As a result the Advaitins' counter-inference *(vyabhicārānumāna)* falsehood which itself is false is too general in regard to truth[27] totally fails and the Mādhva-thesis demanding the truth of the phenomenal appearance might be established.

The Mādhvites' further objections against the Advaitin's falsity of the false silver

Further the falsity of the notion of nonest silver cannot be false. For the silver is false because, it is denied in its substrate and as a result of its denial, the negative judgment 'this is not silver' *(nedam rajatam)* arises and the judgment helps us to come to the conclusion that silver that so long appeared before us is false. Now the silver is negated in its substrate and its falsity is posited by the negation. Thus the silver satisfies the criterion of falsity which itself, however, stands independent of the criterion. So falsity is empirically true even of the silver which is a mere appearance. There is no logic in the argument that falsity must be called false because it has a relation with the nonest silver. The Advaitins take their stand on a so-called universally accepted principle that the things that are related to one another must have the same grade of reality. Such a principle is suicidal. If that law be accepted all the *dharmas* or characteristics which are negated in the pure Being-Bliss Consciousness must be taken as absolutely real because they have been negatively related withAbsolutereality.Againthesubstrate of the nonest silver, mother-of-pearl, which is an empirically valid reality, might be called false or honest for it is in apposition with the nonest silver. And the concrete manifolds which are located in Brahman must be absolutely, true because they have the supreme Being as their substratum.[28] This law is thus Cavidya, untenable. And the interpretation of the said middle *mānadharmikatvāt)* of the Advaita-syllogism as offered in the light of the shown *vyāpti* (things that are related to one another must have the same grade of reality, falsity of the silver is false because it is the charac-teristic *(dharma)* of a false *(dharmin* suffers from a number of defects shown before.

Again if the middle term of the Advaita proposition be interpreted in the given light, the same middle might be applied in establishing the falsity of the Advaita major—*rajata-mithyātva.* The falsity of the false notion of silver is itself false because the said falsity is itself the characteristic mark of the falsity of the nonest silver,[29] and so on *ad infinitum.* Thus the Advaita middle becomes totally invalid in proving the said major. Secondly, if both silver and its falsity be taken as false, the line of demarcation between an illusory percept and the negation of illusion becomes totally obliterated. The judgment, 'this is silver' is called a false percept as its object is false and the negative judgment which arises as contradictory to the illusory percept —'this is not silver but oyster' is not called illusory but an empirically valid cognition because the negative judgment has as its object the falsity of silver which is an empirically valid reality. Now if both silver and its falsity be taken as false as urged by the Advaitins in the syllogism under consideration the illusory percept and its negation which contradicts the false judgment, stand on the same footing which is suicidal to the epistemology of illusion. Again the explanatory instances—barren woman's son, or being and non-being of the dream-elephant, etc., cannot prove the Advaita proposition against the Mādhva thesis (of the two contradictory concepts when one is affirmed, the other is denied and *vice versa).* Phenomenal appearances which can satisfy our pragmatic needs are not nonest but empirically valid realities. Even silver which has an appearance in yonder oyster, totally differs according to the Advaitins' own admission, from the barren woman's son, sky-flower, etc., which have no objectivity at all. Thus the barren woman's son cannot form an explanatory instance to infer falsity of the silver as false. As regards the second instance *(e.g.,* the being and non-being of the dream-elephant), it might be argued that the dream-elephant and its consequent non-existence *(svapnagaja-pratiyogika-dhvaṁsa)* might be called false but its absolute negation *(atyantābhāva)* is not false but true[30] for the negation is not contradicted though its counterpart—the elephant is contradicted at the time we are awakened.

And the instance thus establishes the Mādhva proposition and not that of the Advaitins. From the given dialectics it is definitely proved that the Advaita syllogism which has been advanced to prove the falsity of the silver as false *(rajata mithyātva-mithyātva)* suffers from a number of fallacies and is thus untenable. And the Mādhva syllogism stands true to logic and reason.

Madhusūdana's reply against the Mādhvites

This is, in short, the essense of the Mādhava criticism, Against this Madhusūdana Sarasvatī argues that of the two horns of the Mādhva dialectics, namely, is the falsity of the phenomenal world (*a*) true or (*b*) false, the first position has been thoroughly discarded by the Advaitins and hence the shortcomings pointed out in the former case are not to the point, and require no criticism at the hands of the Advaita teachers. As regards the second alternative, *e.g.*, is falsity itself false, there are two salient points of attack brought forward by the Mādhvites, *viz.*,

(a) the charge of *siddhasādhanatā,* and
(b) the absolute reality of the world order.

This last signal for attack is the mainstay upon which the logical and epistemological dialectics of the Mādhvites takes its stand. Madhusūdana, in order to refute the Mādhva charge, takes it as the main bone of contention and thus repudiates the disputants' criticism. The *vyāpti* or the invariable concomitance upon which the Mādhva syllogism[31] establishing the absolute reality of the phenomenal world is based *(e.g.,* of the two concepts which are *viruddha* in their nature, when one is affirmed, the other is denied and *vice versa),* is not valid. For in an elephant in which both cowhood and horsehood *(gotva* and *aśvatva)* which can nowhere co-exist, might be negated; but when cowhood is negated, horsehood is not affirmed and again when horsehood is denied, cowhood is not posited. Thus the said *vyāpti* fails. But the examination shows that the said *vyāpti* is valid only in cases in which the characteristic marks of falsity do not and cannot reside in the two concepts which are styled contradictory.[32] For example, of the two contradictory concepts, silverhood and its absolute negation or mutual exclusion, when silver is posited or affirmed in the mother-of-pearl, its negation or difference is denied and *vice versa.* Because the basis or the characteristic marks of the things negated *(niṣedhyatā-vacchedakadharma)* differ here. For when silver is negated, silverbood *(rajatatva)* forms the characteristic mark of the counterpart of negation and in the case of its negation, the negation or difference of silver *(rajatatvābhāvatva* or *rajatabhinnatva)* forms the marks of the counterpart. In other words, silverhood and its negation are contradictory and cover the entire universe. Hence the denial of the one is the affirmation of the other and *vice versa.* The Mādhva *vyāpti* is valid only in this sense. But in the case of the elephant in which both cowhood and horsehood are negated, they (cowhood and horsehood) though they cannot co-exist, can be marked out by one common mark, namely the absolute negation of elephanthood *(gajatvātyantābhāvatva).* The *vyāpti* thus does not apply here. Now the truth and falsity of the phenomenal world, though contradictory, both share in the common characteristic mark of objectivity *(dṛśyatva);* they, therefore, are not two contradictory entities bearing two separate marks of negation. The truth and falsity of the worldly existence share in the common determining mark as possessing the character of objectivity; and it is for this mark that both of them are styled false. And the falsity of the phenomenal world being itself false cannot deduce the truth or validity of the phenomenal world. The real logic of Madhusūdana's observation lies in the fact that when two contradictory concepts are of the nature of absolute negation *(parasparaviraharūpa)* or one pervades the absolute negation of the other *(parasparavirahavyāpaka)* as is evident in the case of silver and its absolute negation or mutual exclusion in the mother-of-pearl, the said *vyāpti* of the Mādhvites is valid. But when the two concepts are not so characterised, they are called contrary in the sense that they can nowhere co-exist, but their absolute negation can exist in a third particular substrate or, in other words, the concepts are characterised as '*paraspara-virahavyāpya;*' in such a case, the said *vyāpti* or invariable concomitance totally fails. Such contrary terms being negated in a particular locus, share in the common characteristic, namely the negation in that particular locus as their common determining mark of denial *(ekaniṣedhyatā-vacchedakadharma)*. For example, cowhood and horsehood are contrary because where cowhood is, horsehood is not and where horsehood is, cowhood is not; and again when the negation of horsehood is absent, cowhood is also absent, and when the negation of cowhood is absent, horsehood is also absent. Thus cowhood and horsehood are styled *parasparavirahavyāpya.* But the negation of cowhood and horsehood which is *vyāpaka* or more extensive than its *vyāpya, e.g.,* horsehood and cowhood, can be apprehended in an elephant. Hence the absolute negation of cowhood and horsehood in the elephant *(gajatvātyantābhāvatva)* forms the common determining feature which marks off both cowhood and horsehood and the negation of cowhood or that of horsehood in the elephant cannot, on the strength of the Mādhvites' *vyāpti,* establish validity or truth of horsehood or cowhood. To put simply, the negation of cowhood and horsehood can co-exist and so the negation of the one does not mean the affirmation of the other. Similarly the dual negation of truth and falsity can be cognised in the nonest sky-flower, etc.; thus truth and falsity cannot be styled contradictory, *parasparaviraharūpa* or *parasparavirahavyāpaka.*[33] They are simply contrary because they cannot co-exist in a substrate, but both being negated in the nonest sky-flower they share in the common mark of objectivity or *dṛśyatva* and on the basis of this common mark, Madhusūdana argues that the notion of falsity being itself false cannot prove the truth or validity of phenomenal world. In other words, truth and falsity are contrary but not contradictory concepts. Thus they do not exhaust the entire order of universe as suggested by the Mādhvites. The worldly existence is neither true nor false. It is quite different from such things as sky-flower, hare's horn, etc., which have got no objective validity and are non-existent. It is also different from the ultimate Reality which is pure existence. But it has got an empiric existence of its own. As it is not existent in the pure and absolute sense of the term. it is something false, though it is not false in the sense of non-existence which is the characteristic of sky-flower, hare's horn, etc.

Against this it might be contended that Madhusūdana's logic suffers from self-contradiction. If the notions of truth and falsity be taken as contrary but not contradictory as held by the critics, the question is how the two contrary concepts, truth and falsity, can co-exist in the phenomenal world? For the co-presence of cowhood and horsehood in a particular substrate is a logical absurdity.

Madhusūdana, in support of his position, argues that truth and falsity attributed to the phenomenal appearance do not possess the same form of being or existence; they must differ in their respective value. For it is an universally accepted principle in logic that the two contradictory marks attributed to the same location or *dharmin* must not possess the same degree of being or reality. This *vyāpti* or universal law definitely proves that the notion of validity or reality concerning the empirically false existences must not be empiric or pragmatic. It may either be absolute or imaginary. Now it cannot be absolute for the negation of pragmatic or empiric truth necessitates the negation of the absolute reality as well. Pragmatic validity means the notion of being or reality not contradicted at the time of usage *(vyavahārakālābādhyatva)* in the practical affairs of life. Now when such a notion of uncontradictability is denied, its contradictory, the notion of falsity or contradictability at the time of pragmatic usages is posited or affirmed. And what is contradictable in the pragmatic life is absolutely uncontradictable *(abādhita),* is a logical absurdity. Hence the notion of reality existing in the concrete manifolds must be *prātibhāṣika* or imaginary. Such a position does not suffer from contradiction. Take for example the oyster-silver; the empirically false oyster-silver also appears as real and misleads the man to pick it up. Had there been no notion of reality, the man would not run after it. The silver only appears as real and such an appearance of reality can be assigned to the empirically false silver because the false silver and its notion of reality do not possess the same grade of reality, the one (falsity) is pragmatic while the other, the notion of reality is merely an appearance or imaginary, and they co-exist in the silver.[34]

The Advaitins further establish, against the said *vyāpti*, the co-presence of truth and falsity possessing the same form of empiric being or existence. To support their standpoint the Advaitins contend that the valid conception of unreality or falsity attributed to the phenomenal appearances merely falsifies but does not remove the conception of existent truth, it gives an intellectual assurance and only invalidates the existing notion of reality *(apramātva-niścayo bhavati)* which is, in fact, finally removed at the dawn of supreme consciousness. The notion of truth, attributed to the phenomenal world, is not contradicted by any valid conception other than that of the *Brahman;* hence it cannot be called *prātibhāsika* or imaginary. It is empiric or pragmatic. Both the notions of truth and falsity of phenomenality being denied at the dawn of transcendental consciousness share in the common value of empiric reality. In support of their co-existence, though they are contrary concepts, Madhusūdana argues that as in the theory of the Naiyāyikas conjunction *(saṁyoga)* and its negation, which are of the same nature of being *(samasattāka),* co-exist in the same location, so truth and falsity, the two contrary notions of the same order of being, reside in the same substrate.

It might, of course, be noted here against Madusūdana's observation that conjunction and its negation does not really exist in the same location, for the space-position is not the same but different. Monkey-conjunction *(kapisaṁyoga)* is at the branch of a tree and its negation lies at the root. How then is Madhusūdana's logic justified? It might be argued in his favour that as through different space-position, contradictory notions, *e.g.*, position and negation, may co-exist in one substrate, so in the monistic thesis the contradictory notions of truth and falsity may co-exist as they fall in different orders of time; in other words, they appear pragmatically true and are known to be false only at the dawn of transcendental consciousness. The real logic establishing the equal being or existence of truth and falsity lies in the fact that the two are negated by a single conception, e.g., the knowledge of *Brahman (ekabādhakajñānabādhya)*. When the transcendental consciousness dawns upon us both the notions of falsity and truth of the phenomenal appearance are denied. And such a denial proves that truth and falsity share in equal being or existence, and they, being negated at the dawn of supreme consciousness when all the empiric existences are at nought, are denied in point of objectivity which is the common ground of denial and not merely as true or false. It is an invariable law that two or more notions negated by one contradictive apprehension *(bādhakajñāna)* share in the common being *(samasattā)*. For example, the perception of oyster which negates the idea of silver negates also the exclusion of oyster in the oyster thus both the oyster-silver and the exclusion of oyster in the oyster are called imaginary or *samānasattāka*. Negatively, the pot and the oyster-silver are not negated by one apprehension but by two apprehensions—(a) the trascendental consciousness and (b) the perception of oyster, and they are not called *samānasattāka;* the pot is empirically valid while the silver is imaginary or *prātibhāsika*. The given arguments definitely prove that the world order and its notion of truth and falsity share in the common existence or being. Of the two contradictory marks when the proof of one negates the other, they do not share in the common being and are called *viṣamasattāka* in their nature. In the mother-of-pearls, we have two contradictory concepts, silver and its negation. Of the two the judgment 'this is not silver' which establishes the absolute negation of silver, negates only the notion of silver itself and hence the notion of silver and of its negation do not share in the common being. The oyster-silver is *prātibhāsika* or imaginary but its negation is an empirically valid concept. Truth and falsity of the phenomenal world are, as we have already seen in our previous discussion, *parasparavirahavyāpya* and thus the proof of one does not establish the falsity of the other and they cannot be styled *viamasattāka,* but being negated by the dawn of supreme consciousness share in the same value or being. One supreme consciousness denies the notion of falsity existing in the world order, the world order itself and its notion of validity as well. Thus the Mādhva charge of duality or plurality deduced from the truth or falsity of falsehood totally falls through.[35]

REFERENCES

1. Vimataṁ (jagat) mithyā dṛśyatvāt
2. N. Mr. T., p. 23.
3. Jagat satyaṁ mithyābhūta-mithyātvakatvād ātmavat.
4. Sādhyasya vyāpako yastu hetoravyāpakastathā sa upādhirbhavet. Bh. P. and S. M. on. Śl. 83.
5. Sarve sādhya-samānādhikaraṇāḥ syurupādhayaḥ.
   Hetorekāśraye yeṣāṁ svasādhya-vyabhicāritā.
   Vyabhicārasyānumānamupādhestu prayojanam.
   Bh. P. śls. 87, 88 and S. M. on śls.: 87, 88.
6. Jagat satyaṁ mithyābhūta-mithyātmakatvāt ātmavat.
7. Mithyābhūta-mithyātmakatvaṁ satyatva-vyabhicāri ātmatva-vya-bhicārāt yathā śuktirajatam.
8. Jagat satyam mitbyahhūta-mithyātmakatvāt ātmavat.
9. Svarūpāsiddha, the unreal in itself is that reason which does not exist in the subject and therefore cannot afford the basis of any reasoning, as in the propositions "the lake is a substance because it has smoke. — Bh. P. S.M., śl. 57.
10. The counter-balanced reason *(satpratipakṣa)* is one for which there exists another reason which proves contrary of the consequence. In it the reason is simply rendered inconclusive by the existence of an argument opposed to it of equal weight.
11. The too general reason or *Sādhāraṇa* is found not only in the similar instances, but also in the opposite instances; the possession of horns does not make an animal an ox, nor has the mountain fire because it can be known. —Bh. P. 2, M., śl. 52; T. S. p. 12.
12. Rūpyaṁ mithyābhūta-mithyātvādhikaraṇaṁ na bhavati satyabhūta-(tadviruddha)-satyatvānadhikaraṇatvāt yat satyabhūta-tadviruddhādḥi-karaṇaṁ na bhavati tanmithyābhūta-adadhikaraṇaṁ na bhavati, yathāsatyabhūta-gotva-viruddha-gotvābhāvānadhikaraṇaṁ gauḥ gotvābhāva-viruddha-mithyābhūta-gotvādhikaraṇaṁ na bhavati. Nyāyāmrtataraṅgiṇī, p. 24.
13. Tathā ca rūpyamịthyātvasya satyatvena rūpye hetorevāgamanānna vyabhicāra iti bhāvaḥ, Nyāyāmṛtataraṅgiṇī, p. 24.
14. (a) Nyāyāmṛta, p. 43.
    (b) Rūpyagataṁ mithyātvaṁ mithyā avidyamāna-dharmikatvādi tya-numānamuktaṁ bhavati. —Nyāyāmṛta-Prakāśa, p. 43,
15. Rūpyagatatvena ucyamāne satyatvamithyātve mithyā-mithyātvopeta-dharmikatvāt svapnapratīta-gajarūpavaditi. —Nyāyāmṛtataraṅginī, p. 24.

16. Jagacca satyam syādityuktānumānasya rūpye vyabhicāraḥ tadavastha iti. *Ibid,* p. 24.
17. Suktirajataṁ mithyābhūta-mithyātvādhikaraṇaṁ na bhavati satya-bhūta-(mithyatva-viruddha)-satyatvānadhikaraṇatvāt.
18. Tatra amithyātvamupādhiḥ ataḥ tasya hīnabalatvāt tena na asya sat-pratipakṣ itatvam, ato rūpye hetujñāna-saṁbhavāt vyabhicāraḥ tadavastha iti. —Nyāyāmṛtataraṅgiṇī, p. 24
19. (a) *Vide* Nyāyāmṛta, p. 43.
    (b) Na hi satyabhūtasya gauratvaviruddha-śyamatvasya anadhikaraṇe bandhyāsute tad viruddhaṁ gauratvam mithyābhūtaṁ nāsti kintu satyabhūtaṁ gauratvamastiti yujyate kintu gauratvam tadviruddham śyāmatvañcetyubhayamapi bandhyāsute mithyaiva dhariniṇa eva mithyātvāt. —Nyāyamṛtataraṅgiṇī, p. 24.
20. We have already explained the *vyāpya-vyāpaka* relation in connexion with the definition of truth and falsity or *sattva* and *asattva* in the previous chapter.
21. (a) *Vide* Nyāyāmṛta, p. 43.
    (b) Rūpyagate mithyātva-satyatve mithyā avidyamāna-dharmikatvādityanumānena ubhayorapi mithyātvāvagamena mithyābhūta-mithyātmakatvasya jagatsatyatvasādhakasya rūpye vyabhicāraḥ sustha iti ḥrdayam. Nyāyāmṛta-Prakāśa, p. 44.
    (c) *Vide* Nyāyāmṛtataraṅgiṇī, pp. 24-25.
22. Rūpyagataṁ mithyātvaṁ mithyā avidyamānadharmikatvāt, rūpya-gatatvena ucyamāne satyatva-mithyātve mithyā mithyātvopeta-dharmikat-vāt svapnapratītagajavaditi. *Ibid,* p. 25.
23. Pratipannopādhau traikālikaniṣedhapratiyogitvaṁ mithyātvam.
24. Mithyātvantu dharmibhūta-prapañca-satyatvasya viraharūpam ataḥ dharmisatyaṅ nāpekṣate pratyuta dharmibhūta-prapañca-satyatvaṁ pratikṣipatītyarthaḥ. Nyāyāmṛtaprakāśa, p. 44.
25. Rūpyagataṁ mithyātvaṁ mithyā avidyamāna-dharmikatvāt.
26. Loke atyantābhāvapratiyogitvarūpa-dharmasya dharmisattva-prati-kūlatvasyaiva darśanāt. Nyāyāmṛtaprakāśa, p. 44.
27. Mithyābhūta-mithyātmakatvaṁ satyatvavyabhicāri ātmatva-vyabhicārat yathā śuktirajatam.
28. Pratipannopādhau aniṣiddhaṁ pratyuta bādhakajñānena vihitamapi rūpyamithyātvaṁ yadi prātibhāsika-rūpyasambandhamātreṇa prātibhā-sikam tarhi sati Brahmaṇi niṣiddhā api dharmāḥ santaḥ syuḥ rūpyādhiṣhāriaśuktirapi prātibhāsikī syāt. "Nyāyāmṛta, p. 44.
29. *(a)* Rūpya-mithyātva-mithyātvam mithyā mithyābhūta-rūpyatmithyātvadharmikatvāt. Nyāyāmṛta-prakāśa, p. 45.
    (b) Tvaduktena dharmiṇo mithyātvena hetunā sādhyasya mithyātvamithyātvasyāpi prātibhāsikatvāpattyā hetoḥ atyantāprāmāṇyañca syāt. Nyāyāmṛta, p. 44.
30. Na svapne'pi dvayaṁ mithyā tatraikaṁ satyameva hi.

31. Jagat satynṁ mithyābhūta-mithyātmakatvāt.
32. Tatra hi viruddhayordharmayorekamithyātve aparasatyatvaṁ yatra mithyātvāvaccheda-kamubhayavṛtti na bhayet. Advaitasiddhi, pp. 211-12.
33. *Vide* Viṭṭhaleśopādhyāyī, the gloss on the Gauda Brahmānandī, p. 213. Mithyātvasatyatvayormithyātvasyasvasamānādhikaraṇābhāva-pratiyogitvarūpatvāt satyatvasya kālatrayābūdhyatvarūpatvāt anayośca na paṛasparābhāvarūpatvam, na vā paraspara-viraha-vyāpakatvam; tucche uktamithyātvoktasatyatvayordvayorapi virahāt, kintu mitho viruddhatvamātram; śuktirajatādau mithyābhūte satyatvābhāvāt Brahmaṇi satye mithyātvābhāvāditi.
34. *Vide* Advaitasiddhi, p. 216.
35. Asti ca prapañcatanmithyātvayoreka Brahmajñanabādhyatvam, ataḥ samasattākatvāt mithyātvabādhakena prapañcasyāpi bādhāt na advaitakṣatiḥ. Advaitasiddhi, p. 222.

CHAPTER 7

SUPER-IMPOSITION

We have seen that phenomenal appearances are merely inexplicable forms and not so many realities. They appear as real because they are referred to the Highest Reality which forms their ultimate substratum. It is due to the apparent identity with the permanent substratum that the worldly appearances, though false, appear as independently real in our perception. In perception we cognise only the empirical forms but not the underlying reality which though a-logical, expresses itself as logical, a-material as material, non-temporal as temporal and non-spatial as spatial. This tendency of mistaking the form for reality or reality for the form is commonly called, in the Advaita-Vedānta, *Adhyāsa* or super-imposition. The essence of super-imposition lies in not seeing a thing as it is, and in placing upon it a different interpretation or construction. Super-imposition is thus mal-observation connoting ignorance of something and extension of a false idea to an actual appearance. It is a misjudgment of the data presented to the senses by a pre-conceived idea. It is purely a subjective construction bearing no correspondence to the reality.

An explanation of the position

When in perception, a thing appears to the perceiver as mere existence, a fact whose special nature is for the time being hidden, and it is studied only as a presentation and the mind supplies, on the basis of similarity, some representative elements which are falsely attributed to the presentation where they are really not. This wrong unification of presentation and representation is called *adhyāsa* or a false notion. Presentation or the fact as a mere existence is not screened from the view of the perceiver who mistakes one thing for another. If the thing is totally shut up from the view, no mistake can be committed without any basis or locus. Presentation is the basis of false show upon which on the ground of superficial similarity a wrong notion is apprehended. Presentation therefore cannot altogether be denied but so long as *avidyā* is operative it is falsely interpreted. It being a mal-observation, depends upon the dim or partial perception of an object which forms the basis of mis-judgment. Whenever the object is clearly and distinctly viewed there is no possibility of confusion. It is therefore possible only in the case where the object—the locus of the false show appears only partially as a fact, as a mere existence without its true and distinct characteristics. Vācaspati is therefore right in assuming that *adhyāsa* is not possible when a thing is either distinctly seen or entirely hidden.[1]

On the strength of similarity, the memory-image is revived in the mind of the percipient and memory supplies representative factors of judgment which are erroneously attributed to the presentation. And though the false notion is a creation of mind without any objective validity of its own yet it is quite distinct from memory which is purely mental in its character, having no objective reference outside the mind. In false show though forms of judgment are supplied by the mind as representative elements, the forms are identified with the fact existing outside and as a result some form of *extra-mentality* of the object of false notion is apprehended. In this respect it is quite different from memory. If a memory impression is cognised as a memory impression without any reference to the extra-mental objects, there is no possibility of its confusion with the wrong notion whose extra-mental character cannot be questioned. Herein lies the true essence of super-imposition in which there is a confusion of mental forms as extra-mental facts.

An analysis of the super-imposed idea

To bring out more clearly the nature of super-imposition an instance may be analysed in three stages. The first stage is a stage of pure presentation, the second is one of correction and the last is a stage of confirmation. In the first stage, some thing is presented to the perceiver and the idea of silver in the case of oyster-silver flashes out to his mind and the idea is believed as real though it is not confirmed as real from the standpoint of pragmatic life. Only its reality is not denied for the time being, as no contradiction as yet strikes the percipient subject. In the case of pure presentation, the 'thisness' is a correct perception and remains as correct so long as it is not synthesised with some other predicative idea supplied by the mind to form a judgment. In this judgment construction, the 'thisness' is first synthesised with the predicative idea of silver which is believed as really presented and a judgment is formed. There is as yet no objective reference in the predicative aspect of the judgment and its reality is not questioned. The simple belief underlying this judgment is then corrected by the perception of the oyster as oyster. And the oyster is affirmed as real in contrast with the illusory silver. Silver is illusory because immediate quality of unreality has been attributed to it as a result of its failure to satisfy any pragmatic test. When the correct judgment is affirmed the predicate of the previous judgment is denied as unreal. The perceiver realises that his idea of silver is a pure mental presentation without any objective basis and that the synthesis is wrong. Here the affirmative predicate only proves the unreality of the first impression and the first idea is eliminated. But there is a relation between these two predicates and it is a unique one. The unreal silver by its elimination implies the real oyster, which being an objectively valid entity is in no way affected by the unreality of the silver. The oyster is an entity complete in itself; the false conception of silver has no influence over it.

This is the stage of rectification. In this stage we are directly concerned only with the objective content. In the given example the idea of silver was first presented to the percipient subject and in the next stage when the idea of oyster is affirmed as real the silver though presented becomes illusory. The silver is a mental creation though at the time of perception it appears as an objectively valid entity adequate to satisfy the demand of pragmatic life and when it is negated it becomes purely subjective. Thus the objectivity of silver is beyond question at the time of appearance so long as it is not corrected. It is not presented as a merely subjective fact but as an objectively presented reality. As an object of past perception its objective character cannot be questioned. Falsity arises as a result of wrong identification of silver with the 'thisness.' And when the idea of oyster is affirmed the illusory character of silver is established. Silver which was perceived as an objectively valid existence, is now cognised as non-existent not only for the present moment but also when it happened to be perceived as real. Thus the non-existence of illusory silver on the 'thisness' is proved in the case of the past as well as the present presentation and it might very well be inferred therefore that it will be non-existent also in the case of future presentation of the 'thisness.' And its unreality is established as the silver did not exist, does not exist and will not exist. The test of workability comes next and determines its validity from the practical standpoint. The silver being a mere subjective contribution cannot satisfy any demand of practical life, for when the percipient wants to deal with it in any manner, it fails to work. In this stage also facthood of silver as an object of remembrance is not denied even when unreality is attributed to it. Hence the unreal silver is not a merely subjective fiction in so far as it is based on the memory of past perception. Thus the illusory silver is neither really subjective as hallucination having its basis in the remembrance of past experience, nor really objective having failed to satisfy pragmatic demands and cannot consequently be covered by either category. It should therefore be placed in a separate category which the Advaitins call inexplicable or *anirvacanīya*. The unreal silver is neither a positive nor a negative entity. It is neither an absolute nought *(tuccha)* like the sky-flower, hare's horn, etc. nor absolutely real. It appears in the first stage and is negated in the second and does not therefore come within the categories of existence or non-existence *(sadasadvilakṣaṇa)*. It is a new category which shares in the characteristics of both position and negation and therefore a middle category between the two, positive-negative in its character. The illusory silver is perceived and hence distinguished from the absolute nought *(tuccha)* which cannot be perceived as object of experience. Again it is not an absolute reality as it can be negated and absolute reality can never be negated. The silver is perceived as well as negated it is therefore neither absolute nought nor an absolute reality.[2]

Illusory objects are entirely new creation due to Avidyā

The presentation of silver on the locus in oyster-silver super-imposition is not a mere objectification of a memory-image. It is, on the contrary, an entirely new creation due to the operation of *avidyā* which has a twofold capacity—screening and creation. If the silver were an objectification of a past memory-image the form of judgment-should have been 'this is that silver,' instead of the form 'this is silver' and in this very illustration, this twofold capacity is equally patent, *Avidyā* here screens the real nature of the 'this' or locus which is oyster by shutting out from view its special features and creates a new silver which the percipient cognises. The silver we see in erroneous perception, says Vācaspati, is not that of the market but is an entirely new creation on the mother-of-pearl—a novel appearance in a definite point of time and space and this spatial and temporal mark is sufficient to indicate its existence as different from a similar object perceived in a different place at a different time. When however this particular appearance is declared false, it is never intended to deny the existence of silver as such elsewhere. All that is implied is that in this particular spatio temporal reference, *i.e.,* on this locus, the elsewhere-existing silver is not negated. From this it is not however to be understood that the silver of this false appearance is purely imaginary *(alīka)* like hare's horn, sky-flower, etc., for it appears in consciousness with a particular spatio-temporal reference which is wanting in purely imaginary ideas. And this screening operation of ignorance or *Avidyā* may be interpreted, without affecting the final result, from two different points of view. From the objective side, which has been emphasised by *Sarvajñātmamuni* in his *Saṁkṣ-epaśārīraka,* it is argued that ignorance or *Avidyā* which is the substance-stuff of the false appearance, hides the determinate qualities of the 'this,' *i.e.*, the underlying oyster and so long as the specific ignorance of the determinate qualities of oyster remains, the illusory perception of silver continued. From the subjective side *Nṛsiṁha Bhaṭṭa* contends that illusory perceptions are due to the defects in sense organs resulting from association and other causes. He however does not deny the presence of *Avidyā* or ignorance as a substance-stuff of illusory perception. On the contrary, he shows that as soon as the *Avidyā* inherent in the 'this' comes into contact with the defective sense organ, the real cause of false perception, it undergoes a vibratory modification and transforms itself into the silver.[3]

If the illusory silver is a new creation as is admitted by the monistic teachers, the question inevitably arises—of what stuff is the new creation made or in other words what is the material cause of it? It is, of course, *Avidyā* and we have to determine what must be the nature of *Avidyā* if it is to be the material cause. *Ānandabodha Bhaṭṭarakācārya* in his *Nyāyamakaranda* has given an account of *Avidyā* as the material cause of the illusory perception; This *Avidyā* cannot be mere false knowledge, nor absence of knowledge nor both; for it would then be without substantiality, implying mere absence, and the, effect, *i.e.*, the false appearance having objectivity the unsubstantial *Avidyā* cannot be its material cause. *Avidyā,* therefore, has to be conceived as something unique, beginningless and indescribable having substantiality of its own because the existence of such a material cause is testified to by its effects, for it won't do to argue that mere instrumental cause can produce an effect without a material cause; all effects except *dhvaṁsa* or destruction must be produced by material cause. Further the material cause of illusory perception cannot be absolutely real; for the effect, *i.e.*, illusory perception, would then be real; nor can the material cause be absolutely unreal, for the latter being devoid of any capacity of its own cannot produce the illusory object even. Hence the material cause of illusion must be something which is neither absolutely real or absolutely unreal.[4]

To sum up, the real essence of the *Anirvacanīya* theory of the Advaita-Vedānta as propounded by Śaṁkara in his exposition of *Adhyāsa* and developed by other advocates of the monistic school, is that appearances are inexplicable and mysterious as their *causa materia avidyā* is inexplicable and mysterious in its character. *Avidyā* as becoming principle creates new appearances in erroneous conception. Objects of normal perception as well come under this category; as the time-space-cause world also owes its origin to the mysterious power of *Māyā* and is super-imposed on the Absolute Being. The principle therefore is the same in the normal and abnormal perception. But the *Advaita-Vedānta* draws a distinction between the false percept and normal percept, the normal percept though super-imposed persists to the last while the abnormal one is denied in our pragmatic life.

Śaṁkara's theory is a *via media* between the rigorous idealism of the *Vijñānavādi-Buddhists* and the extreme realism of the Nyāya and Vaiśeṣika systems. And though Śaṁkara and his school strenuously fought against the *Vijñānavādins,* a close examination of the two positions strikingly reveals an agreement and parallelism between them in some important respects as will appear from an analysis of the *Vijñānavādins'* view as explained in the *Laṅkāvatārasūtra,* an authoritative literature of this school. Thus we get the view of *Māyā* characterised as *anirvacanīya,* unambiguous declaration of the reality of consciousness, the invalid character of the external world, the emphasis laid on *adhyāropa* (super-imposition) and *apavāda* (elimination) and a gradation of reality and so forth, equally fully developed in both schools. It will therefore be interesting to note the development of these ideas according to the *Ātmakhyātivādins* or *Vijñānavādins* who hold that both normal and abnormal perceptions are the result of a modification of consciousness.

The Ātmakhyātivāda or Vijñānavāda

Vijñānavādins[5] maintain that there is neither any necessity nor any justification for upholding the existence of an external world of objects either as directly perceived or as indirectly inferred from the diversification of our ideas. They argue that logical knowledge or knowledge necessitated by our practical life results as a consequence of the activity of the understanding. When anything is taken cognizance of by the understanding, knowledge diversifies into a knower *(pramātā),* known *(prameya)* and instruments of knowledge *(pramāṇa),* and experience arises; where there is no cognizance by the understanding no cognition is generated. For instance, of the things outside the understanding, only those that come within its grasp can occasion any idea or cognition. Hence, it follows that it is the understanding which is the creator of this diversification of experience and the objects revealed in or by it have no existence apart from the understanding. The understanding or, as they put it, *Vijñāna,* therefore, only is real and not the so-called external objects. If it is objected that the understanding by itself alone is not adequate to explain the manifold nature of experience without the assumption of external objects or *grāhyavastu,* it can be demonstrated to be so by reference to dreams or illusions where the same diversification of the knower, known and knowledge as in waking experience is generated by the activity of the understanding without the presence of any objects, *i.e., grāhyavastu.* This fact is bound to be admitted on all hands. It is therefore clear that the understanding alone might be responsible for the distinction of knower, known and knowledge. Knowledge or *pratyaya* is thus produced without the help of external objects.[6] The problem therefore now resolves itself into the question as to whether there is any distinction between waking experience and dream experience. It might be said that waking experience has got what may be called *samvādakatva, i.e.,* the power of enabling us to attain the object perceived; while the objects of dream experience are admittedly illusory and unreal, as they might be contradicted. The real problem therefore is what is to be understood by the *saṁvādakatva,* or what does constitute the validity of waking experience?

A close consideration of this question shows that waking experience is to be admitted as valid because its objects are real; whereas dream experience is invalid because its objects are unreal. This leads to an examination of what is meant by objects of waking experience being real. What then are we to understand by the reality of the external objects? From the Vijñānavādins' standpoint, nay, from the point of view of all Buddhistic metaphysics, only momentary existence is real and everything else is unreal. Hence how can, for example, the steady appearance of things be taken as real, seeing that it is the result of taking the series of momentary vibrations which alone are real, as non-momentary or *sthira?*

Thus objects cognised as non-momentary or *sthira* are merely false appearances.[7] Knowledge derived from waking experience being vitiated by the false appearance of objects is therefore of the same category as dream experiences.

Moreover it might also be said that idea and its objects being always cognised together are not two different things but are one and the same thing; for it is a universally accepted principle that things experienced and cognised together always and invariably, such as blue and idea of blue, are identical and not different.[8]

Finally, it is also clear that the diversification spoken of is nothing but a mere modification of consciousness. In other words, we are not aware or conscious of any diversification beyond the range of consciousness. So it is but natural and inevitable that we should identify this diversification with the form of consciousness or understanding. Hence the object so called is not something outside the consciousness or understanding but a mere modification of it. Jayanta Bhaṭṭa also explains the view thus : since nothing outside the range of the understanding is cognisable and since knowledge always assumes diverse forms of necessity, it is to be concluded that it is understanding which gives or generates those diverse forms without any so-called external objects outside the under-standing.[9]

Jayanta Bhaṭṭa further explains that even admitting for the sake of argument that there are external objects, it is to be noticed that cognition or *jñāna* is capable of giving diverse forms of itself; for it is cognition which first gives rise to the idea of the object and it is through this definitely formed idea that we can know or speak of the object, and not that the so-called object comes first to give shape and form to the idea. Cognition or knowledge is thus not without form of its own. Hence, according to the logical law of 'parsimony,' it is unnecessary and wrong to assume that it is the so-called objects which give rise to different forms of cognition. An example perhaps will make this clearer : when it is said, "I have known the pot" it is the cognition which comes first and gives definite shape to the idea of the pot. So the assumption of the external objects is redundant and unnecessary.[10]

The author of *Śāstradīpikā* also in explicating the position appeals to popular verdict. A man ordinarily speaks of an object as blue because his cognition has the form of blue. If, however, cognition is supposed to give its own form, the question is bound to arise as to how the distinction between cognition and the thing cognised is felt in the very act of perception The author of *Sāstradīpikā* and his commentator answer this question by saying that there being no external objects cognisable beyond the range of cognition, it is cognition itself which appears to us in the shape or form of external objects. In other words, the relation between cognition *(grahaṇa)* and the thing cognised *(grāhya)* is one of *tādātmya* or identity. But owing to non-apprehension of this identity, they appear as two distinct and different things.[11]

According to the *Vijñānavādin's* position, there are two aspects of knowledge—one referring to what might be called its '*samāropa,*' super-imposed or phenomenal aspect, *i.e.,* the aspect in which knowledge ordinarily appears to us; the other aspect might be called its '*apavāda*' or real or metaphysical aspect in which it appears in its true nature rising superior to the false notions or super-imposition.[12] The two aspects might also be called the *khyāti* aspect or the aspect in which knowledge appears to us only, and the *nirodha* aspect or the aspect in which it returns upon the ultimate reality which is its true nature. These two aspects of knowledge have been very elaborately dealt with by the author of the *Laṅkāvatārasūtra*.

Perception does not give us the true nature of reality of objects. This happens as a result of what the author of the *Laṅkāvatārasūtra* calls *samāropa* or super-imposition which consists in taking one thing for another as when we mistake a rope for a snake or the illusory world for reality. What then is the nature of the *samāropa?* It consists of four forms of varieties according to the *Laṅkāvatārasūtra, viz.,* (a) *Asattrikṣaṇasamāropa* or the super-imposition of *trikṣaṇa* or trimomentary existence of the object though it is really momentary or *kṣaṇika*. In other words, this means that though the object, and for the matter of that, reality is momentary, still it is cognised as enduring for at least three moments or stages such as origination, duration and destruction, as admitted by all Indian systems holding external objects to be real. But this is not true according to the nihilistic school of Buddhism, *(b) Asaddṛṣṭi-samāropa* or the super-imposition of a wrong notion of things. Thus there is here a false appearance of something steady though really it is momentary, (c) *Asaddhetu-samāropa* or the super-imposition of a cause falsely. This means that though really, according to this school, knowledge or cognition is without any cause being itself the only beginningless reality, still particular perceptions falsely appear to be caused or occasioned by such and such organs of sense, conjoined with representative elements supplied by memory, etc. This ascription of cause to something causeless is thus a false super-imposition, *(d) Asadbhāva-samāropa* or the false super-imposition of existence *(bhāva)* and non-existence *(abhāva)* to things. For, according to this school, the visible manifoldness of this world is as false as the ascription of horns to a hare. Still people are apt to classify things falsely under either existence or non-existence though really things are beyond the range of both existence or non-existence.[13]

Analysing deeper and more closely, the author of the *Laṅkāvatārasūtra* classifies twelve varieties of cognition called *vikalpas* which arise as a result of the super-imposition already discussed. Thus there are the *Abhidheya-vikalpa, Lakṣaṇavikalpa* and *Abhilāpavikalpa* and so on which by their separate and conjoint action make the world appear to us falsely as a manifold variety.

This false super-imposition together with all these *vikalpas* is due to the beginningless desire or what is also called by him *Māya* or *Avidyā.*[14] The relation of this Māyā to the manifold universe is neither identical nor different; it cannot be altogether different and distinct from the universe for the manifold universe itself, as already shown, is the result of this Māyā; nor can it be identical with the universe seeing that it is something over and above this manifoldness. It is therefore *anyānanyavivarjita,* is something beyond identity and non-identity. Hence it cannot be regarded as either existent or non-existent or in other words, it is something which is inexplicable.[15]

This aspect is what is called *khyātivijñāna* or *samāropa, i.e.,* phenomenal aspect of knowledge by means of which the affairs of practical life are carried on. The other aspect of knowledge is what is called *apavāda, i.e.,* metaphysical aspect or knowledge which consists in turning away from or realising the false character of knowledge as generated by *samāropa* or, as Śaṁkara would put it, *adhyāsa* described before. *Apavāda* or metaphysical knowledge eliminates falsely super-imposed knowledge and turns the mind towards reality; for *apavāda* means literally that something is *apavādyate, i.e.,* eliminated. It is only when there is nothing to be eliminated as due to super-imposition or *vikalpa* that true knowledge or intuitive vision of the Buddha *(Buddha-netṛtva)* might be said to be attained. Thus when there is a complete destruction of the mental modifications or super-imposition that *Nirvāṇa* is attained. The final result of the *Vijñānavādins'* position is that according to it the empirical knowledge, such as 'this is oyster' is as much the creation of consciousness *(Ālayavijñāna)* as the so-called objects of false knowledge, *e.g.,* silver in mistaking oyster for silver. Thus normal (empirical) and abnormal (illusory) perception is on the same level, the *Ālayavijñāna* itself appearing as the object in both. The falsity of erroneous perception consists in the wrong objectification or spatio-temporal reference of the purely mental image of silver. For the silver as idea is real and cognising of this real mental image as something external constitutes error of false perception and though the silver might be negated in the 'this' or locus, its reality as a mental image is unquestionable. Thus contrary to the generally accepted view they hold that it is really the thisness of appearance which is false and not the idea *(i.e.,* silver) whose reality as a form of consciousness cannot be gainsaid.

Refutation of the Vijñānavāda or Ātmakhyātivāda

Against this fundamental position of the *Vijñānavāda* that knowledge is without any corresponding reality *(vijñānaṁ niralaṁbanam)* all Brahmanical schools of Philosophy direct their attack. They all argue that particular forms of perception or cognition are all due to external objects. Śaṁkara, Rāmānuja and other Vedāntic schools argue that in cognition, the objects such as the pot, cloth, etc., are always perceived as something external and not as a mere form of cognition. In other words, no one cognises those objects as cognition itself, but only as objects of cognition having extramental reality. Moreover, the very arguments that cognition itself takes on forms of objects and that cognition itself appears as something external or extramental, presuppose or imply that there are objects which are external or extramental; for in the absolute absence or non-existence of external objects, how is it possible to speak or conceive of them? Besides, the argument that the simultaneous presence of the perception and its objects implies their non-difference or identity has not much force in it; for *abheda* or non-difference itself means that there is a prior difference, since if there be not two separate things how could you speak of their non-difference or identity? The explanation of the manifold variety of consciousness as being due to different desires is also unsatisfactory, for in the first place the whole position is directly opposed to all experience. Experience shows that the different desires are excited or evoked by different objects. And it is a reversal of the true order of experience to maintain that it is the desires or *vāsanās* which arouse or excite a consciousness of manifold objects. Lastly, the analogy of dream consciousness is not applicable to perceptual or cognitional knowledge. For dream consciousness is contradicted and falsified by waking consciousness and is due to certain faults in its causation such as sleep, etc. But true perception or cognition as distinguished from false perception is never contradicted or falsified and is free from any fault in its causation. Thus there is a fundamental difference between dream consciousness and waking con-sciousness and it is not permissible to infer on the dream analogy that there are no extramental objects in cognition just because there are no such objects in dream consciousness. Moreover, dream consciousness is not without objects as maintained by the Vijñānavādin. There are undoubtedly objects present in dream consciousness though these objects have not the same vividness as the objects of waking consciousness. Besides mere idealism as advocated by the Vijñānavādin is unable to explain worldly activity or practical life; for in life external objects play an important part and, as has been already shown, such idealism is contrary to all facts of experience. Hence it is to be concluded that no experience or knowledge is possible without extramental reality or objects.

An estimate of the Ātmakhyātivāda of Vijñānavāda

The main points of attack against the Vijñānavādin' s position advanced by all the orthodox Brahmanical schools including the Advaita Vedānta might be reduced to two. Firstly, that external objects cannot be regarded as mere forms of consciousness in so far as in cognising them the form of consciousness is not that they are cognitions but that they are something beyond and other than cognition, having an outward reference; secondly, that in the Vijñānavādin's view the broad and unmistakable difference between dream and waking consciousness would altogether be obliterated, both being forms of consciousness only. It might be, however, noted in passing that it is not merely the Brahmanical schools which attack the Vijñānavādins in this way. Another school within Buddhism itself, *viz.*, the *Sautrāntikas* [16] also made these two weak spots in the Vijñānavāda epistemology the target of their attack. With regard to the first point, the *Sautrāntikas* hold that it would not do to say that because cognition and the cognised object appear simultaneously in consciousness, there is no difference between the two, for to argue thus would be against all canons of proof or reasoning. If there were no difference, the form of cognition would be 'I am blue' and not 'this is blue.' Moreover the cognition is inward-looking while the object has outward reference. Nor would it suffice to hold that owing to mistake, the blue appears as if it were modification of consciousness. For, if there be nothing external, how can you say "as if it were an external object?" It would be as absurd as to say that Vasumitra appears to be the son of a barren woman. The very fact that you have to speak of 'as if it were external' implies a real external world and your denial of it returns upon and hits you like a boomerang.[17] Again to maintain this non-difference between cognitions and the cognised would lead to a logical fallacy. For identity or non-difference can be proved only when the manifestation of difference is shown to be illusory. In other words, identity postulates a prior difference.[18]

A close examination of the Vijñānavādin's position however shows that the above criticism is based on a misunderstanding or distortion of his position. It is as a reaction against the crude materialists, dualists and realists that the Vijñānavādins develop their theory of idealism and therefore appear to fall into the opposite error of solipsism or mentalism. This however is not the true position of *Vijñānavāda* or *Yogācāra* school of Buddhism The Vijñānavādins argue against the easy-going assumption of the realists that the mind is a self-contained reality confronted in experience by other self-contained things. Going behind the two substances of mind and matter they try to discover a comprehensive reality embracing the two. Like Kant in the West, with true philosophic insight, the Vijñānavādins urge that the whole objective world cannot exist without a transcendental apperceiving intellect or *Vijñāna* which is more than merely individual. Within this '*Vijñāna*' arises the distinction of subject and object. Hence the '*Ālayavijñāna*' of the Vijñānavādins is a fundamental fact of reality revealing itself in individual minds and things; for, all the manifold distinctions of experience such as subject and object, etc., appear in it because of the beginningless series of dualistic desire.[19] Thus the phenomenal existence of the world with its distinctions of subject and object is accepted by them. As Mādhavācārya in his *Sarvadarśanasaṁgraha* writes : "Nor must it be supposed that on this hypothesis, the juice, the energy and the digestion derivable from an imaginary and actual sweetmeat will be the same.[20] The Vijñānavādins therefore do not reduce the external world to an absolute nought but go further along with most other Buddhistic schools to discriminate between the threefold nature of knowledge or *Vijñāna* implying three grades of reality corresponding to them : *(i)* imagined nature *(Parikalpita), (ii)* dependent or caused nature *(Paratantra)* and *(iii)* absolute or metaphysical nature *(Parinispanna)*. In *Parikalpita,* the imagination is active without being controlled by the categories in the Kantian sense, *e.g.*, when a rope is mistaken for a snake. It cannot stand critical judgment and has no practical efficiency. *Paratantra* is empirical knowledge and is the work of the understanding, its categories having validity within experience. But the absolute reality cannot be known through this categorised knowledge.[21] *Parinispanna* is metaphysical insight through which it is possible to rise to the universal which exists as whole and undivided *Vijñāna* or consciousnesss. Plurality is due to subjection to space and time which are the principles of individuation. The highest stage of knowledge is thus the '*Ālayavijñāna*' which though not yet phenomenalised into the manifold by beginningless desire, is still a concrete reality according to the *Yogācāras;* for they admit only the reality of intellect with forms.[22] Moreover, in explaining the experience of the manifold the *Yogācāras* divide all things into two groups—*saṁskṛta* or composite and *asaṁskṛta*' or non-composite and admit such things as five '*skandhas*' or constituents, four '*dhātus*' or bases, and six '*āyatanas*' or locations, though the emphasis is laid by them on '*citta*' or mind and not, like the realists, on '*rūpa,*' *i.e.*, matter. Nāgārjuna reduces the first two to one'*saṁvṛtisattā,*' the other name of *Avidyā,* and calls the third '*paramārtha*' or the highest reality.[23]

The criticism of Śaṁkara and others would seem to be based on a misunderstanding; and the misunderstanding itself was generated by the fact that the Buddhistic writers and their Brahmanical expounders used language and illustrations which were liable to misinterpretation. Thus it is said that the waking consciousness is just like dream, that the distinction of knower, known and knowledge is false like the illusion of the double moon, etc.[24] Now this is surely apt to suggest that no distinction is drawn between dream and waking life. Moreover, in other places the Buddhists have emphasised the false character of all existence consistently with their view of the non-validity of all knowledge *(svataḥ aprāmāṇya);* for if normal knowledge is naturally invalid, it stands to reason that the so-called universe is unreal. All this led to the impression that the Vijñānāvādins do not distinguish between waking consciousness and dream. But a closer scrutiny of their position would show that the criticism is misapplied and beside the point. The Vijñānavādins took care to emphasise that due to the activity of '*saṁvṛti*' or *avidyā* the waking consciousness is as much unreal as the dream consciousness. This is almost identical with the position of the Advaitins who also hold the same view and as we have seen the Vijñānavādins differentiate between '*parikalpita*' (imaginary or dream) and '*paratantra*' (empirical) knowledge. The only question is—is the criterion of differentiation an adequate one? Śaṁkara thinks it is not; the dream consciousness is sublated or negated while waking consciousness persists, *i.e.,* the one is *bādhita* while the other is *abādhita.*[25] It may be noted here that according to the Advaitins' own true position this is not just, for from the standpoint of the Advaita-Vedānta, both dream and waking consciousness are unreal, being the product of *Māyā,* and capable of annihilation on the dawn of true knowledge. We have therefore to admit that in levelling this criticism Śaṁkara forgets his own position as an absolute idealist, and becomes more of a realist. The poor Vijñānavādins have done nothing else except emphasising that from the metaphysical standpoint both waking consciousness and dream are unreal being the product of '*saṁvṛti*' or *avidyā.* It is only from the standpoint of the ultra-realists, such as materialists and dualists who hold the reality of both the subject and object as eternal, that a real criticism of the Vijñānavādin's position might be maintained. For if both subject and object are equally real eternally how can we speak of one as more real than the other? To this the Vijñāñavādins can reply along with the Advaitins that duality or plurality necessarily implies unity, that the distinction of subject implies something that transcends both and that the distinction of waking and dream indicates a continuity of consciousness which comprises both. The only real question is what is the nature of this unity? The Vijñānavādins hold that it is the *Ālayavijñāna* which is the highest form of reality. But what is this *Ālayavijñāna* and can it be conceived as the highest reality? The Vijñānavādins explain *Ālayavijñāna* as the concrete intelligent principle of consciousness which underlies all experience; it is identified with the self and diversifies itself into the manifold forms. It is thus not without a form or feature. A question may, therefore, be asked how are the forms generated? Are the forms in *Ālayavijñāna* due to the activity of beginningless desire? If so, what is the exact relation between the two? The Vijñānavādins cannot satisfactorily answer these questions. If beginningless desire is regarded as the cause of these manifold forms in *Ālayavijñāna,* the *Ālayavijñāna* itself is reduced to unreality. The Vijñānavādins cannot escape from the charges like the Advaitins to whom also the same questions about the relation of *Brahman* and Māyā might be put. For the Advaitins can answer by saying that their *Brahman* or highest reality is without any form or feature and whatever forms appear are the workings of Māyā which can in no way affect the nature of *Brahman,* the evolution of forms being of the *'vivarta'* type or an evolution without substantial mutation. Hence we have perforce to conclude that the *Ālayavijñāna* cannot be the highest form of reality. Besides this, the Vijñānavādins use *Ālayavijñāna* in a rather ambiguous sense making it difficult to say what they exactly mean. Sometimes they use it to mean universal consciousness which diversifies itself into different minds and things and sometimes they imply by it rather the empirical ego. Lastly, though *Yogācāras* did not altogether intend to make the world of space and time depend on individual consciousness, it cannot be denied that in their eagerness to refute crude realism they sometimes made a confusion of psychological and metaphysical points and thus arrived at a crude mentalism. The confusion is worse confounded by the employment of the same term *'vijñāna'* to indicate both changing and unchanging aspects of mental life.

Asatkhyātivāda or Śūnyavāda and an estimate of the position

Śūnyavāda or *Asatkhyātivāda* might be regarded as the logical culmination of the Vijñānavāda epistemology. If *vijñāna* is the only reality and outward objects are unreal as the Yijñānavādin holds, the *vijñāna* itself becomes unreal. For we cannot have consciousness without an object of which we are conscious. And when the Vijñānavādin accounts for the empirical world by posting a continuous subject, the *Śūnyavādin* or *Asatkhyativādin* pushes the argument a step beyond and "the very shadow of the soul" is discarded. If the Vijñānavādins are right there can be no objects to be known and no object implies no subject. Thus the *Śūnyavādins* do away with the constant *ālaya* and set our ideas adrift. If there are no extramental relations there can be no world. External objects and internal states are both *void or śūnya.* According to the *Śūnyavādins* we are dreaming even when we are awake. Besides the *Ālayavījñāna* of the *Yogācāras* cannot be the highest form of reality, for there being no object, what is it that gives it form? In other words, it cannot be *akārasahita* or with forms, *i.e.,* relational. Thus the highest reality must be non-relational there being no possibility of distinction between subject and object and this can only be called *Śūnya* as void. Therefore the question naturally arises as to what it is that the *Śūnyavādins* or *Asatkhyātivādins* mean when they speak of the highest reality as *Śūnya?* Do they imply by it absolute void or nothingness as the orthodox Brahmanical schools, nay, even the Vijñānavādins themselves, represent, or does it mean something positive though no definite attribute or qualification can be ascribed to it? Thus Śaṁkara, Kumārila[26] and Udayana all take this *Śūnya* to mean absolute nothingness leading to the complete unreality of the world. Udayana therefore queries: "Is the conception of *Śūnya* or void a fact or not? If it is not a fact that is per-ceived by and through one, how can you say that the world is *'śūnya'?* If it is a fact, is it selfevident or perceived by and through some one else? Then, the existence of some one else and what he perceived must both be admitted." The Vijñānavādin goes further and argues that 'If all is nothing, then nothing itself becomes the criterion of truth and the *Mādhyamika* or *Asat-*

khyātivādin has no right to discuss with others of a different way of thinking. He who accepts nothing as real, can neither prove his position nor disprove his opponent's case.[27] Again a still more formidable objection against the *Mādhyamika* position is that nothingness or ultra-void fails altogether to explain the causal connexion in the cosmic evolution. If nothing is the reality, how are we to explain the process of the universe? Nāgārjuna frankly admits the validity of this objection and holds that causation or change itself and along with it the empirical world is unintelligible; for the very conception of change or causation is full of contradiction or antinomy. As Nāgārjuna puts it "a thing is born neither from itself nor from another nor from both or without cause. Production seems to be logically impossible. What is non-existent cannot be produced by any cause such as a square circle. If origination is admitted to be desirable in the case of what is existent, then it "produces only that which has been already produced. One and the same thing cannot be both existent and non-existent, Nor can we say that one and the same thing is distinct from both existence and non-existence. Nothing real can be spoken of as coming to existence, nor can it be said that the pot, this moment non-existent, next moment becomes existent. That will be to assert a contradiction. When we know that things have no absolute existence we see that they cannot produce others with such existence. If we speak of causes, we do so at the expense of logic indulging in makeshifts of subject and object, substance and attribute, space and time. Absolutely speaking there is no cause or effect, no production or cessation.[28] The *Śūnyavādins* further elaborate this idea of causation in their theory of *'Pratītya'samutpāda'* or dependent origination according to which a thing is a mass of *"dharmas"* following one another in a continuous succession. The individual human being -is a collection of *'dharmas'* since every thought, sensation or volition is a *'dharma.'* A. carriage is a name of a collection of material *'dharmas.'* Apart from the *dharmas* the carriage and the man have only an ideal existence, an existence of designation *(prajñapti)*. *Dharmas* alone exist though they are liable to destruction. Every thought or thing may have as its determining cause or *pratyaya* a great number of *'dharmas'* more or less external to itself, such as object of vision, visual organ, etc., but its real *hetu* or cause is the thought immediately preceding it, even as every moment of the duration of the flame depends on the oil, wick, etc., though it is truly a continuation of the preceding moment of the flame. Thus the Śūnya-vādins do not dismiss the *'dharmas'* as wholly unreal. Only they consider them to be phenomenal and momentary. Nāgārjuna further admits the *Yogācāra*-objection that what is inexplicable is unreal and only adds that on this principle *vijñāna* itself is unreal since we cannot say anything consistent about it. He also agrees with the *Yogācāra* in holding that the world is constituted by relations but goes further in maintaining that these relations are only hypostatization or abstractions, being wholly unintelligible. All we can say is that the whole world, matter, soul, space, time, cause and substance, etc., are without substance and therefere only appearance. Though the *Śūnyavādins* thus speak of the world as mere appearance, they however maintain that there is something which underlies this appearance. For even when we wrongly superimpose the notion of a serpent on the rope, the rope exists though the serpent does not. The rope is only void of serpent. Similarly the qualities, characteristics such as form, etc., commonly attributed to things may not exist. Though the denotable properties may not exist, the substratum exists. The distinctions of *'jñāna'* and *'jñeya,'* knowledge and knowable, etc., are based on something. As *Bodhisattvabhūmi* puts it: "For Śūnya (vacuity) to be a justifiable position, we must have firstly the existence of that which is empty, and then the non-existence of that by the absence of which it is empty; but if neither exists, how can there be a vacuity?" In other words, vacuity or void implies something which is void or vacuum. Thus the void or the *Śūnya* of the Śūnyavādins is not something negative but seems to be positive. They speak of it as *tathāta* and in their description of *talhāta* as the highest reality they speak in terms almost similar to the description of Brahman of the Advaita-Vedānta. The *tathāta* or the metaphysical absolute of the Buddhists is in its essential nature real and eternal but we mistake it as absolute nothingness, it is called *'bhāva'* or existence, though its true nature cannot be expressed by means of language. For as Asaṅga says, "It can neither be called existence or non-existence. It is neither such nor otherwise. It is neither born nor destroyed. It neither increases nor decreases. It is neither purity nor filth. Such is the real *lakṣaṇa* or nature of the transcendental truth—"There is then neither that which speaks nor that which is spoken of; neither that which thinks nor that which is thought of; when you conform to *tathāta* and when your subjectivity is completely obliterated, it is then that you. will he said to have insight."[29] The absolute is free from relativity, individuality and conditionedness, though it is self-existent and the source of all. More positively it is the effulgence of great wisdom; the universal illumination of the *dharma-dhātu* (universe), the true and adequate knowledge, the mind pure and clear in its nature, the eternal, the blessed, the self-regulating and the pure, the immutable and the free.[30] It is now clear that the highest reality of the *Mādhyamikas* is almost identical with the Brahman of the Advaitins; and Mādhavācārya makes it still clearer by quoting from *Vivekavilāsa* that *Mādh-yamikas* admit only the featureless self-subsistent consciousness as the highest reality.[31] It has been probably called 'Śūnya' by the *Mādhyamikas* because no proof can be applied to it as it is totally featureless. Hence it is that Ānandatīrtha in his *Tattvodd-yota* points out that there is no difference between the *Sūnya-vāda* and the *Māyāvāda*.[32]

Though there is a striking similarity between the *śūnyavāda* and the *Māyāvāda* in respect of the nature of their ultimate reality and various other points as noted by Ānandatīrtha, the former, on closer examination, will be found to fail in the explanation of the cosmic evolution. As we have seen, the Śūnya-vādins explain the cosmic process by reference to what they call cyclic origination. But the question is this : If their ultimate reality is totally featureless how is its modification or appearance as the basis of the manifold world to be explained? If it is said that appearance or cyclic process of cosmic evolution is generated by the working of the beginningless desire in it, the ultimate reality will no longer remain featureless. If, on the contrary, the beginningless desire has no relation to the absolute reality, the world process itself becomes an inexplicable enigma and again this will lead to dualism, the desire being an independent reality. Hence as we saw in the case of the *Yogācāra* school, the problem of the relation of the ultimate reality to the world-process remains as unsolved as ever.

The Satkhyātivāda of Rāmānuja

As regards the objective implication of knowledge Rāmānuja's view-point is known as *Satkhyātivāda.* All so-called appear-ances forming the object of knowledge exist as objectively valid entities. Objects are regarded as prior to knowledge and the act of knowledge functions to bring them into relation with the knowing subject. Appearances even in false perception are valid, implying objective reality. This reality is not merely objective or relative but absolute. Rāmānuja has tried to bring out this realistic aspect of knowledge from the Vedas. Even in erroneous perception whatever is cognised is something existent; knowledge in the absence of corresponding object is an impossibility. "In other words, the agreement between knowledge and its object should extend from the 'that' *(prakārin)* to the 'what' *(prakāra)* also of what is presented." Rāmānuja is thus an advocate of extreme realism. The time-space-cause world, to him, is an absolute reality endowed with real qualities. And it is the real world that forms the object of our knowledge. Every appearance has a value and validity of its own, and whatever appears and forms the object of experience is *(sat)* truth. As regards normal perception Rāmānuja's position is not very difficult to follow but so far as erroneous perception or illusion is concerned the position is somewhat difficult. For illusory percepts cannot satisfy the pragmatic test which may be accepted as the real mark of empiric truth. To establish his position on the philosophic basis Rāmānuja argues that the main function of consciousness is to enlighten experience and it would be the height of folly to go against the evidence of self-consciousness. Self-consciousness cannot go against its own revelation and commit suicide and self-negation. The evidence of self-consciousness even in false perception cannot be doubted for even in illusion, there can be no question about the appearance of something as also that this form of consciousness can be embodied in a judgment. The difference between an illusion and an empirically valid perception consists in this, that while the object of the former can be negated or proved false as a result of practical endeavour, the latter cannot be gainsaid as it satisfies all pragmatic demands. As a form of consciousness both are on the same level and valid. The facthood or theoretic assuredness of false percepts is not denied in the system of Rāmānuja. False appearances also have materialistic value and validity and are real in our experience. They are not totally false though they cannot satisfy demands of practical life.[33] Even in false perception, between the presented datum and the cognition, there is no difference of materials, for when we perceive the oyster as silver, the perception of silver in the oyster is occasioned by the element of silver it contains. Rāmānuja corroborates this epistemological realism by a reference to the metaphysical theories of *Pañcīkaraṇa* or *Trivṛtkaraṇa*[34]—the former holding that all the cosmic manifolds are mixed substances, containing all the five *bhūtas* or gross elements and the latter implying that the cosmic world is made tripartite and this tripartite constitution is apprehended even in all valid perceptions. For example, "the red colour sensation in the burning fire comes from primal elementary fire, the white colour from water, the black colour from earth."[35] The threefold nature of the burning fire is thus proved and the same principle holds good in the case of all things, everything being composed or compounded of all the three primary elements. On the basis of this theory Rāmānuja gives a materialistic interpretation of many cases of false perception.

(1) In the erroneous perception of mirage, the cognised water is really there in the overheated sandy waste which has a tripartite constitution or is a product of the five cosmic *bhūtas* and not merely of pure earth though the earth constitutes the preponderating part of it. The other primary elements are however there in small quantities. Here the perception of water is thus a presented datum actually existing in front of the particular percipient and the cognition is of the something that is really existent or *sat*.

(2) In the case of oyster-silver Rāmānuja similarly argues that the illusion of shell-silver is due, among other causes, to the similarity between the two substances, *viz.*, their peculiar lustre. This similarity means, to Rāmānuja, the presence in the 'shell' though only to a very limited extent, of the very material which constitutes silver. Likeness is to him only another term for partial identity and so even here what is perceived is what is actually presented.[36] Only it is not the *bhūtas* as such that are brought together here, but what are derived from them— *bhūtas*. The shell is a compound not of *pṛthivī, tejaḥ,* etc., in their premitive form, but of certain differentiations of them, the 'shell' being a particular modification of *pṛthivī* and silver, as indicated by the lustre of *tejaḥ.*[37]

This realistic explanation of Rāmānuja on the basis of the primitive elements and the structural affinity of the physical world, may hold good only in cases where the objects of illusory percepts are made of *bhūtas* or gross elements. But in other cases, when the white conch is seen as yellow by a person with a jaundiced eye, a different explanation has to be given to establish his theory of *Satkhyātivāda* or that which exists is alone cognised. In explaining the erroneous perception of the white shell being seen as yellow Rāmānuja in his Bhāṣya argues that the visual rays issuing from the eye come in contact with the bile—the element of which is already existent in the eye—kiss the shell, and the result is that the whiteness of the shell being suppressed by the yellowness of the bile is not apprehended; the shell thus appears as yellow just as if it were gilded. The bile and its yellowness is, owing to its exceeding tenuity, not perceived by the standers; but thin though it be, it is apprehended by the person suffering from jaundice, to whom it is very near, in so far as it issues from his own eye, and through the mediation of the visual rays, aided by the action of the impression produced on the mind by that apprehension, it is apprehended even in the distant object, *viz.*, the shell.[37]

The explanation advanced by Rāmānuja cannot satisfy the philosophic thought. It is arbitrary and fanciful. And the unsoundness of his explanation may be clearly brought out by examining further his interpretation of some instances of the erroneous perception. The cognition of one's own face in the mirror or in some other reflecting surface is, according to Rāmānuja, true in its character. The fact as explained by him is that the motion of the visual rays coming forth from the eye towards the mirror, is reversed by the mirror, and the rays in their reverse order apprehend the person's own face, subsequently to the apprehension of the surface of the mirror. Owing to the rapidity of the process there is no apprehension of any interval between the mirror and the fact, and the fact presents itself as being in the mirror.

(a) In the case of one direction being mistaken for another, *e.g.*, when the south is taken as north, the object of perception as such, Rāmānuja says, is true. For the idea of direction such as south, north, etc., being relative to the difference of spatial position, the percipient actually cognises the north as such, for with reference to another percipient occupying a different space-position it is really north and it is only owing to the operation of an unseen principle *(adṛṣṭa)* that the particular percipient mistakes the south as north. Space as such is one indivisible who learned if reference to any particular percipient is overlooked or ignored, every direction might be regarded as any direction since potentially every direction is all other directions. And it is owing to the operation of the unseen principle that all other elements of direction are screened up from the view in the case of any particular percipient when he mistakes the south as north.

(b) The valid nature of the double-moon perception has been justified by Rāmānuja. On the basis of his own principle he argues that either through the pressure of the finger upon the eye or owing to some abnormal affection of the eye the visual rays are divided, and the double, mutually independent apparatus of vision thus originates and becomes the cause of a double apprehension of the moon. One apparatus apprehends the moon in her proper place, the other which moves somewhat obliquely touches at first a place close by the moon, and then the moon itself, which thus appears somewhat moved from her proper place. Although what is presented is the one moon distinguished by the apprehension in two places at the same time—an apprehension due to the double apparatus of vision—and since the cognitions are distinct, the objects, apprehended, must also be taken as true inasmuch as there is no cognition of identity between the two moons. Thus a double moon presents itself to perception.

(c) In the same way the 'fire-brand circle' *(alātacakra)* perception may also be explained as true. The fire-brand swings round very rapidly. Its cognition as a fiery wheel explains itself through the circumstances that moving very rapidly it is in conjunction with all points of the circle described without our being able to apprehend the intervals. The case is analogous to that of the perception of the real wheel in which case no intervals are apprehended because there are none; while in the case of the fire-brand none are apprehended owing to the rapidity of the movement. Therefore in the latter case also the object of the cognition is true, being really presented.

(d) In explaining the valid nature of the dream-consciousness where at least we seem to have experience without corresponding objects existing at the time, Rāmānuja, on the authority of the Upaniṣads, argues that the divinity creates, in accordance with the merit and demerit of the individual, things of unique nature subsisting for a certain time only and perceived by the individual for whom they were created as objectively real entities. In agreement herewith the scripture says—"There are no chariots in that state, no horses, no roads, then the Almighty creates chariots, horses and roads. There are no tanks, no lakes, no rivers, then the God creates tanks, lakes and rivers. For He is the maker."[38] It means that although there are no chariots, horses, etc., to be perceived by other persons, the Lord creates such things to be perceived by the dreaming person only. And such creative agency is possible only for Him who possesses the wonderful power of making all his wishes and plans objectively real.

God is the creator, says Rāmānuja and adds that the reason of his creating such unique things is the same as in the case of objects of waking state, *viz.*, the providing of suitable means for the individual to experience pain or pleasure according to his past *'karma.'* The author of the *Brahmasūtras* also in his *sūtras,* discussing the possibility of the individual soul creating the objects appearing in dreams, finally decides that the wonderful creation is produced by the Lord only for the benefit of the individual dreamer.[39] For so long as the individual soul is in the *'saṁsāra'* state, its true nature comprising the power of making its wishes come true—is not fully manifested, and hence it cannot practically exercise that power.

Explanation of true and false knowledge in Rāmānuja's Satkhyātivāda

According to the *Satkhyātivāda* of Rāmānuja, whatever we may think of its scientific value, true or false *(pramā* or *bhrama)* cannot be divorced from reality and even in the case of objects whose existence cannot be vouched for only by individual experience, there is no ideal or purely subjective element. If all knowledge is equally valid, it may be pointedly asked how the universally recognised distinction between the truth *(pramā)* and error *(bhrama)* is to be explained? The doctrine postulates that only what is given is known, it does not however imply that all that is given is cognised. Knowledge, no doubt, is always of the given and of nothing but the given; but it need not be of the whole of what is given. This is evident from the example cited above. Besides the 'water' and the silver for instance there is much in the sandy 'waste' and the 'shell' that is left unapprehended. Rāmānuja bases his explanation of error on this feature of knowledge. The real implication of *Satkhyātivāda* is this : there can be no error of commission, all errors are those of omission, for all knowledge, though invariably valid, may be incomplete and incomplete knowledge *(agraha)* may give rise to errors of this kind. Thus in the case of the "yellow conch" it is the failure to comprehend its whitensss that causes the error. In dream-objects again, the fact that they are private to the particular dreamer is ignored and they are confounded with the corresponding objects of normal waking life. That error is consequent of omission is made clearer still in the case of another example cited—the fire-brand circle *(alātacakra)* where a point, owing to its rapid movement, is mistaken for its locus; for while the fact of its occupying every point on the circumference is apprehended, the other fact of its occupying them successively and not simultaneously remains completely unperceived.

These illustrations and the statement that error is due to incomplete knowing may possibly lead one to think that truth is complete knowledge. But that would not be correct, for according to *Satkhyātivāda* there may be an element of omission even in the so-called true perception. When, for instance, we perceive shell as shell there is present in it silver, but it is overlooked quite as much as the shell aspect is, when the same shell is mistaken for silver. Similarly in the case of desert when we cognise it as such, our mind fails to perceive the element of water in it. Thus completeness, like validity, fails to distinguish between truth and error; Rāmānuja therefore propounds a new principle, *viz.,* that of pragmatism which means that knowledge to be true, in its commonly accepted sense, must in addition to agreeing with outside reality be serviceable in life. When the mirage and the shell silver are described as false, what we mean is not that water and silver are not present there, for in that case there could have been no cognition of them at all; but that they are not such as can satisfy any practical use. The distinction between truth and error is thus significant only from the pragmatic stand-point; from the theoretical point of view the distinction does not exist. All knowledge without exception is valid and necessarily so, but such validity need not postulate that what is known is enough to satisfy a practical requirement. True knowledge according to the Rāmānujists, is not only '*yathārtha*' or agreeing with outside reality but also '*vyavahārānuguṇa*' or conforming to *vyavahāra* or practical interest in life.[40] In order that knowledge may conform to *vyavahāra,* it should in the first place refer to objects of common or collective experience. It is deficiency in this respect as implied in their private character, which makes the yellow conch and the dream elephant false, and it is that very deficiency which reveals their falsity. In the second place knowledge to conform to '*vyavahāra*' should comprehend the preponderating element in the object presented. The object we call shell may contain silver but the shell part predominates in it and it is this predominance that explains its being put to use as the one and not as the other; 'silver,' though certainly present, is of no account practically because of its *alpatva* or smallness; and it is this very feature, when discovered, that changes the erroneous knowledge of silver into the true one of shell. *Pramā* or true knowledge consists not only in correct apprehension so far as it goes, but also implies further that it can be of service in life. *Bhrama* or false knowledge also is right so far as it goes; but it does not go far enough and therefore fails to help us in the manner in which it may be expected to do. So when erroneous knowledge disappears and truth flashes forth as Rāmānuja's commentator says, "the *artha* (object) is not negated but only *pravṛtli* (activity) is arrested."[41]

An estimate of Rāmānuja's view-point

A close examination of Ramānuja's theory of *satkhyāti* reveals that false knowledge or '*mithyājñāna*' might be classified or studied under two headings, *viz.*, *(i)* general or common, *(ii)* private or individualistic. The yellow conch appears to a person with a jaundiced eye and the dream chariot is a fact which flashes out to a particular dreamer; they are therefore objects solely of individual experience. The mirage, the oyster-silver and such other illusory percepts are instances of common errors which any and every individual may commit in the practical affairs of life. The mirage-water and shell-silver, etc., are perceived by particular individuals and in this sense they are also objects of individual experience but yet they constitute a different grade of erroneous percepts and are not on the same level with the former instances, as they are subject to common test or verification unlike the yellow-conch and dream-chariot percepts. These latter are individual experiences and are perceived as absolutely real by the individual and only he can testify as to their validity. It would thus appear that Rāmānuja is forced to admit two classes of erroneous perception. And the inevitable implication of this distinction is that Rāmānuja has to accept different grades of being—an admission which would place his doctrine epistemologically on the same footing with the Advaitins.

Further in explaining the valid nature of the objects of dream consciousness, Rāmānuja was compelled to say that these objects are created by the Almighty in accordance with the *adṛṣṭa* or merits and demerits of the particular dreamer. A question may pertinently be asked as to what is the stuff out of which these objects are created. They cannot obviously be explained by the *Pañcīkaraṇa* theory as the dream chariot and actual chariot are of different orders, the former being unable to satisfy any pragmatic requirements while the latter can. It might be said that the will of the Almighty is the stuff out of which they are newly created, these unique creations being for a particular dreamer and only for the time being. This would amount almost to the new creations of Māyā of the Advaitins, for the divine will is itself an inexplicable mystery, which is further mystified by the statement that the creations are for the time being and for the particular dreamer.

Again the *Satkhyātivādins* explanation of the false perception of shell-silver implies that the perception of silver is *yathārtha* or real, though the element of silver present is too small to be of any practical utility. Now, if practical utility or serviceableness is the test of reality, as admittedly it is, it may be contended that the silver in the shell, serving no practical purpose at any time anywhere, may as well be nonest. Moreover how is it that the small element of the silver makes itself felt in the illusory perception while the preponderant element, of shell is altogether hidden from view? It stands to reason that the preponderant element should make itself felt rather than the insignificant element of silver. Besides if, as explained by the Rāmānujists, omission and commission be the criteria of falsity and truth, it might be argued that in false perception the doubtful silver (the existence of which is questioned) is perceived while the shell constituting the name and form of the presentation fails to be apprehended. This is equivalent to saying that the real object fails to be perceived and something else as a new creation is apprehended. And this is what the Advaitins maintain. Lastly, if the metaphysical theory of *Pañcīkaraṇa* is admitted, how is it that, though all other elements are present in the object, only the element of silver is perceived to the entire exclusion of other elements? Instead of silver, why do we not perceive some other lustrous substance?

The *akhyātivāda* of the Mīmāṁsists

Closely allied to the above view of the Rāmānujists is the view of the Mīmāṁsists known as *Akhyātivāda*. They maintain that the object of all knowledge is true *(yalhārthaṁ sarva-vijñānam)*. The main difference between the two however is that, in explaining the true nature of the object of perception the Rāmānujists or *Satkhyātivādins* fall back on their metaphysical presupposition of *Pañcīkaraṇa,* while the *Akhyātivādins* rely chiefly on psychological analysis. The metaphysical explanation, as we saw, led to some serious difficul-ties, and it has now to be seen how far the psychological explanation is satisfactory. The view is known as *Akhyātivāda* because, according to this view, the cognition of shell as silver is due to the non-apprehension of the difference between the presented object, *viz.,* the 'this' and the represented idea, *viz.,* the silver. In this illusory perception there is a confusion of memory (representation, *e.g.,* silver) with presentation (e.g., the this). Each of these elements taken by itself is true : the presentation as such is there and the memory-representation of silver also is valid, and it is only the non-apprehension of the difference between these real elements that leads to the false perception of shell as silver.[42] Memory and presentation are opposed to each other both in their nature and object. Thus the form of memory is 'this is that silver' while presentation implies immediate apprehension. How is it then that these two diametrically opposed elements are confounded with each other? The Mīmāṁsists explain this in the following way : They maintain that owing to some defect of sense-organs, the real nature of the something presented *(i.e.,* the this) is not apprehended; but because of its similarity in lustre it excites the mental residuum or *saṁskāra* and revives the memory of silver seen before. Again owing to some further fault or defect the representative character of this silver (*i.e.*, the thatness) is not apprehended and the silver is cognised as presented; and the non-discrimination gives rise to the false perception which seems to be as real as an empirically valid cognition of a piece of real silver, and leads to appropriate activity.[43] In further explanation of this view Śālikanātha, the author of the *Prakaraṇapañcikā,* points to the fact that in many cases, elements admittedly due to memory appear in consciousness as immediate presentation shedding the form 'this is that.' Thus, for example, in the continuous consciousness *(dhārāvāhikajñāna)* of something such as a pot or apprehension of meaning from a word, the memory elements due to previous presentation shed their form of' this is that' and are apprehended as immediately presented.[44] Again that the silver in the present case is due to memory cannot be gainsaid. For it can neither be perceptual cognition, there being no immediate contact of the eyes with it, nor an inference, there being no middle term or *hetu* to make the inference possible. Nor can it be argued that silver in the present case is an immediate perception due to the similarity of the 'this' with the silver in lustre. For the function of knowledge is to enlighten the real character of objects and it would be against universal experience to hold that one thing can cause the presentation of another in the way suggested; for this would be to make life impossible, there being no certainty about the objects of knowledge which alone can ensure practical success. It has therefore to be concluded that the silver here is a representative or memory element.[45] Similar explanations apply to the stock examples of dream-consciousness, yellow-conch perception of the jaundiced, mistaking directions, etc. In dreams, the objects though supplied by memory are perceived as presented owing to the non-apprehension of the 'that' element of memory, memory itself being roused to activity on account of some unseen principle *(adṛṣṭa)* of the dreamer. Against this it may however be urged that memory objects such as a golden palace in the air might appear in dreams though the dreamer might have no previous experience of them in order to have a memory of them. How are these extraordinary dream-phenomena to be explained? The *Akhyātivādins* would find great difficulty in answering this question by their own principle. The Rāmānujists however can escape this by referring to these objects as the new creation of God at the time of perception.

In the case of the perception of conch as yellow by the jaundiced, the same principle on non-apprehension of the difference is operative. In shell-silver perception there was non-apprehension of the difference between memory (silver) and the shell (the this) while in this case, there is the non-apprehension of the difference between two perceptions (conch and yellowness). The way in which it happens is this : Due to jaundice only the colour' yellow' is perceived and not the coloured bile, the real seat of the colour, and owing to some other organic defect the white colour of the conch is screened from view and it is perceived only as something without colour. And as a quality cannot subsist apart from a substance nor a substance without qualities, though the locii of the two presentations are different owing to a non-apprehension of difference, the two are perceived as one.[46] In the double-moon-perception the visual apparatus, due to some defect or other, is bifurcated into two and cognises the same moon as two and this is possible because of the non-apprehension of the identity of the two moons.[47] In illusion of direction the mistake lies in the fact that the subject fails to cognise the distinction between the real direction and the remembered direction and this happens just in the same way as in the case of shell-silver. There is only perception of direction as such without its real character (as east) *plus* the remembered direction (south) without the elements of remembrance, and the illusion lies in the non-apprehension of the distinction between the two (perception and remembrance).[48] Again in the case of fire-brand circle, the illusion of a continuous circle arises in consciousness owing to the non-apprehension of the different moments of space and time through which the lighted body passes very rapidly.[49]

It is now clear that this psychological explanation lays great stress on the element of memory in the genesis of false perception and it further emphasises that false perception is really due to the non-apprehension of the difference between memory and presentation. That in so doing the Mīmāṁsists have come upon a real core of truth is abundantly clear in so far as all theories of false perception have to admit that in the stock example of mistaking the shell for the silver, the element of silver is due to memory and the false perception is the result of the non-discrimination between the presentation (shell) and the memory (silver). Further, the contention of the Mīmāṁsists that the element of memory *(i.e.,* silver) in false perception sheds its representative character and appears as a presentation is unassailable; for the judgment in the case of shell-silver is not that 'I remember *(smarāmi)* the silver' but that I see or know it *(jānāmi);* and it might also be further conceded as an admitted fact that in continuous consciousness also the element of representation (memory) loses its remembered character and appears as present apprehension. Jayantabhaṭṭa, however, here raises a very pertinent query. He says that all this might be perfectly true, but not from the Mīmāṁsist's standpoint. He urges that the Mīmāṁsists maintain that knowledge is self-luminous and self-valid *(svataḥ-pramāṇa)* and if this is so, how to explain the suppression of its remembered character in the case of silver? It cannot be due to memory for then there would be no non-apprehension between the silver and the shell, nor can it be a present cognition, for then it should mean the admission of the Naiyāyika theory that something appears as somthing else or what is called *Anyathākhyāti* or *Viparītakhyāti.*[50] Further as already pointed out, the *Ākhyātivādins* have no satisfactory explanation to offer in those extraordinary cases where memory is lacking, for the simple reason that such experiences are impossible. Thus in dreams one might see his own head cut off though obviously he cannot have any such memory for the obvious reason that he had no such experience.[51] Again in the perception of double moon how are we to explain the false character of the perception seeing that according to the Mīmāṁsists the objects of all knowledge are true? The non-apprehension of identity of the two moons might explain the perception but that does not sufficiently explain the falsity of the perception according to the Mīmāṁsaka theory of reality of all knowledge.[52]

Against this theory of false perception Gaṅgeśa, the father of the Navya-Nyāya school, urges a most formidable objection. He argues that non-apprehension of the distinction cannot account for the activity to which the person subject to false perception is prompted.[53] Vācaspati in his *Bhāmatī* urging the same objection develops it further. He argues that the activity of the conscious agent must be due to knowledge and since the activity is directed towards the object *(e.g.,* the this, implying shell) it is clear that after the non-apprehension of the difference between the this (presentation) and silver (memory) there are intermediate stages which the Mlmāṁsists or the *Akhyātivādins* overlook.

The stages are *(i)* identifying the silver with the this (shell), *(ii)* the consciousness that silver is of practical use, *(iii)* the cognition that yonder object being silver will serve a practical need. It is only when all these stages are gone through that activity is possible. For the mere non-apprehension of the remembered character, without its identification with the 'this' (shell) cannot lead to practical endeavour on account of its inability to create a consciousness of the utility of the 'this.'[54] If the silver has to be superimposed on the shell, it implies that different attributes other than its own are ascribed to the shell. This means that something appears as something else; in other words, it is the *Anyathākhyāti* or appearance of something as something else which it is really not.

Anyathākhyativāda

The theory of illusion known as *Anyathākhyātivāda* is held by the Naiyāyikas. They develop the theory in the following mannu; As already sherm practical endeavour in relation to the perception cannot be explained without the identification of the silver with the shell. If however it is said that silver is altogether negated as soon as the percipient discovers that yonder object is shell, the Naiyāyikas reply that absolute negation of silver does not follow from the cognition that the shell is not silver. All that this implies is that silver is not present in the shell. It does not imply that silver as such is nowhere to be found. Again if it is asked how is it that the silver though not present is perceived as a presentation, the Naiyāyika explanation is that yonder object (shell) by its superficial quality of brilliancy excites in the mind the residual impression of the silver through similarity and as soon as the connotation of silver is thus revived in the mind, we have the perception of silver as the underlying substance of the connoted quality; for the quality of a thing and the thing itself are inseparable. Thus though the silver is not presented to the senses, it has become an object of knowledge inherent in self connected with the mind and the senses and the falsity lies in perceiving silver not where it really is but in yonder object (shell), *i.e.,* falsity lies in taking one thing for another.[55] Hence as Jayantabhaṭṭa in his *Nyāyamañjarī* says, it is not enough to stop short by saying, as the *Akhyātivādins* do, that the silver is a pure memory-image with the element of remembrance dropped. We have to go further and say that the silver is a presentation, for the form of the perception is 'this is silver.' The memory serves as the exciting cause of the perception of silver as a presentation.[56] The only question is how the silver can be a direct perception in the absence of sense-contact as, in the present case, the shell and not the silver is in contact with the eyes. The Naiyāyika answers this by saying that there is such a thing as perception through the mind even without sense-contact. This he calls *Jñānalakṣaṇasannikarṣa* in which there is direct perception, for example, of the fragrance of sandal wood *(surabhicandanam)* when we only see it.[57]

A close scrutiny of the different theories of false perception reveals the fact that the *Anyathākhyātivāda* of the Naiyāyikas as a principle underlies all other *khyātivādas* or theories of false knowledge. Thus according to the *Ātmakhyātivādins* ideas or *vijñānas* appear as other than ideas, *i.e.,* as outward objects though, they are not really so; to the *Asatkhyātivādins* that which is purely non-existent appears as '*sat*' or existent; to the *Akhyātivādins* memory-element appears as presentation; to the *Satkhyātivādins* though the appearance is true yet the shell with its preponderating elements hidden, appears as silver; to the *Advaitins* the appearance is something other than what is there.[58] The only point of controversy in their explanation of false perception among the different schools is about the nature of the object that is apprehended. The Naiyāyikas hold that it is a mental perception *(jñānalakṣaṇa)* without any sense-contact. If it is so, it may be asked why it is that the silver which is a mental perception is identified with the 'this' (shell) which is an object of direct perception being in contact with the eyes? Mental perception, *e.g.*, of the fragrance of the sandal wood is obviously indirect while the silver in this false perception of shell-silver is cognised as direct presentation. Hence Śaṁkara and the Śaṁkarites maintain that there is no doubt about the direct presentation of the silver. And this presentation being there, it cannot be called unreal nor wholly real as it cannot serve any practical need; it is mysterious or *anirvacanīya.*

REFERENCES

1. Atyantagrahe atyantāgrahe na cādhyāsaḥ.
2. (a) Nātyantāsato naraśṛṅgāderāvabhāso nāpi atyantasataścidātmanaḥ bādhagocaratā tadiha ubhayānyathānupapattyobhayaviiakṣaṇatā rajatāderāvedyata iti—Ny. M. K., p. 113.

   (b) Tasmāt na *sat* nāpi sadasat parasparavirodhāt ityanirvācyameva āropaṇīyaṁ marīciṣu toyamāstheyaṁ na toyaṁ pūrvadṛṣṭam kintvanṛtamanirvācyam. Bh., p. 21.

   (c) V. K. P., p. 21.
3. Idamaṅśāvacchinna-caitanye rajatapariṇāmini avidyā duṣṭendriya-samparkarūpād adhyāsakāraṇabhūtāt kṣobhaṁ kāryābhimukhaṁ prāpnoti uttarakṣ aṇe ca rajatarūpeṇa parinamate.
4. Avidyālakṣaṇamatra kāraṇamāśriyate avidyā hi vidyābhāvaḥ mithyā jñānaṁ vā na cobhayaṁ kasyacit samāvayikāraṇamadravyatvāt, na ca asatyasya kāryasya sākṣāt satyopādānatā yuktā, tathā sati satyatāpātāt, na ca atyantāsataḥ nirasta-samastasāmarthyasya upādānatā yuktimatī yattadanirvācyaṁ rajatādyupādānaṁ saivāsmākamavidyā sidhyantī rajatādyupādānatayaiva svapramāṇasiddheti na rajatādeḥ tadupādānatāyāmapi vivaditavyam. Ny. M. K., p.p. 122-124.
5. The school is also called 'Yogācāra,' since it declares that the absolute truth or Bodhi manifested in the Buddhas is attainable only by those who practice 'Yoga' and 'ācāra.' Yogācāra brings out the practical side of the Philosophy, while Vijñānavāda brings out its speculative features, *Asaṅga* and his younger brother *Vasubandhu* founded the idealistic view of the 'Yogācāra.'

   S. D. S., p. 30.
6. Vijñānameva khalvetad gṛhṇātyātmānamātmanā
   vahirnirūpyamāṇasya grāhyasyānupapattitaḥ
   buddhiḥ prakāśamānā ca tena tenātmanā bahiḥ
   tadvaḥatyarthaśūnyāpi lokayātrāmihedṛṣīm. Nyāyamañjarī, p. 178.
7. Nairantaryāvabhāsasya bhrāntatvāt tasmādārāt santareṣu vṛkṣeṣvekaghanavana-pratyayavadeṣaḥ sthūlaḥ pratyayaḥ. Bh., p. 543.

8. Yad yena saha niyatasahopalaṁbhanaṁ tattato na bhidyate. Bh., p. 544.
9. Jñānañca gṛhyamāṇamākārahitaṁ grahītumaśakyamiti balāt sākārameva tad grahītavyaṁ sākāre ca jñāne gṛhīte sati dvitīyakāraṇābhāvāt kuto jñānātirikto vāhyo rthaḥ? Ny. M., p. 538, Benares Edition.
10. *Vide* Nyāyamañjarī, pp. 538-39, Benares Edition.
11. *Vide* Śāstradīpikā and Siddhāntacandrikā, p. 52, Bombay Edition.
12. *Cf.* Adhyāropa and Apavāda theory of the Advaita-Vedānta—*vide* Vedāntasāra, p. 16.
13. *Vide* Laṅkāvatārasūtra, pp. 73-74.
14. Svataḥ svacchamapi Jñānam anādyavidyāvāsanāvibhavena tattadanekākārakāluṣyaruṣitavapuriva prakāśate jñānavāsanābhedasantāna-yośca bījāṅkuravadanāditvāt nāsya paryanuyogasyāvasaraḥ kuto vāsanā pravṛtta iti. Nyāyamañjarī, p. 539, Benares Edn.
15. (a) *Māyā* ca vaicitryānna anyā na ananyā yadi anyā syāt vaicitryaṁ māyāhetukam na syāt atha ananyā syāt vaicitryānmāyā vaicitryayorvibhāgo na syāt sa ca dṛṣṭo vibhāgaḥ tasmāt na anyā na ananyā ata eva māyā na nāstyastitvena abhiniveṣṭavyā.
    Vide Laṅkāvatārasūtras, p. 118.
    (b) *Cf.* Sadasadvilakṣaṇā avidyā of the advaita-Vedānta,
16. The second school of the Hīnayāna is called the Sautrāntika. The Sautrāntikas, unlike the Vijñānavādins, admit the extramental existence of the phenomenal world which, according to them, is not directly perceived but inferred from the diversification of cognition. In support of this theory Madhavāçāryya in his Sarvadarśana-saṁgraha writes: 'Cognition must ultimately have some object since it is manifested in duality. If the object proved were only a form of cognition it should manifest itself as such, and not as an external object.' Of the origin of the term 'Sautrāntika' Mādhavācāryya says: "The name Sautrāntika arose from the fact that the venerated Buddha called some of his disciples Santrāntikas who asked what was the ultimate purport *(anta)* of the aphorism *(sūtra).*"

    It may well be noted that the Sautrāntikas are so because of their adherence to the 'Sutta Piṭaka' or the section consisting of the discourses of Buddha to the rejection of the two other Piṭakas.
    (a) *Vide* Sarvadarśanasaṁgraha, p. 43.
    (b) Sūtrasyāntaṁ pṛcchatāṁ kathitaṁ bhavantaśca sūtrasyāntaṁ pṛṣṭavantaḥ sautrāntikā bhavantviti bhagavatā abhihitatayā sautrāntikaṭsaṁjñā sañjāteti. *Vide* Sarvadarśanasaṁgraha, p 43.
17. Ato bahirvaditi vadatā bāhyaṁ grāhyameveti bhāvanīyamiti bhavadīyavāṇo bhavantaṁ praharet.—*Vide* Sarvadarśanasaṁgraha, pp. 35-36.
18. Bhedapratibhāsasya bhrāntatve abhedapratibhāsasya prāmāṇyaṁ tat prāmāṇye ca bhedapratibhāsasya bhrantatvamiti parasparāśrayaprasaṅgācca, —*Vide* Sarvadarśanasaṁgraha, p. 36 (Abhyaṁkara's Edn.).
19. (a) Atrāpi anādiravicchinnapravāhā bhedavāsanaiva nimittam—*Vide* Sarvadarśana-saṁgraha, p. 32. (Abhyaṅkara's Edn.)
    (b) *Vide* Nyāyamañjarī, p. 536.
20. Na ca rasavīryavipākādi-samānamāśāmodakopārjita-modakānāṁ syāditi veditavyam—*Vide* Sarvadarśana-saṁgraha, p. 32.

21. *Cf.* Kantian Phenomenalism and Agnosticism.
22. Ākārasahitā buddhiryogācārasya sammatā.
Vide Sarvadarśana-saṁgraha, p. 45.
23. *Vide* familiar Buddhistic verses quoted by Ānandatīrtha in his Tattvoddyota 2. 2. 29:
(a) Satyantu dvividhaṁ proktam
saṁvṛtam pāramārthikam
saṁvṛtam vyavahāraṁ syāt
nivṛttau pāramārthikam.
(b) Dve satye samupāśritya Buddhānāṁ dharmadeśanā,
Loke saṁvitsatyañca satyañca paramārthataḥ
Cf., Pāramārthika-sattā and vyavaḥārika-sattā of the Advaita- Vedānta.
(c) Vicāryamāne no'satyaṁ satyañcāpi pratīyate
yasya tat samvṛtam jñeyam vyavaḥārapadañca tat.
24. *Vide* Sarvadarśanasaṁgraha, p. 29, Abhyaṅkara's Edn.
(a) Dṛṣṭārthavyavaḥāraśca svapnavyavahāravat saṁvṛtyā saṅga cchate.
(b) Yaścāyaṁ grāhyagrāhakasaṁvittīnāṁ pṛthagavabhāsaḥ sa ekasmin candramasi dvitvāvabhāsa iva bhramaḥ, atrāpi anādiravicchinna-pravāhābhedavāsanaiva nimittam. *Ibid,* p. 32.
25. *Vide* Śāṅkarabhāṣya, 2. 2. 29. Bādhyate hi svapnopalabdhaṁ vastu pratibuddhasya mithyā mayā upalabdho mahājanasamāgama iti, naivam jāgaritopalaṁbhaṁ vastu kasyāñcidapyavasthāyām bādhyate.
26. *Vide* Ślokavārttika, 115.3.10.
27. *Vide* Sarvasiddhāntasāra-saṁgraha, Chap. 3.3.4.
28. *Vide* Sarvasiddhāntasārasaṁgraha, Chap. 21.
29. *Vide* Suzuki, The Awakening of Faith, p. 58.
30. *Ibid*, p. 96.
(a) *Vide* also the Buddhist verse quoted by Ānandatīrtha—Nāsya sattvamasattvaṁ vā na doṣo guṇa eva vā, 2. 2. 9.
Heyopādeyarahitaṁ tat śūnyaḥ padamakṣayam. *Cf.* the Advaitic conception of Brahman.
31. *Vide* Sarvadarśana-saṁgraha, p. 46. Kevalāṁ saṁvidaṁ svasthāṁ manyante Madhyamāḥ punaḥ.
32. *Vide* Tattvoddyota (Mādhvavilāsa Book Dep., Sutra, 2. 2. 29) Na ca śūnyavādinaḥ sakāśād vailakṣaṇyaṁ māyāvādinaḥ. The following resemblances have also been pointed out by Ānandatīrtha in his *Tattvoddyota :* *(i)* The Brahman is *nirdharmāka, nirguṇa, nirākāra,* etc. so is the Śūnya of the Śūnyavādins. (ii) The Brahman is *niṣkriya,* devoid of all activity, the Parmenedian Being, so is the Śūnya. (iii) The Brahman is indescribable, and cannot be squeezed, into conceptual categories, so is the Śūnya. *(iv)* The Brahman manifefts itself as the phenomenal universe, so does the Śūnya. *(v)* The Brahman is the goal of the Advaitin's spiritual and metaphysical endeavour, so is the Śūnya the goal of fhe moral and metaphysical endeavour of the Buddhists.

33. *Vide* Śrutaprakāśikā, p. 185 (Bombay Edition).
34. *Vide* Yatīndramatadīpikā (p. 12 Ānandāśrama Edn.)
35. *Vide* Chāndogyopaniṣad, 6. 3. 2.
36. *Vide* Śrutaprakāśikā (Bombay Edn.), p. 185. Sadṛśe sadṛśāntarabud dhiryāthārthyam nirūpyate.
37. *Vide* Śrībhāṣya, pp. 22-3 (Lalus L. Edition),
38. *Vide* Bṛhadāraṇyaka Upa., 4.3.10.
39. *Vide* Brahmasūtra with Śrībhāṣya.
    Sandhye sṛṣṭirāhahi, 3.2.1.
    Nirmātārañcaike putrādayaśca, 3.2.2. Māyāmātrantu kārtsnenānabhi vyaktasvarūpatvāt, 3.2.3.
40. *Vide* Yatīndramatadīpikā, p. 3, Ānandāśrama Edition.
41. *Vide I.* Ph. C. L., p. 83.
42. Evaṁ svarūpatoviṣayataścāgṛhītabhedaṁ jñānadvayameva visaṁvādipravṛttihetuḥ. T. C., p. 475, Bib. Ind. S.
43. Sannihitarajataśakale rajatamatirbhavati yādṛśī satyā bhedānadhya-vasāyād iyamapi tādṛk parisphurati. T. C., p. 776, Bib. Ind. S.
44. *Vide* Prakaraṇapañcikā, p. 33, Benares Edition.
45. *Vide* Nyāyamakaranda, pp. 59-60.
46. *Vide* Prakaraṇapañcikā, p. 35, Ch. 4, Kārikās 48, 49, 50.
47. *Vide* Prakaraṇapañcīkā, p. 36, Kārikās 58, 59.
48. *Vide* Prakaraṇapañcikā, p. 36, Kārikā 61.
49. *Vide* Prakaraṇapañcikā, pp. 36-37, Kārikās 62-63.
50. *Vide* Nyāyamañjarī, pp. 180-81, Benares Edition.
    Svaprakāśā ca saṁvittiriti bhavatām darśanam, tatraiṣā rajatasaṁ-vittiḥ kena rūpeṇa prakāśatāmiti cintyam, yadi smaraṇātmanā kaḥ pramosārthaḥ, atha anubhavātmanā, tadiyaṁ viparītakhyātireva smṛteranu-bhavatvena pratibhāsāt.
51. *Vide* Nyāyamañjarī, p. 182, Benares Edition. Svapne tu svaśiraśchedāderatyantānanubhūtasya smṛtiriti kathyamānameva trapākaram.
52. *Vide* Nyāyamañjarī, p. 183, Benares Edition.
    Suṣirabhinnā nayanavṛttirekatvena grahītuṁ na śaknoti śaśāṅkamiti tādṛśī dṛśo vṛttirekatvamindormā grahīt dvitvānubhavantu bhrāntaṁ kva pracchādayāmaḥ.
53. (a) Na ca bhedāgrahāt pravṛttyupapattirapi viparītacatuṣke yugapatpravṛttinivṛttyāpatteḥ. T. C., pp. 486-87, Bib. Ind. S.
    (b) *Ibid,* pp. 499-501, 505.
54. *Vide*
    (a) Bhāmatī, p. 28, Bombay Edition.
    Tathā hi bhedāgrahād idaṁkārāspade rajatatvaṁ samāropya, tajjātīyasya upakārahetubhāvam anucintya, tajjātīyatayā idaṁkārāspade rajate tamanumāya, tadarthī tatra pravartate ityānupūrvyaṁ siddhaṁ, na ca taṭastharajatas mṛtiridaṁkārās padasya upakārahetubhā vamanumāpayitumarhati.

(b) *Vide* Nyāyamakaranda, p. 81.
(c) *Vide* Nyāyamañjarī, p. 185.
(d) *Vide* Nyāyavārttika Tātparyaṭīkā, p. 189, Benares Edition.

55. (a) *Vide* Nyāyamakaranda, p. 81. Śuktiśakalameva kāmalādidoṣadūṣ italocanālocitamarthāntaraṁ rajatātmanā avabhāsate, na ca, nedaṁ rajatamiti bādhāvabodhavaśād asattai-vātyantikī rajatasyeti sāṁpratam, sa khalu sannikitedaṁkārāspada-tādātmyaniṣedhād asannihitatāmevāsy-ārthādāyāti na punarātyantikīmasattām.
(b) *Vide* Nyāyamañjarī, p. 182.

56. (a) *Vide* Nyāyamañjarī, p. 182.
Sāmānyadharmasahacaritapadārthāntaragata-viśeṣasmaraṇopakṛtād bhavati viparītapratyayaḥ.
(b) *Vide* Nyāyamañjarī, pp. 185-86.
Vayantu smṛtyupārūḍharajatādyākāra-pratibhāsamabhivadanto bādḥaṁ smṛtipramoṣ mabhyupagatavantaḥ, kintu na tāvatyeva viśrāmyati matiḥ, api tu, rajatādyaṇubhavo'pi, saṁvedyate iti na smṛtipramoṣamātre eva virantavyam.

57. "*Jñānalakṣaṇasannikarṣa* occurs when we perceive the fragrance of the sandal wood. When we only see it, the visual presentation recalls the fragrance with which *manas* comes into contact. It is indirect perception. The Jainas think that it is a mixed mode of consciousness in which the visual presentation of the sandal and the idea of fragrance are integrated. The Vedāntaparibhāṣā holds that the presentative and the representative elements do not lose their identity in the mixed mode of consciousness. The Naiyāyika does not admit mixed modes of consciousness. Every psychosis is single, and the atomic nature of *manas* makes two simultaneous psychoses impossible. So he regards the visual perception of fragrant sandal as a simple psychosis, though it is preceded by the visual presentation and the recollection of fragrance. Modern Psychology accounts for this phenomenon by the doctrine of the association of ideas.".

58. (a) *Vide* Śāṅkarabhāṣya (Introduction), pp. 18-32.
Taṁ kecidanyatra anyadharmādhyāsa iti vadanti kecittu yatra Sdadhyāsastadvivekāgrahanivandhano bhrama iti, anye tu yatra Sdadhyā-sastasyaiva viparītadharmakalpanāmācakṣate, sarvathāpi tu Syasya anya-dharmāvabhāsatāṁ na vyabhicarati.
(b) *Vide* Rāmānuja-bhāṣya, p. 195, Lotus L. Ed.
Khyātyantaravādināñca sudūramapi gatvā anyathāvabhāsaḥ avaśyamāśrayaṇīyaḥ Asatkhyātipakṣe sadātmanā, Ātmakhyātipakṣe ca arthātmanā; Akhyātipakṣe anyaviśeṣaṇamanyaviśeṣaṇatvena, jṇānadvayamekatvena ca, viṣayāsadbhāva pakse api vidyamānatvena.
(c) *Vide* Bhāmatī, p. 38, Bombay Edn.

CHAPTER 8

NESCIENCE

Phenomenal appearance as explained by the monistic philosophers is the creation of *avidyā*. The world of experience, subjective and objective, is a false show on the locus consciousness. *Ajñāna* screens the locus and creates implications of practical and theoretical reason. *Avidyā* is the *causa materia* of the world illusion, inexplicable in its nature. It has no beginning in time and is located in *Brahman* and as a screening principle it hides the true nature of *Brahman* and creates this phenomenal appearance. The position of the monists has been seriously questioned by all the theistic schools of Vedānta. A good number of objections has been raised by the Rāmānujists, Mādhvites and other theistic teachers against the monistic interpretation of *avidyā*. An attempt is made to give here a glimpse into the dialectical search of the different Vedāntic schools with their different standpoints.

Rāmānujists and Mādhvites urge that *avidyā* as an existence as held by the monists escapes logical and categorical determination. It cannot be logically defined. And there is no logical proof to satisfy the position of the monists. The author of Nyāyāmṛta contends that the Advaita-Vedānta as an epistemological inquiry admits of three categories, *viz.*,

(a) the pure consciousness,
(b) the knower, and
(c) the knowables.

Pure consciousness alone exists and the other two categories are relatively real. *Avidyā* cannot partake of the permanent character of the pure consciousness because the pure consciousness is alone real and *ajñāna* does not share in the true character of *Brahman*.

Again it can neither be knower nor knowable, for they are due to *avidyā* or nescience and what is due to nescience cannot be nescience itself. Moreover if it falls in the purview of nescience, then something else in the shape of nescience is necessary to account for its existence and so on. This leads us to the fallacy of infinite regress.

In order to refute the objections that have been raised by the Mādhvites, Advaita-Vedānta defines that "*Avidyā* as the *causa materia* of all illusions is without a beginning and positive and yet removable by pure consciousness."[1]

This *ajñāna* has no definite origin, but has got a definite end. The author of Nyāyāmṛta asserts that in the case of the rope-serpent, etc., the above definition does not hold good. Nescience has been defined as beginningless, but as applied to rope-serpent has a beginning in point of time.

The Śaṁkarites, refuting the objection of the Mādhvites, divide *ajñāna* into *(i) Tūlā* and *(ii) Mūlā,* secondary and primary. *Tūlā,* the secondary *avidyā* is the concrete form of the *mūlā* the primary *avidyā*. *Avidyā* is one in essence and manifests itself in and through phenomenal appearances of this worldly existence. It also works in and through the manifold objects of senses. They are but the concrete expressions of the one beginningless primary *avidyā*. Just as pure Consciousness, though eternal and indeterminate, appears limited and determinate in the knowledge of the concrete manifold, so *avidyā* though without a beginning manifests itself through limitation in the concrete worldly expression.

Again the positive character of *avidyā* has been seriously contended against by the Mādhvites. The Advaita-Vedānta asserts that *ajñāna* is positive in its character as indicated by the definition itself. But this nescience, the Mādhvites argue, is the material cause of both positive and negative phases of the world. So it militates against the law of causation which implies that the material cause and effect must be of the same nature.

If position can give rise to negation, then reality can cause an illusion.[2] Reality is never destroyed because it is eternal and permanent. Illusion will thus never be destroyed because it will also share in these qualities. To meet the objection the Śaṁkarites maintain that the term 'positive' is wider in its connotation as applied to *avidyā*. It is a category which is neither positive in the ordinary sense nor negative but a third something which is different from both position and negation. As the cause of both the positive and negative phases of the world, it is at once positive-negative in its nature or more truly it is inexplicable and mysterious.

It has been further objected that as nescience is neither positive *(sat)* nor negative *(asat)* but a third something, it cannot be the cause of the world which possesses positive and negative characteristics.

But this is to be refuted thus—though nescience is a third something yet it partly shares in the characteristics of the *bhāvatva* and *abhāvatva*. While possessing the former it can be the cause of the positive phases of the world, while sharing in the latter, it can be the cause of the negative phases. The law of causation does not imply that the effect must partake of the character of the cause in all points. It should be similar to the cause in certain essentials. So there arises no violation of the doctrine of causality. The world appearance in itself is inexplicable as its cause nescience is inexplicable. This point will be illustrated later on in connexion with the inexplicability of *avidyā*.

In order to meet the objection raised by the Mādhvites that if reality be the cause of illusion the latter must also be something real, the Śaṁkarites argue that perfect community of identity between cause and effect would make any transition from the one to the other impossible. Law of causation therefore implies no such community between cause and effect which however may agree in their essentials. Again an illusory effect, though illusory in appearance, is grounded on the locus-consciousness which admits of no change. The Śaṁkarites maintain that what is illusory in an appearance originates from nescience but for the *is-ness* which runs through it, it is to be referred to the locus-consciousness which though unchangeable shines in and through all appearances. Yet *Brahman* which is unchangeable cannot itself be the cause of something which undergoes changes constantly. We must therefore seek for causality of this world in something else. So *avidyā* which is false and inexplicable is the *causa materia* of the manifold whose nature is shrouded in a mystery.

Inexplicable character of nescience

Ajñāna or Nescience neither partakes of the character of being nor non-being. It is a third something mysterious in its character. Rāmānuja contends that from experience we find two categories, *viz.*, *sat* and *asat,* real and non-real, the world of objects must be included either in the former or in the latter, according as it possesses the quality of existence or non-existence. But *ajñāna* which Advaita-Vedānta defines as positive-negative, can be subsumed in neither of the two. Hence the inexplicable character of the world, on which the Śaṁkarites take their stand, has been assumed against all logic. The existence of such an inexplicable category is contradictory to experience and what is not in experience does not exist and cannot be true. The Śaṁkarites are guilty of begging the question, for the inexplicable nature of *ajñāna* involves them in the difficulty of defining something which can by no means be logically and categorically determined. The assumption of such a possibility not only goes againts the validity of experience but undermines the very foundation of knowledge by creating a mental confusion.[3] The Śaṁkarites maintain that we can realise in our experience a third something inexplicable in its nature, a factor which has been left out of account by the Rāmānujists in their categorical determination of the entire existence into *sat* and *asat*. So they have analysed the entire existence into three categories, *viz.*,

(1) transcendentally real,
(2) empirically real,
(3) *tuccha* or imaginary.

According to them *sat* and asat, judged by their connotations, represent the two extreme poles. The one (sat) is transcendental reality and the other (asat) is *tuccha* or imaginary in character.

The division of the Rāmānujists into *sat* and *asat* is faulty as it does not cover the entire existence. Room must be found for a third category in the shape of positive-negative occupying a middle position in order to account for the concrete manifold which, though phenomenal, has a relative validity. The world is neither *sat* nor asat. It stands midway between the two extremes, *sat* and *asat*. It is *sat* because it partially shares in the quality of existence and *asat* because it partially partakes of the character of non-existence, for though without a beginning, it has an end and will die out. The world is, because it appears to us, and also is not, because it will cease to exist ultimately. It follows also that *avidyā,* the *causa materia* of this world exists because it appears to us, and at the same time it does not exist because it ultimately dies out of existence. So we find that both the world and its *causa materia, avidyā,* are neither being nor non-being but inexplicable in their nature. Madhusūdana Sarasvatī thus maintains that the inexplicable character of nescience is neither *sat* nor *asat* nor both.[4] From the assertion that the world is neither *sat* nor *asat*, it clearly follows that it can neither be *sadasat*. Madhusūdana's answer is that he has used the third alternative in order to prove clearly the mysterious character of this worldly existence.[5]

The charge that avidyā cannot have a locus

Now the question is, if such an inexplicable nescience exist where does it exist? What is the seat of nescience? Nescience is not a self-existent entity in the Advaita-Vedānta, for it brings in the charge of dualism. *Avidyā* must have a substrate for its existence, *avidyā* without a locus *(āśraya)* and object *(viṣaya)* is inconceivable.

Jīva cannot be the substrate of nescience

Jīva or finite self is a. creation of *avidyā* and cannot therefore be the seat of *avidyā.* Finitude is a mode of the measuring principle. All finite selves and finite existences have their characteristic, *viz.,* finitude due to *avidyā* which limits the unlimited, features the featureless; and as a result of the limiting activity of *avidyā,* consciousness which has no inherent limitation in itself appears as limited and finite intelligence. Everywhere in the Advaita-Vedānta finitude or limitation is due to the operation of *avidyā* and what is a product of *avidyā* cannot form the support or substrate of *avidyā*.

Īśvara-consciousness also is not beyond limitation and on the same ground it cannot also be the locus of *avidyā*. If it be argued that the nescience which has finite intelligence as its locus, is quite different from the measuring principle which originates *Jīva* and Īśvara-consciousness, it leads to the fallacy of infinite regress, for the originating principle also requires its locus and so on.

Brahman cannot be the seat of *avidyā*

Brahman which is pure, self-luminous consciousness is opposed to *avidyā* which is sublated by knowledge and cannot be the support of *avidyā*.

Against these charges of the critics the Advaitins argue that both finite and infinite consciousness may form the substratum of *avidyā*. As regards the seat of *avidyā* there are chiefly two theories. Vācaspati and his school hold that *avidyā* is located in the finite *Jīva*-consciousness. Sarvajñātmamuni, Prakāśātman and Ānandabodha, who belong to the old school of the Advaita-Vedānta, maintain that *avidyā* is located in the absolute consciousness.

Vācaspati's position considered

The charge of begging the question levelled against Vācaspati's position is refuted by Madhusūdana Sarasvatī on the ground that both finite consciousness and *avidyā are* without a beginning in time, both exist simultaneously from eternity—one is the principle of modification and the other is the subject modified. They are not interdependent entities. Madhusūdana further observes that the percipiency of *Jīva* is not dependent upon *avidyā* and the charge—*avidyā* creating *sākṣi* or witness intelligence and *sākṣī* revealing *avidyā* does not stand. The percipiency is a potent fact and can in no way be affected by its association with *avidyā*. And *avidyā* is revealed by this percipiency of witness intelligence.[6] Again nescience and consciousness are not exactly interdependent because nescience has its locus in consciousness and depends upon consciousness for its existence but consciousness is not located in nescience, and does not depend upon *avidyā* for its existence.[7] *Avidyā* cannot totally eclipse *Jīva* or the percipient subject but can put a limitation upon its being. Now though the charge of interdependence cannot be brought forward here yet the question of inter-subordination *(anyonyādhīnatā)* of *avidyā* and *Jīva* cannot be denied. Inter-subordination means a relation between *avidyā* and *Jīva* and the relation is explained as one of container and the contained. In support of this relation Madhusūdana contends that just as one conceives a pot enclosing the sky, similarly *avidyā* is conceived as the limiting principle or vessel enclosing within it consciousness, which is thus turned into *Jīva* or finite self.[8]

Madhusūdana's explanations of Vācaspati's position shows that *Jīva* has two aspects—consciousness and finitude; as consciousness, it is eternal and unlimited as the sky enclosed in the pot in the given example and its finitude is only due to *avidyā*. Hence like the pot, *avidyā,* though it limits the *Jīva,* cannot completely affect its whole nature and *Jīva* as percipient subject can be the seat of *avidyā*.

Brahman or pure consciousness is the seat of avidyā

The old school of the Advaita-Vedānta holds that *Brahman* is the seat of *avidyā*. Against the objection of the critics that Pure Consciousness which is of the nature of light cannot sustain and support *ajñāna* which is of the nature of darkness and as such quite opposed to consciousness, Madhusūdana argues that the charge of contr-adiction is not to the point. The locus of *avidyā* and its destructive factor are not one and the same thing; what reveals *ajñāna* is undivided Pure Being-Bliss-Consciousness and what destroys and removes it is the modified consciousness reflected in the psychosis *(vṛttipratiphalita-jñāna)*.[9] Operation of *avidyā* emerges through subject-object differentiation and is opposed to knowledge which is characterized by the same subject-object reference. Absolute consciousness is neither a thought activity nor a judgment construction. It is a super-logical reality. It is not con-tradictory to *avidyā*. Consciousness as a process is contradictory to *avidyā*. Thus the opposite capacities of knowledge as intuition and judgment are supported by Madhusūdana by a commonplace example. The sun which lights up cotton, straw, etc., burns them when his rays are focussed through a lens. Similarly knowledge which sustains *avidyā* destroys it when knowledge is reflected in mental *vṛtti* or psychosis.[10]

The position of the old school of the Advaita-Vedānta has been criticised by the Mādhvites on the ground that the old-school theory goes against perception and thus involves contradiction. In the perception of *ajñāna* which is evident in the judgment construction—I do not know, etc., the Mādhvites contend that nescience is cognised as posited not in the *Absolute Brahman* but in the limited I-consciousness. I-consciousness implies egoistic feeling or *ahaṁkāra* which is inherent in the subject of judgment. Now judged from the perceptual standpoint *ajñāna* is supported and sustained by I-consciousness and not by *Brahman*.

The Advaitins refute the charge of the Mādhvites by pointing out that the Mādhva position involves a *petitio principii*. The limited I-consciousness is the result of the operation of *avidyā* and cannot, as we have seen, be the support of *avidyā*.

It is also to be noted in this connection that *avidyā* which has a beginning in point of time as applied to rope-serpent, oyster-silver, etc., is not something different from the primary *avidyā*. It is the concrete form of the primary one known as tūlā or secondary *avidyā*. It manifests itself through limitations of the concrete manifold and appears finite and limited. In essence avidyā is one and occupies the some locus though in the case of secondery *avidyā* the subjective self appears as its support, it is a wrong notion due to super-imposition or adhyāsa. It is not the limitation which is a creation of avidya sustains avidyā but consciousness itself under limitation supports it. Pure consciousness plus limitation creates a false notion impl-ying that the subjective consciousness is the support of avidyā[11] All limitations being the product of avidyā cannot sustain *avidyā*.

Thus something unlimited and infinite transcending all operation of *avidyā* must be sought for as the locus of avidyā and it is the Pure Being-Bliss Consciousness which is taken as the seat of avidyā in the Adaita-Vedānta.

Answer to the charge that Brahman cannot be concealed by nescience

We have seen that *avidyā* is located in Brahman or pure consciousness and it also conceals its real nature *Avidyā's* function is to conceal the nature of *Brahman* which is thus known as the object of *avidyā*. The result of *avidyā's* thus functioning is that the real nature of Brahman is not revealed to the percipient subject. *Avidyā* presents *Brahman* as different from what it is. The Pure Being-Bliss-Consciousness thus appears to the percipient as Non-Bliss-Consciousness. The percipient or *Jīva* is identical with this Being-Bliss-consciousness. But owing to the operation of *avidyā* the Jīva forgets his nature and appears to himself as finite, ignorant, etc., and at the dawn of consciousness *avidyā* is sublated and Jīva realeses his identity with Brahman. Avidyā as a screening principle only veils the real nature of *Brahman* which is not in any way modified or affected by its operation. The disappearance or non knwledge of self-luminous consciousness as Jīva's own essential mark is what is meant by concealment of *Brahman* by *avidyā*; and its reapearance or cognition on the destruction of *avidyā* is what is called revelation of *Brahman*. Or in other words, concealment means the forgetfulness of identity of *Jīva* with *Brahman* and revelation means identity with *Brahman*. Thus Rāmānuja's charge based on the contention that con-cealment means either obstruction of origination of luminosity *(prakāśotpatti-pratibandha)* or the destruction of existing lumi-nosity *(vidyamānasya vināśo vā)* falls to the ground.

The Advaitin's perception of *ajñāna* as a positive entitiy

This positive and inexplicable character of *ajñāna* is apprehended through perception, inference and some other logical proofs That *ajñāna* becomes directly cognisable to internal perception is patent enough from such judgments as I do not know, 'I do not know either myself or others.' In fact, such a judgment presents itself directly to the mind. It must not be regarded as a case of antecedent non-existence of knowledge which is presented to the mind not immediately, but mediately through *Anupalabdhi* an indirect proof. Even if it be admitted that negation is immediate in its perception,[12] the position does not improve. For, the experience under discussion presupposes that there is always a cognitive element in the self which recognises the negative character of the judgments.[13] The consciousness of the non-existence of knowledge is some kind of knowledge and as such cannot be explained away as mere negation for it leads to an apparent self-contradiction.

To draw out the fallacious logic of its opponent schools the Śaṁkarites analyse the judgment 'I do not know,' and pointedly ask whether or not in the above judgment the subjective self, on the one hand, is conceived as the locus or substrate of non-knowledge and the predicate of the judgment and knowledge, on the other—is conceived as the counter-entity of non-knowledge as implied in the predicate. If answered in the affirmative, the judgment can form no valid conception as the subject and the predicate are contradictory in their import and as such cannot be joined by a copula. The other alternative remains and it may be argued that in the judgment there is no apprehension of knowledge. In that case the very conception of the non-existence of knowledge becomes impossible, for knowledge stands as the counter-entity of non-knowledge in the predicate of the judgment and no conception of negation is possible without the conception of its counter-entity.[14] If, on the other hand, non-knowledge be viewed not as a negative, but as a positive entity, there arises no contradiction even if there is (as there is in fact) at the same time knowledge of self as qualified by non-knowledge, and of knowledge as the counter-entity of non-knowledge. We therefore must accept the conclusion that the state of knowledge expressed by the judgment 'I am non-knowing,' has for its object a non-knowledge which is a positive entity.[15]

The Rāmānujists' criticism against the Śaṁkarites's view

The theory of the Advaitins to propound *ajñāna* as a positive entity has been criticised by the Rāmānujists. They argue that no perception based on sound principle reveals criticism against the *ajñāna* to be positive in nature. In such judgment constructions as I am not knowing, I know neither myself nor others,' the contradictions, which are said to vitiate the antecedent non-existence view of knowledge, equally affect the position of the Advaitins who explain *avidyā* as a positive entity. The objections raised by them are equally destructive of their own theory. Thus it may be questioned whether or not the inner Reality is known as the object and substrate of *avidyā*. If known, it leaves no room for nescience which must die out by the cognition of the true nature of the inner reality. On the other hand, if it be not known, how can there be any possibility of nescience without its objects and locus?[16] Now the answer given by the Ādvaitins to meet these objections, equally redeems the position of the Rāmānujists. The Advaita-Vedānta, for example, explains that what really is contradictory to *ajñāna* is the pure presentation of Self or Reality but not the limited I-consciousness which is but an obscure presentation of reality. So in the judgment construction there is in fact no contradiction between the cognition of the substrate and the object on the one side and knowledge of *ajñāna* on the other, for, the Ī-consciousness, the subject of judgment, is not pure but an obscure presentation of reality. The Rāmānujists may acquit themselves with the same answer. No contradiction is involved if *ajñāna* be viewed as antecedent non-existence of knowledge. For it may be contradictory to the pure presentation of Reality but not to the limited presentation of I-consciousness. So *ajñāna,* as antecedent non-existence of knowledge, may have its object and locus in the self in its obscure presentation. Hence the Advaitins make no real advance by framing a new theory on the positive nature of *avidyā*.

Moreover, whether viewed as a positive entity or as the prior non-existence of knowledge, in either case it comes out, as its connotation indicates, as non-knowledge or negation of knowledge, *i.e.,* as that which is other than knowledge, or that which is contradictory to knowledge; and in each one of these cases it is admitted that non-knowledge implies pre-conception of knowledge. So non-knowledge as held by the Advaitins also suggests its relativity to the cognition of knowledge as much as the antecedent non-existence of knowledge implies the pre-existence of knowledge as its counter-entity. The Advaitins, therefore, in their imputation and refutation have indeed argued for both the schools. They have gained nothing by ascribing a positive character to non-knowledge. So antecedent non-existence of knowledge, whose entity is admitted by both the schools should be accepted for the explanation of the judgments discussed above.[17]

Advaitin's answer

Against this contention of Rāmānuja, the Śaṁkarites argue that antecedent non-existence of knowledge *(jñānaprāgabhāva)* is not admitted as a distinct category by the Advaitins. Even admitting for argument's sake that there is such a category as antecedent non-existence, the *ajñāna* of the Advaitins is very different from it, for it is not of the nature of non-existence; it is a distinct category different from both positivity and negativity as we have seen in our previous discussion. If *ajñāna* meant antecedent non-existence of *jñāna* then it would have been negation of knowledge and contradictory to it. But according to Advaitins *ajñāna* is not admitted as contradictory to *jñāna* or knowledge, for it resides there, *i.e.,* in pure consciousness, and conceals its real nature and as such it is not something negative. It is said to be of the nature of darkness and darkness is, according to the Advaitins, a positive entity. Again since *ajñāna* is perceived, it cannot be something negative, for Advaitins do not admit that anything negative or non-existent can be perceived, and that is why the Advaitins regard *anupalabdhi* as a separate logical proof.

Advatin's inference to prove *ajñāna* as a positive entity

Again, the Advaitins argue that *ajñāna* as a positive entity is also proved by inference in the following form:

"Just as the first rays of a lamp, which light up and illuminate objects not already illuminated, annihilate darkness having the following four characteristics, *viz.* :—

(1) that the darkness is not merely the negation of light, but has, a positive existence—a concrete content;
(2) that the darkness had been screening the objects which are afterwards illuminated by the rays of light;
(3) that the darkness is capable of being annihilated by the rays of light; and
(4) that the darkness was located in the locality now occupied by the rays;

so the knowledge established by one of the different means of proof *(pramāṇa-jñāna)* which lights up or intellectually illuminates the objects of knowledge, which were not known before, annihilates ignorance having four similar characteristics, *viz.*,

(1) that ignorance is not merely the negation of knowledge, but has a positive existence;
(2) that ignorance had so long been screening the objects which are afterwards intellectually illuminated by the *pramāṇa-jñāna* or knowledge established by the valid means of proof;
(3) that this ignorance is capable of being annihilated by the act of intellectual illumination; and
(4) that the ignorance was located in the locality of the said illumination.[18]

To put the argument in the form of a syllogism : —

All instances of lighting up or illumination (whether intellectual or otherwise) of objects not already illuminated are instances which are invariably accompanied or preceded by the annihilation of a substance having four characteristics mentioned before (1, 2, 3, 4).

All instances of knowledge established by one of the different means of proof are instances of lighting up or illuminating objects not already illuminated.

All instances of the knowledge of proof are instances which

are invariably accompanied or preceded by the annihilation of a substance (ignorance) possessing the above four characteristics.

The *vyāpti* or the universal concomitance in this syllogism is established by the observation of the single instance of physical or material illumination of objects by the rays of light. It is worth notice here that the physical illumination of material objects by means of the light of a lamp and the intellectual illumination, *i.e.*, the apprehension of objects of knowledge by means of perception, inference, etc.—these two entirely different kinds of illumination—are treated as belonging to the same category.

The above argument may be put also in the form of a hypothetical-categorical syllogism as follows :—

In all cases if there is any lighting up or illumination of objects not already illuminated there is an antecedent or concomitant annihilation of substance having the above four characteristics.

There is a lighting up or illumination of objects (not already illuminated) in the knowledge of the valid means of proof.

There is an antecedent or concomitant annihilation of a substance having the said four characteristics in knowledge.

Here also the major premise—the *vyāpti*—is a general proposition the truth of which is established by the observation of a particular instance, *viz.*, that in the case of illumination of objects by rays of light there is an invariable antecedent or concomitant phenomenon, *i.e.*, the annihilation of darkness which is a positive form of being.

Rāmānuja's criticism against the view of the Advaitins

Rāmānuja raises the following objections against the above inference of the Advaitins : —

The instance of physical illumination is not a relevant instance at all and does not establish the universal relation of concomitance between the phenomenon of illumination and the phenomenon of annihilation of ignorance as a positive form of existence, because intellectual illumination is quite different from physical illumination.

The term *prakāśa* is used here in two different senses. *Prakāśa* as intellectual illumination means apprehension of objects of knowledge in perception, inference, etc. This intellectual illumination is due, not to light, but to consciousness alone *(vijñānasyaiva prakāśakatvam)*. Light cannot produce intellectual illumination or apprehension of objects of knowledge, it simply helps the operation of the organ of vision by removing the obstacle, *viz.*, darkness which stands in the way of visual perception. Intellectual illumination *(prakāśa)* consists in apprehending the objects of knowledge and not in simply removing the obstacles thereto *(na hi virodhinirasanamātraṁ prakāśakatvam)* . Hence the relation of sequence or concomitance between the physical illumination by light and the annihilation of darkness cannot establish a similar relation between intellectual illumination and annihilation of ignorance as a positive form of being.There being no resemblance in kind between the two entirely different types of illumination the instance of physical illumination is an irrelevant instance.[19] The fallacy of false analogy therefore vitiates the whole body of the argument. The fallacy of ambiguity in respect of the term *prakāśa* (illumination) is equally worth notice.

Even assuming for argument's sake that illumination *(prakāśa)* means not only intellectual illumination, *i.e.*, apprehension of the objects of knowledge, but also any function which helps or facilitates the act of intellectual illumination (such as the operations of the sense organs, light, etc.) it follows that in every instance of illumination in this wide sense there must be present as an invariable antecedent or concomitant a substance bearing the four characteristics mentioned above. Just as in the instance of the rays of light which illuminate the objects net illuminated already the annihilation of darkness is present as an invariable antecedent; just as in the instance of intellectual illumination of the objects of knowledge the annihilation of a positive substance, *viz.*, ignorance is present as an invariable antecedent; similarly in the instance of illumination *(i.e.,* operations helping apprehension of objects) effected by the organs of senses, the annihilation of a similar substance, *another* ignorance *(ajñāna)*—must be present as an invariable antecedent or concomitant.

And again we can infer another non-knowledge as an invariable antecedent or concomitant to this *ajñāna,* which this inference aims at; for this *ajñāna* under discussion also being based on a valid inference comes under the head of *pramāṇa-jñāna* or knowledge established by valid means of proof.

Now if another *ajñāna* be established as an antecedent to this *ajñāna* which this inference tries to prove, that *ajñana* must hide, as the inference implies, the non-knowledge which is located in the *Brahman* and veils it and not the *Brahman* itself. And as the second *ajñāna* has *avidyā* the screening principle of *Brahman* as its locus and object, it has no bearing upon *Brahman.* It, therefore, has got no utility in the range of our philosophic speculation as the supposition of such an *ajñāna* stands without any purpose. *Ajñāna* is cognised as a screening principle in our philosophic conception. It hides *Brahman* the locus-consciousness and as a becoming principle it produces this cosmic manifold. If no such purpose be served by admitting a second *ajñāna* as an antecedent to the positive *avidyā* proved by the said inference, it is completely useless to suppose such an entity.[20] And from this supposition this inference involves as well the fallacy of infinite regress. But the instance of these two separate ignorances which may be proved by the same logic advanced by the opponent himself, would be contradictory [21] *(viruddha)* to the conclusion drawn by him. The fallacy therefore lies in the universal major premise—that all instances of illumination are preceded by the annihilation of a positive form of existence having certain characteristics, which is not only materially false but also, when closely examined, is found to be contradictory to the conclusion drawn by the opponent himself.[22]

If the opponent argues that in the instance of intellectual illumination alone ignorance having the said four characteristics is present as an invariable antecedent, but in the instance of illumination effected by the organs of senses and also in the instance of illumination indicated by the opponent's inference of *ajñāna,* no separate ignorances are present as invariable antecedent or concomitant, then it amounts to a denial of the *vyāpti*—a denial of universal relation of invarible concomitance between the phenomenon of illumination and the phenomenon of annihilation of ignorance. Thus the universal premise which states this relation of universal concomitance would be false; or in other words, if the phenomenon of illumination is sometimes preceded by the annihilation of ignorance and sometimes not, then there can be no generalisation at all of any relation of invariable concomitance between the two phenomena and therefore the existence of ignorance on the basis of the said inference would not be established at all. The *vyāpti* or the general proposition is materially true when the invariable concomitance between the two phenomena is established by observation of an adequate number of instances. But if there be some instances in which this concomitance fails, *i. e.,* in which the phenomenon implied by the middle term does not accompany the phenomenon implied by the major term, the result is that there can be no *vyāpti,* no generalisation of the relation of invariable concomitance between the two phenomena and any syllogism based upon this wrong generalisation is fallacious; this fallacy is known as *Anaikāntika hetu* in Indian logic. An illustration will make it clear. Sound is eternal for it is devoid of tactual properties. In the instances of jars and other things it is observed that there is a relation of co-presence or concomitance between tactual properties and destructibility. From these instances one may generalise that all things having tactual properties are things which are liable to destruction; with this universal proposition as the major premise a syllogism may be thus constructed—

All things having tactual properties are things which are liable to destruction.

Sound is not a thing having tactual properties.
Sound is not a thing which is liable to destruction.

This inference is fallacious; apart from other fallacies it is subject to the fallacy of the falsity of the major premise. It is not true that in all instances without any exception the presence of tactual properties invariably accompanies the presence of destructibility. There are negative instances in which tactual properties are not accompanied by destructibility. It is found that atoms though they possess tactual properties are not liable to destruction *(dṛśyate sparśavāṁśca aṇur nityaśca iti)*. These negative instances must not be neglected. Hence if the *hetu,* or the phenomenon implied by the middle term, is found in some instances to accompany and in some other instances not to accompany the phenomenon implied by the major term *(sādhya),* then there can be no *vyāpti*—no universalisation of the relation of concomitance between the two phenomena. This fallacy of inference is ultimately based upon a fallacy of non-observation, *i. e.,* neglect of negative instances which should have been taken notice of.[23]

To judge the inference under discussion from this standpoint the opponent is placed between the two horns of a dilemma.

If in all instances, without a single exception, illumination is preceded by the annihilation of ignorance then in the instance of the particular inference of the opponent and also in the instance of the operation of sense organs the existence of different ignorances as separate substances would be established —which is contradictory to the position of the opponent.

Again if there are some exceptions in which illumination is not preceded by annihilation of ignorance then the relation of concomitance would not be universal and consequently the opponent's conclusion would be false, being based on a false major premise.

Illumination is preceded by ignorance either in all cases without exception or there are some exceptions.

So, the opponent's position is either self-contradictory or subject to the fallacy of the falsity of the major premise.

Hence the inference as advanced by the Advaitins for the establishment of *ajñāna* as a positive entity is fallacious in more ways than one; and on the basis of this inference, says Rāmānuja, positive character of *ajñāna* cannot be established.

Again to prove the untenable character of the Advaitin's inference Rāmānujists advance the following counter-reasonings:

1. *Ajñāna* which is a matter of dispute, is not located in

Brahman which is pure consciousness, because it is *ajñāna* like the *ajñāna* seen in oyster-silver. *Ajñāna* can reside in a conscious being or knower and not in absolute consciousness. *Ajñāna* in the knower veils the true nature of the oyster and makes it appear as silver.

2. *Ajñāna* being *ajñāna* cannot veil knowledge, it can veil only an object as seen in the case of oyster-silver. *Ajñāna* veils oyster shells which is an object to the perceiver.
3. *Ajñāna* cannot be sublated by knowledge because *ajñāna* cannot veil knowledge; *ajñāna* that is sublated by knowledge veils the object of that knowledge. Thus *ajñāna* of oyster is sublated by knowledge because oyster is an object of knowledge. If the *ajñāna* regarding *Brahman* be removable by knowledge, then *Brahman* becomes an object of knowledge.
4. *Brahman* cannot be the location of *ajñāna* because *Brahman* is not a knower as the pot is not a knower.
5. Inferential knowledge cannot have an antecedent *ajñāna* other than its own antecedent non-existence, because it is knowledge derived from valid proofs. The inference which has been advanced by the Advaitins to establish *ajñāna* proves the existence of another *ajñāna* veiling this *ajñāna* established by the Advaitin's inference. Thus the Advaitin's inference leads to the establishment of *ajñāna,* which goes against the Advaita position. To avoid this, it is better to deny *ajñāna* as a positive entity; *ajñāna* can only be antecedent non-existence of knowledge.
6. Knowledge cannot destroy an entity *(vastu)*. For this knowledge is mere knowledge without being endowed with special powers. Knowledge and that which is other than knowledge can destroy a substance only when endowedwithspecial powers, such as the knowledge of *yogins* and the club.
7. *Ajñāna* which is a positive entity cannot be sublated by knowledge because it is positive in its character like the pot.[24]

Advaitin's reply

Against these objections of Rāmānujists the Advaitins contend that they do not admit an *ajñāna* which veils ajñāna. The inference is not intended to establish *ajñāna;* it is established by *sākṣicaitanya* or witness intelligence and is without beginning. The inference and other proofs are advanced to establish its positive character and not existence.[25] No further elaboration is necessary here as this point has been already discussed at length in connexion with the question of the seat of *ajñāna.* Thus the charge of inconclusiveness of the middle term or *hetu* is not to the point. As regards the instance of lamp as revealing what was concealed, the charge is that knowledge is the only revealing factor, and so the analogy of the lamp and knowledge fails. In answer to this objection, the Advaitins say that by the expression revealing factor as applied to lamp in this particular example they mean what is contradictory to non-revealing factors *(aprakāśa-virodhi)* and so helping agents such as the sun, light, sense organs, etc., are included by the term *prakāśaka.* They however differ in their distinctive functions.

Thus, knowledge is contradictory to nescience which veils an object, so it is an illuminating principle, spiritual in nature, which is self-revealed and self-evident. Light is contradictory to darkness which screens an object from the view of the perceiver. It is an illuminating principle but is inert in its nature. The eye is a primary instrument in visual perception. It is thus an illuminating principle but only as an instrument.[26]

As regards the counter-arguments advanced by the critics the Advaitins observe that the first, second, and third inferences in which *ajñāna* is the minor term or *pakṣa* and the *ajñāna* in the case of oyster is an explanatory example, are faulty because they are conditional or (*sopādhika*). Condition or *upādhi,* in short is that which is present in the explanatory example but not in the minor and thus accompanies the major and is not invariably accompanied by the middle.[27] In the inferences under consideration the explanatory instances may be characterised by secondary ajñāna or *pallavājñāna* as distinguished from the principle of cosmic illusion or *mūlājñāna*. The *ajñāna* residing in oyster can be explained as *pallavājñāna,* but *ajñāna* the minor or *pakṣa*, which means *mūlājñāna* cannot be so explained.

The fourth inference again is conditional because the explanatory example, the pot, can be characterised as *phalavyāpya* but not *Brahman,* the minor term in the syllogism.

The fifth inference does not affect the Advaitin's position, for they do not prove by their inference the existence of nescience but only its positive character, nescience being established by *Sākṣicaitanya,* or witness intelligence.

In the sixth inference the middle is unreal in itself because knowledge is a self-luminous, self-evident entity in which there can be no addition or subtraction of power. Thus the middle as determined by the absence of special power cannot be established. The middle is called *viśeṣaṇāsiddha* or is not established in respect of its qualifying adjuncts.

In the seventh inference the *vyāpti* or invariable concomitance fails in the case of the *ajñāna* of oyster-silver which *(ajñāna)* is positive according to the standpoint of Advaita-Vedānta and yet is sublated by the true knowledge of oyster.

This dialectic we have so far followed removes the doubts and refutes the charges of the opponents of Advaita-Vedānta and establishes *avidyā,* or the principle of cosmic illusion, as a positive entity which is inexplicable in its nature. This *avidyā* is beginningless and being the principle of cosmic illusion introduces multiplicity, subject-object relations, individuality, etc., where there is but one undifferentiated Being. Pain, sorrow, grief and all other evils of life arise from a consciousness of multiplicity. To one who sees one in the apparent many no sorrow or no evil can come. But the knowledge of the absolute one-ness and the illusory character of this world does not dawn so long as *avidyā* persists. It is only when the veil of *avidyā* or nescience is removed, that we can realise the utter hollowness of this world; we become conscious that this phenomenal world is superimposed on the Being whose nature is Being-Bliss-Consciousness. The study of the Vedānta removes *avidyā* and reveals true knowledge completely disentangled from the accidental impurities. It is in absolute monism, where all multiplicity vanishes and where knower, knowledge and known are all merged in one undifferentiated Being, that we find ineffable Bliss. It is to this end, to the removal of misery and to the attainment of Bliss, that the study of the Vedānta tends.

REFERENCES

1. (a) Advaita-siddhi, pp. 544-45. Bombay Edition.
   (b) Anādibhāvarūpaṁ yadajñānena vilīyate
   Tadajñānamiti prājñā lakṣaṇaṅ sampracakṣate.
   Citsukhī, p. 57, Bombay Edition.
   (c) Bhāmatī, p. 333, Bombay Edition.
2. Abhāvasya bhāvopādānatve asatyasya satyopādānatvāpātāt. N. Mr., p. 99.
3. *(a)* *Vide* R. Bh., p. 175, Lotus L. Edition.
   (b) *Vide* Śrutaprakāśikā, p.170.
4. Sadvilakṣaṇatve sati asadvilakṣaṇatve sati sadasadvilakṣaṇatvam. Sattvāsattvābhyāṁ vicārāsahatve'pi sadasattvena vicārāsahatvaṁ vā. Sattvarahitattve sati asattvarahitattve sati sadasattvarahitatvamityapi sādhu. Adyaita-siddhi, p. 621, Bombay Edition.
5. *(a)* Tattatpratiyogidurnirūpatāmātraprakaṭanāya.—Ad. S., p. 621.
   (b) *Ibid,* pp. 620-25.
   (c) Citsukhī, pp. 54-57 and 74, 82, Bombay Edition.
   (d) E. Bh., p. 170.
   (e) *Vide* Śrutaprakāśikā, p. 170, Bombay Edition.
   (f) *Vide* Nyāyāmṛta, p. 99, Bombay Edition.
   (g) *Vide* Khaṇḍanakhaṇḍakhādyam, p. 137, Discussion on the positive and inexplicable character of *avidyā*.
6. *Vide* Ad. S., p. 585, Bombay Edition.
7. Ajñānasya cidāśrayatve cidadhīnasthitikatve'pi citi avidyāśritatva-tadadhīnasthitikatvayorabhāvāt. Ad. S., p. 585.
8. Svenaiva kalpite deṣe vyomni yadvad ghaṭadikaṁ
   tathā jīvāśrayāvidyāṁ manyante jñānakovidah.—Ad. S., p. 585.
9. Nanu kathaṁ caitanyamajñānāṣrayaḥ tasya prakāśarūpatvāt, tayoṣ-ca tamaḥprakāśavad viruddhasvabhūvatvāditi cenna, ajñānavirodhijñāṁ na caitanyamātraṁ, kintu vṛttiprativiṁbitaṁ tacca nāvidyāśrayaḥ yaccāvidyāṣ rayaḥ tacca nājñānavirodhi. Ad. S., p. 577
10. Svatastṛṇatūlādibhāsakasya saurālokasya sūryakāntāvacchedena svabhāsyatṛṇatūlādi-dāhakatvavat svato'vidyātatkāryabhāsakasya caitany-asya vṛttyavacchedena taddāhakatvāt. Advaita-siddhi, p. 577.
11. Vide Advaita-siddhi, p. 577.

12. The Naiyāyikas and some other philosophers, who hold that *Anupalabdhi* is not a separate means of proof, include it under perception.
13. Abhāvasya pratyakṣatvābhyupagame api ayamanubhavo nātmajñānā-bhāvaviṣ ayaḥ anubhavavelāyāmapi jñānasya vidyamācatvāt avidyamānatve jñānābhāva-pratītyanupapatteśca. R. Bh. 169.
14. (a) Ahamajña ityasminnanubhave ahamityātmanaḥ abhāvadharmitayā, jñānasya ca pratijogitayā avagatirasti na vā, asti cet virodhādeva na jñānābhāvānubhavasaṁbhavaḥ, no cet dharmipratiyogijñānasavyapekṣo jñānābhāvānubbavaḥ sutarāṁ na saṁbhavati. R. Bh , p. 171.
    (b) *Vide* Śrutaprakāśikā, p. 171.
15. Asya ajñānasya bhāvarūpatve dharmipratiyogijñānasadbhāvo'pi virodhābhāvādayamanubhavaḥ bhāvarūpājñāna-viṣaya eva abhyupagantavya iti. R.Bh., pp. 171-72, Bombay Edition.
16. Pratyakṣeṇa na bhāvarūpamajñānaṁ pratīyate, yastu jñānaprāga-bhāvaviṣ ayatve virodha uktaḥ sa hi bhāvarūpajñāne'pi tulyaḥ viṣayatvena āśrayatvena ca ajñānasya vyāvartakatayā pratyagarthaḥ pratipanno vā apratipanno va, pratipannaścet tatsvarūpajñānanirvartyaṁ tadajñānaṁ tasmin pratipanne kathamivatiṣṭhati, apratipannaścet, vyāvartakāśraya-viṣayajñāna-śūnyamajñānaṁ kathamanubhūyeta. R.Bh., pp. 173-70, Bombay Edition.
16. (a) *Vide* R. Bh., pp. 174-75, Bombay Edition.
    (b) *Vide* Śrutaprakāśikā, pp. 174-75, Bombay Edition.
18. *(a)* Pañcapādikā-vivaraṇa, p. 13, Benares Edition.
    (b) Vivādādhyāsitaṁ pramāṇajñānaṁ svaprāgabhāva-vyatirikta-svaviṣ ayāvaraṇa-svanivartya-svadeśagata-vastvantara-pūrvakaṁ aprakāśitārthaprakāśakatvāt andhakāre prathamotpannapradīpaśikhāvat. Advaita-siddhi, p. 562, Bombay Edition,
    (c) R. Bh., pp. 172-73, Bombay Edition.
    N.B.—Those who hold such inference accept the view that darkness is a positive entity first from its being more or less dense, and secondly from its being perceived as having colour, activity, etc. Tamaḥ tamāla-varṇābhaṁ calatīti pratīyate, rūpavat vat kriyāva tvāt dravyantu daśamaṁ atamḥ.
    (d) Advaita-siddhi, pp. 562-63.
    (e) Vedānta-kalpataru, 1. 3. 3.
    Amalānanda in his Vedānta-Kalpataru, in order to establish the positive character of *ajñāna* on the basis of dialectical logic says : —
    Yadyapi śuktiṁ svata eva jadāmavidyā nāvṛṇoti tathāpitatsthānirvācya-bhāvarūparajatopādānatveneṣṭavyeti, bhāvarūpāvidyā saprayojanā pramāṇantu Ditthapramā Ditthagatatve sati yaḥ pramābhāvaḥ tattvānadhikaraṇānādi-nivarttikā pramātvāt Dapittha pramāvat.
    (f) Vedānta-kalpataruparimala, p. 333, Bombay Edition.
19. R. Bh., p. 179, Bombay Edition,
20. Pramāṇajñānasya aprakāśitarthaprakāśakatvat svaviṣayāvaraṇajñānāntara-sādhakatve sati tadajñānaṁ Brahmasvarupacchadakam siṣādhayiṣita-majñānamāvṛṇoti, tenāvrtatvāt tadajñānaṁ Brahmaṇā na sākṣāt kriyate,

aparamārthasya apratīyamānasya kāryakaratvāyogāt ajñānakalpanā niṣpha-lā tirodhānarūpakāryārthaṁ hi tat kalpanā. Śrutaprakāśikā, p. 178.

21. *(a)* When the phenomenon implied by the middle term, instead of invariably accompanying the phenomenon implied by the major, is not at all found to occur along with it we have a fallacy called *viruddhahetuḥ,* According to Vātsyāyanabhāṣya *viruddhahetuḥ* means a reason which contradicts the final conclusion. Thus it may also be taken as a fallacy of self-contradictory reasoning.
(b) *Vide* Vātsyāyanabhāṣya, 1.2.6:
(c) Siddhāntamabhyupetya tadvirodhī viruddhaḥ.
(d) *Vide* Nyāyavārttika, p. 172, Benares Edition.
(e) *Vide* Indian Logic and Atomism by A. B. Keith, p. 146.

22. *(a)* *Vide* R. Bh., p. 178, Bombay Edition.
(b) *Vide* Śrutaprakāśikā, pp. 178-79, Bombay Edition.

23. (a) Anaikāntikaḥ savyabhicāraḥ nityaḥ śabdaḥ asparśatvāt sparśavān kumbhaḥ anityaḥ dṛṣṭaḥ, na ca tathā asparśavān śabdaḥ tasmāt asparśatvāt nitya śabdaḥ sparśavān aṇuḥ nityaśca, asparśā buddhiranityā ca. Vātsyāyanabhāṣya, 1.2. 5.
(b) Yat khalu sādhyatajjātīyavṛttitve sati anyatra vartate tad vyabhicāri tatra yo heturupātta bhāvantāvāśritya vartate saḥ anaikāntikaḥ. Nyāyavārttika, pp. 169-70, Benares Edition.
(c) R. Bh., p. 188, Lotus Library Edition.
(d) Śrutaprakāśikā, pp. 178-79, Bombay Edition.
(e) Indian Logic and Atomism, by A. B. Keith.

24. (a) Vivādādhyāsitamajñānaṁ na jñānamātra Brahmāśrayaṁ ajñānatvāt, śuktikādy ajñānavat.
(b) Vivādādhyāsitatnajñānaṁ na jñānāvaraṇam ajñānatvāt śuktikādya-jñānavat, viṣayāvaraṇaṁ hi tat.
(c) Ajñānaṁ na jñānanivartyaṁ jñānaviṣayānāvaraṇatvāt—yajjñānani-vartyamajñānaṁ tajjñānaviṣayāvaraṇaṁ yathā śuktyādyajñānam.
(d) Brahma na ajñānāspadaṁ jñātṛtvavirahāt ghaṭādivat.
(e) Vivādādhyāsitaṁ pramāṇajñānaṁ svaprāgabhāvātiriktājñāna-pūrvakaṁ na bhavati pramāṇajñānatvāt bhavadabhima-tājñānasādhanapramāṇa-jñānavat.
(f) Jñānaṁ na vastuno vināśakaṁ, śaktiviśeṣopabṛṁhaṇavirahe sati jñānatvāt yad vastuno vināśakaṁ tacchaktiviśeṣopabrmhitaṁ jñānamajñānañca dṛṣṭaṁ yathā yogiprabhṛtijñānaṁ yathā ca mudgarādi
(g) Bhāvarūpamajñānaṁ na jñānavināśyaṅ bhāvarupatvāt ghaṭādivat. Rāmānuja-Bhāṣya, p. 178, Bombay Edition.

25. *Vide Cit,*, p. 60: asmanmate jñānasya sākṣisiddhatayā pramāṇā-bodhyatvāt.

26. Yadyapi anubhava-cakṣurālokānāṁ ghaṭādivyañjakatvaṁ samānaṁ tathāpyanubhavasya viṣayājñānavirodhitvāt cit-prakāśatvam ālokasya viṣ ayagata-tamo-virodhitvāt jaḍāprakāśatvam cakṣuṣaśca aparokṣānubhavaṅ prati sākṣāt sādhanatvāt ajñātakaraṇatvamiti saṅbhavatyeva vaiṣamyam.
Vivaraṇa-prameya-saṅgraha, p. 56.

27. The nature of *upādhi* and how it invalidates inference has been discussed in Chapter VI.

INDEX

✧✧✧